LEN SILVER

As Luck Would Have It

A Cockney's Tale

LEN SILVER

As Luck Would Have It

A Cockney's Tale

RETRO*SPEEDWAY*

First published in England in October 2009 by

RETROSPEEDWAY

Tel: 01708 734 502
www.retro-speedway.com

Printed in Great Britain by the MPG Books Group, Bodmin and King's Lynn

Distributed by Retro Speedway
103 Douglas Road, Hornchurch, Essex, RM11 1AW, England
Email: editorial@retro-speedway.com

ISBN 978-0-9559340-3-2

The champagne flows after another England victory – this time in 1981, Len's last season as national manager.

ACKNOWLEDGEMENTS

I couldn't have written this book without the help of the following people and I'd like to personally thank them all:

Gareth Rogers, who typed up all my hand-written words and compiled most of the contributions to the Tributes section of the book, plus Peter Oakes, Tony Hurren and the Silver Ski office staff.

My publishers, Retro Speedway, and I would also like to acknowledge and thank the following for their assistance:

Pete Sampson and staff at Paradise Wildlife Park, Jeff Brown, Pete Jackson, Matt Jackson, Allen Trump, Phil Rogers, Bob Ferry, Ray Collins and Paul Tadman.

Photography: Alf Weedon, Wright Wood, Peter Morrish, Ian Bush, the late Don Ringrow, The John Somerville Collection and Retro Speedway.

With sincere apologies to anybody who we may have overlooked.

CONTENTS

Hazal and me on our wedding day in July 1979.

INTRODUCTION

THIS autobiography was written in the past two years when I was between the ages of 75 and 77 and, in part, I simply wrote things down as I remembered them. So much of the book tells the story of my life but not necessarily in chronological order.

I dedicate this book to the person who has been the greatest influence in my life and who I met when she was 14-years-old. She has been at different times, and sometimes all at once, my best friend, my lover, my greatest advocate and supporter and one who does all the hard work simply so that I can get the praise.

Her name is Hazal and I love her dearly.

All my net proceeds from this book will be donated to my favourite charity, the Speedway Riders' Benevolent Fund, who do such good work supporting riders with permanent injuries and those who have fallen on hard times.

My philosophy of life can be summed up in two of my favourite expressions:

'You catch more flies with honey than you do with vinegar' and . . .

'Be nice to people you meet on the way up, for be sure you will meet them on the way back down.'

Len Silver
Maidstone, Kent
September 2009

Chapter 1 – Early days
WAR-TIME ADVENTURES

I WASN'T aware of it at the time, of course, but it was on a cold morning on February 2, 1932 that I was introduced into the world. The startling event took place in a nursing home on the East India Dock Road in London's East End. I'm sure the first sound I heard was the ringing of Bow Bells to celebrate the occasion.

The family home was in the bottom half of a big four-storey house at 504, Old Ford Road and the Gilhams lived upstairs. Eliza Swettenham, my gran, lived in the front room and brewed her own beer, although that didn't stop her from spending most evenings in the Volunteer Pub on the corner of Milton Road! She was a tiny woman, tough as nails, who'd bred five children. The youngest of which was my mum, Grace Lilian, who first saw light at the turn of the century in 1901. She married Fred Silver, my dad, around 1925 and bore her first son, my brother Ron, in 1928.

Dad was a costermonger, as they were called in those days. He sold fruit and veg from a barrow which he pushed every day from Stepney to Stoke Newington, while mum was a trouser machinist working at home on a foot-operated treadle sewing machine for her Jewish boss who had what we'd now call a 'sweat shop' in Bethnal Green. All of her sisters did the same so that the family, on the whole, had enough money to live without too much hardship. Unlike most of our neighbours, we had no 'tally men' knocking on the door each week, collecting money for goods acquired 'on tick'. My mum never bought anything she couldn't pay for and raised me and my brother to follow the same path.

That philosophy lives with me to this day.

Every Sunday I was sent, when I was old enough, to the Methodist Church for Sunday school on the corner of Parnell Road, opposite the Lady Franklyn, where the number eight buses turned around. My cousin Irene, seven years my senior who lived opposite, used to take me out to play in Victoria Park on the other side of the canal that we used to call 'The Cut'. One of my earliest memories is of her setting me off with a shove in my pushchair down the hill of Gunmakers Lane (the entrance to the park) and chasing after me as I bounced and hurtled over the cobblestones toward the main Old Ford Road at the bottom – hoping to stop me before I ran under a number eight bus! It was hugely exciting and I loved it.

My brother and me were forbidden to go into the park on days when the 'Blackshirts', led by Oswald Moseley, held their rallies there to rouse anti-semitism among the Cockneys. It was the time of the rise of Adolf Hitler in Germany and Moseley was one of his followers. As a small child, of course, I had no concept of what it was all about, although I knew the 'Blackshirts' were not very nice people.

Mum and Dad in the 1970s. *Cousin Irene, who used to push me around.*

At the infant's school I attended from the age of four, all of us kids paraded around the Union Jack on Empire Day – Britain still had an Empire then – and the maps of the world were coloured in huge areas of red to signify where our colonies were. If I suffered any bullying at school, which I did from time to time 'cos I was smaller than most of the other kids, it was no good running home to mum or dad. I'd be told in no uncertain terms to go and fight my own battles. It was, as I came to realise in later life, a wonderful lesson, learning to stand on my own two feet, facing realistically all that life could throw at me.

For some curious reason, known only to himself, when I was nearly four years-old dad took me to the funeral of King George V, carrying me on his shoulders so that I could see the coffin being borne on the gun carriage covered with a Union Jack. The crowd was huge and everyone, except me it seemed, was very sad. Soon after we all got mugs given to us with the picture of the new King Edward on them, to celebrate his coronation, and they were placed with pride on the mantelpiece above the black stove in the kitchen, which doubled as our tiny living room.

Sometimes that room was full of grey trousers and cloth pieces when mum was working. I would sit on the floor, turning the band linings inside out with a tool the shape of a long finger. The room was always cleared and spotless before dad came home from selling his fruit. When he arrived he always hung a bag of specks (slightly damaged or over-ripe fruit) on the handle of the kitchen door and my brother Ron and me were encouraged to dip into the bag whenever we wanted. I learned to love bananas that were almost black – and I still do!

Roman Road market was just a short walk away. A busy and bustling place, full of stallholders selling anything from live eels or pickled cucumbers (wallies) to boots

Elder brother Ron and me.

and shoes or overcoats. Everything in the house came from there and on Saturdays mum would buy a sheep's head and cook it for dad's tea. Ron and me used to get to pick at the leftovers and we loved it! We never went hungry and mum took pride in making our clothes to keep us 'respectable'.

I never understood at the time but I remember the abdication of the new King Edward (due to the 'Mrs Simpson affair') in December 1936 and very soon we were given another coronation mug showing King George VI and his Queen. They had two daughters – the Princesses Elizabeth and Margaret – and when we went to the 'pictures' they were always shown on the newsreels. Everybody loved them and somehow the world seemed OK simply because they were there.

But, as I grew older, trouble was brewing and the Blackshirt rallies in Victoria Park were becoming more frequent and the threat of war, as Hitler became more powerful, was in the air. The Prime Minister, Neville Chamberlain, tried to make a pact with the Nazis but failed, even though he thought he'd succeeded.

So, at the age of seven years and seven months, on September 1, 1939, me and Ron, who was four years older, were taken to Mile End underground station. There we joined thousands of other East End kids, all carrying gas masks in brown cardboard boxes strung around their necks, to be evacuated from London. Lots of people were crying and making a fuss but Ron and I were on a great adventure! No tears from mum and dad – only a stern warning to behave ourselves, as we shuffled off in the queue to board the train.

We were given a brown carrier bag and inside was a huge bar of chocolate, some fruit and a bag of crisps. We'd scoffed the lot before an hour had passed so that by the time we arrived at Swindon railway station many hours later, we were starving hungry. The sausage rolls and cakes waiting for us there vanished without trace in a flash. East End kids never stood on ceremony!

An old rickety bus took some of us to a Wiltshire village called Aldbourne, about nine miles from Swindon. There we were shepherded into the church hall at the top of The Green. We all stood in a rough circle while big ladies with red faces and hair done up in buns walked around slowly, choosing children to take back to their homes. The girls were all picked first and then the single young boys. Ron and me were the only brothers and all the others had disappeared by the time we were picked – reluctantly – by Mrs Giles. She then took our hands and marched us off to her cottage at the bottom of The Green.

There was no Mr Giles and the old house with tiny doors and a narrow wooden staircase smelled slightly of mothballs. Strangely, my most vivid memory of the house was an apple tree which appeared to grow out of brick paving just outside the back garden door. It didn't stop us nicking the apples when Mrs Giles wasn't looking!

Two days after we arrived, on Sunday September 3, a bright sunny day, some of us kids had walked to a big country house up a hill called – we thought hilariously – Upper Upham. On the way back we were passing a house at the top of The Green and its windows were open. The wireless was on loud enough for us to hear and we listened to the voice of Neville Chamberlain and his famous speech declaring war on Germany. God knows why we did it but all of us Cockney kids cheered as loudly as we could!

We didn't know then that all our lives would never be the same. Some of them had seen their parents for the last time and most would live in the homes of strangers for a long, long time.

We didn't stay in Aldbourne for very long and many of us were taken to Frome, in Somerset, where we were billeted with various families all over the town. Me and Ron ended up with a newly-married couple who lived on a new housing estate on the edge of town. They lived on rabbits' food and had no idea how much grub East End kids needed. We were constantly hungry and went 'scrumping' for apples and other fruit whenever we could, while often being chased by square-shaped men in leather gaiters intent on bashing us with a big knobbly stick! We were never caught and we thought it really exciting.

My brother went to a senior school with the pupils of the evacuated Coopers Company School from Mile End. We were all taken to Frome together but I wasn't old enough to join them, so instead I was sent to all kinds of buildings where temporary classes were being made up.

One day our parents came down to see us and we laughed uncontrollably as we saw dad get off the train with a walking stick and his leg in plaster. We didn't realise he'd broken his ankle and thought that he'd dressed up to make us laugh. It was the sort of thing we knew him to do.

Soon after that day mum arranged for me to come back to London while Ron stayed with his school in Frome to complete his education. He was there for most of the war. When I got back to the big house in Old Ford I was sent to Lauriston Road School in Hackney on the other side of Victoria Park. I had a long walk every morning and afternoon.

Not too long after I arrived back home the Germans sent their bomber planes over the East End and the Blitz began. Wailing air raid sirens would warn us of the coming horror and we'd hurry down the garden into the Anderson shelter that my dad and uncle Jim had installed, like all their neighbours, just before war started. By that time, dad had given up being a 'barrow boy' and was an ambulance driver. He was never in the shelter with mum and me. His job was to rescue injured people while the bombs dropped all around us. I didn't realise as a child what danger he was in or how brave he was. He didn't speak about it much and we got used to the weird existence of nightly explosions, the noise of the ack-ack guns in the park, and finding the next morning that another house in our area had virtually disappeared.

For a little while, when I was eight-and-a-half I went to live with my Aunt Liz and Uncle Will in their bungalow in Hornchurch, right next to the fighter aerodrome in the Essex town. Spitfires and Hurricanes would almost knock the chimney stack off the roof as they took off to face the Battle of Britain made famous in Churchill's great speech about 'The Few'. I loved it there and got a huge thrill out of watching the aircraft circling overhead day after day. But it didn't last all that long and I was back in the East End by 1941.

When I was 10 I got a sore throat and I can remember dad declaring that I had

'Dip' as he carried me to an ambulance which whisked me off to Homerton Hospital in Hackney, where I stayed for 10 weeks. Forced to lie without raising my head from the bed, I had the then dreaded disease of diphtheria – a serious child killer in those days before antibiotics were available. At the end of the 10 weeks the doctors removed my tonsils, which seemingly had become the seat of the disease. Soon afterwards I returned to the big house in Old Ford and life got back to normal.

I sat and passed my exams to attend grammar school and I was due, after another entrance test, to attend Dame Lady Owen School in Islington, North London. This was a famous centre of excellence at the time. However, it was not to be. Mum and dad bought a little terrace house at 18, Wingfield Road in Stratford and my father, as well as driving the ambulance, started up business as a window cleaner. This at a time when most windows were either missing, boarded up or plastered with sticky tape to stop them being shattered when bombs dropped nearby. Not the most astute move, you'd think, but it typified my dad, who was the most optimistic man I ever knew in my life. I probably inherited some of his attitude and it has stood me in good stead in times of trouble.

I became a pupil at Stratford Grammar School and rode my bike to and from there every day with my satchel strapped to the crossbar.

Night-time air raids were still interrupting our sleep but we were kept cheerful by listening to Tommy Handley in I.T.M.A. *(It's That Man Again)* on the wireless every evening and I acquired the knack of reading a book and enjoying the radio shows at one and the same time. 'Doodle Bugs', the strangely comic flying bombs, became a constant feature of our lives and the sound, like a motorcycle engine, heralded their arrival. When the noise of the engine stopped we dived for safety and held our breath until we heard the crunch as the bomb exploded onto some unfortunate victim – thankful that it wasn't us. No-one let them upset their life and everyone was upbeat, particularly when we listened to Winston Churchill make his famous speeches on the wireless. There is no doubt that he was an inspiration to us all and I admired him greatly. To this day, he remains an absolute idol to me.

We nearly always went to the pictures once a week and watched newsreels of the great war events and images of the King and Queen picking through the bombed rubble in the East End, particularly around the docks, and chatting to the Cockneys on the mornings after raids. Everyone loved them dearly and admired the fact that none of the Royal family had evacuated to safety. The Princesses Elizabeth and Margaret were old enough to join the forces, which they did, and we would see newsreels of the future Queen driving an army lorry. This only endeared them to all of us even more.

But the optimism of that era was soon to end. The Nazis had invented the V2 rockets and these were aimed at London with devastating effect. Suddenly there was genuine fear in the atmosphere. The rockets came without warning, no sound of aero-engines or the buzz bombs' motorbike noise, just a huge crunch of an explosion as whole blocks of houses were flattened in one enormous devastation. Even the normally cheerful Cockneys became strangely silent as fear gripped us all. I was then 11 and mum decided to take me out of the immediate danger zone. She

Dressed up in my favourite cowboy outfit. I couldn't halt the Germans invaders but this picture remained on display in the window of our local photographic shop in the Old Ford Road for many years!

sent me for a short while in the summer to live with my rich Aunt Vi who'd bought a house in a village just outside Bedford, near Wootton Army Barracks.

As a grammar school boy, I was sent to continue my education at the very posh school next to the River Ouse in the town centre of Bedford. There the boys wore straw boaters and striped blazers and went punting on the river. I felt right out of it, I can tell you, but no-one took the mickey. They didn't fancy facing me with my boxer's nose, thinking that a Cockney kid might just be able to look after himself.

Two things stood out in my mind from my short stay in Bedford. The first was a very pleasant experience. It was the end of term, probably July 1943. All the boys, wearing their straw boater hats, lined up, myself among them, in the grand hall. Each of us was given an envelope containing 'Maundy Money', apparently donated by the King. I couldn't believe my luck! When I opened the envelope, inside were brand new coins – a half-crown, a florin, a shilling and a sixpence – all shiny silver. It was more money than I'd ever had in one go – six bob! It seemed like a fortune and it went in my pocket very quickly, just in case someone asked for it back.

The other incident was so ridiculous it was laughable, but it ended my stay with Aunt Vi. Like many other schoolboys there, I had become a 'train spotter'. We would go to a field alongside the railway lines just outside Bedford mainline station. There we'd note in a book the numbers or names of all the train engines which passed by. The most valued were the big engines with names and we were careful not to miss those.

On this particular day one of the trains passed me and I missed its name. But it had stopped just up the line before entering Bedford station, so I upped and ran along the lines to where it stood blasting out steam all over the place. Having noted its name in my book, I then slowly walked back to my position in the field. There were quite a number of parallel train lines running into the station and this particular train was about four or five tracks out. When I got near the back of the train there was a man leaning out of a window in the end carriage. 'Hey son,' he called to me. 'What's that on the rail down there? Is it a bomb detonator? Crikey – what's that? Come and have a look,' he demanded.

So I stepped across several railway lines until I was just below him. Looking at where he was pointing, there, sure enough, was a round red object rather like a big mushroom but made of metal, sitting on the railway line. I was astonished. I had no idea what it could be and bent down for a closer inspection.

Then, suddenly, I was grabbed from behind. Big hands and arms circled my waist and lifted me clean off my feet. I wriggled and squirmed to get away but the grip of this big man in a blue denim shirt was too powerful. He carried me clear of the ground, over the lines, across the field and onto the roadway. He kept a firm hold of me, ignoring my shouts.

Very soon a Wolseley police car pulled up and the man opened the door and climbed inside, still holding me firmly. I was terrified and didn't know what to do. Quickly, the car with me inside zoomed off and eventually arrived at a police station in the town. There I was carried out bodily, feet not touching the ground, into the station. 'Hey,' called out the huge man, gripping me tightly. 'We've caught a midget spy here. You'd better lock him up!' I nearly died with fright. Midget Spy? What was he talking about? 'I'm Lennie Silver. And I'm 11-years-old.'

They took me into a small room and kept firing questions at me. I was totally confused and probably didn't say all the right things. It seemed to go on for hours although it probably didn't. Anyway, eventually my Aunt Vi arrived and I was crying my eyes out. She told them who I was but in the meantime it seemed that the police had been in touch with my parents in London. They wouldn't allow me to leave with my aunt, so I had to wait until mum and dad arrived on the train. When they eventually came it was a huge relief to feel mum's arms around me. After the police had satisfied themselves that I was not a 'Midget Spy' they let my parents take me home to London.

But I still wonder to this day what that small round metal object was on the line. I've had many a laugh over it since.

Very soon after returning to Stratford my mum and I went to live at Alsager, just on the edge of the Potteries in Stoke-on-Trent. We lived with the kindly Mrs Millard who had a heart of gold but looked just like the witch in *The Wizard of Oz* – mum boxed my ears soundly when I told her so!

Every day I went on a double-decker bus to Hanley High School and I was thrilled to discover that Mitchell, the designer of the Spitfire, was educated there. The propeller from the first plane was on the wall at the end of the main school hall and it made me feel very special at the time.

It was there that I suffered the penalty of having to stay after school when I'd been misbehaving in class – a common occurrence! – and was forced to do what was called 'long tots'. These were enormous lists of numbers that had to be added up and I hated it. Later in life I was grateful, because it made me able to do mental arithmetic very quickly, an ability I have found invaluable throughout my business life. During my years as a speedway promoter I always knew what a rider's costs would be and whether I could afford them, without having to write down the calculations. My speedy responses often acted to my advantage – so I'm most grateful to Hanley High School!

With D-Day and the allied invasion of occupied Europe, the V2 rocket attacks stopped and England became a comparatively peaceful place again. The Luftwaffe ceased appearing over our skies and the Home Guard (immortalised by TV comedy *Dad's Army*) spent their time marching behind military bands, staffed by white-haired men who stuck out their chests proud in the knowledge that they'd been through all the dark days to repel the enemy. Although we've all laughed at the antics of Captain Mainwaring and his *Dad's Army* crew for the last 20 years, we didn't laugh at them during the war. They were 'doing their bit' just like everyone else.

V.E. Day (Victory in Europe) came and London went mad. There were parties in every street with bonfires that made big black patches in the tarmac roads. Long tables filled with cakes and sausage rolls were laid out between the rows of houses and we all had a good old knees up. The relief and joy of that time was greater than anything I've experienced since. Winston Churchill and the Royal Family waved for hours to the crowds flocking around Buckingham Palace and all was well with the world.

Not long afterwards the Yanks dropped two atomic bombs on Nagasaki and Hiroshima in Japan. V.J. Day followed, giving us all an excuse to party in the streets yet again.

It was 1945 and I was 13.

Chapter 2 – Teenage years
WHEN HOSKINS SAW RED

THE euphoria of winning the war against Adolf Hitler and the Nazis kept everyone's spirits up in spite of severe food rationing and shortages of practically everything. Most East Enders kept chickens in their gardens while many had hutches full of rabbits – all to supplement the meagre meat supplies which were available via coupons in the ration book.

Like all the other houses in East End streets we had no bathroom or inside toilet, so it was once a week to the local bath house in the Romford Road. There we would call out in a loud voice whenever necessary: 'More hot in number six' – at which the bath house attendant would swing his lever and gushes of steaming water roared into the bath. It was sixpence (2.5 pence in modern money) and for that you were give a towel and soap. If you timed your weekly bath to Saturday afternoon, you would feel lovely and fresh to go out that evening.

One of my pals at the local youth club, just off Water Lane in Stratford, taught me how to play the ukulele banjo and I quickly became a George Formby fan and learned a lot of his slightly saucy songs. It wasn't long before I started performing in public and joined a concert party doing shows for charity all over East London and Essex. Sometimes I got paid 30 shillings (£1.50) to perform at a working men's club and once I appeared at the New Cross Empire as one of (New Cross promoter) Fred Mockford's 'Speedway Discoveries'. But I wasn't much good.

In the spring of 1946 – it may well have been at Easter, though I'm not positive – a school pal named Sands asked me if I wanted to go to the local speedway with him. 'Speedway?' I asked. 'What's that?'

'Motorbike racing,' he said. Like most teenage boys, I found the idea of watching motorbikes highly attractive, though I was totally ignorant about what I was going to see at West Ham Speedway on that first visit. However, as a young boy, I'd collected cigarette cards depicting speedway riders – 'Stars of the Dirt Track' as they were known – such as Tom Farndon, Bluey Wilkinson and Phil Bishop. But at the time I didn't know what they actually did to warrant such fame.

That evening after school, we both took the 699 trolley bus down Prince Regent Lane to Custom House, joining a long queue before the turnstile gates were open. The meeting was due to start at a quarter-to-eight and at around six o'clock they opened the gates. We paid about nine pence each (the child's price) which is less than four new pence.

Once inside I followed Sands as he made a mad dash to get inside the stadium proper. It was a huge place with a double-decker grandstand along one straight, riders' pits at the far end and terraces to hold 100,000 people. Around the pits area, a section which had suffered bomb damage was closed off. We both sat on a concrete wall that surrounded the dog track which was, as usual, on the outside of the speedway track.

We sat at the end of the back straight, facing the riders head-on before they veered left into the corner. After what seemed like an eternity the 'March Past of the Royal Air Force' was played over the loud speakers and at the far end a small army of men in red sweaters, carrying rakes and flags, followed by countless St. John's uniforms, marched into view with military precision worthy of the Grenadier Guards. Not surprising really since all of them had been soldiers during the war just ended.

Very quickly afterwards, four riders dressed in black leather suits cruised out of the pits towards us, riding quite slowly. I remember turning to Sands to say that if this was motorbike racing, I didn't think much of it!

But moments later a huge roar deafened us as the four riders lined up at the start, over to our right. I couldn't see clearly as the four figures dashed into the first corner at the far end. Suddenly they were screaming towards me with the certainty that I'd be knocked for six when they hit me. I ducked to one side, expecting the worst, but as I watched out of one eye they all suddenly turned left and huge plumes of dirt sprayed spectacularly into the air as they slid around the bend. Some of it landed on us but I didn't care.

My eyes were deceiving me – these supermen were steering their front wheels to the right yet their bikes were turning left! By the time that first race was over, and it only took just over a minute, I was totally hooked and intrigued about the spectacle that I was watching.

I learned that West Ham was a team and they had riders like Colin Watson, Eric Chitty, Malcolm Craven and Bob Harrison among them. My life was to change forever as I became an avid fan, never to miss a Tuesday night's racing in that vast West Ham arena at Custom House in the heart of East London's docklands.

To pay for my entertainment at the speedway I did two things. On Saturday mornings I helped dad to clean windows for half a crown (12.5 pence) and every morning I delivered newspapers using a massive and heavy old bicycle supplied by the old lady who ran the paper shop by Maryland Point.

Very soon after that first trip to the speedway I was riding this old bike by Deanery Road, near Stratford Broadway, and on a bomb site there I saw a few boys riding their bikes around a makeshift track, imitating the stars of speedway. Without further ado I was on the track with them riding the heavy old bike, speedway-style, by sitting on the low carrier over the back wheel. It was awkward but effective and I loved it.

The track, if you could call it that, was almost circular and had several hills and dips in it. Soon I chatted with the other kids and they told me about another track at Janson Road. This happened to be opposite where I lived, just off the Leytonstone Road, only about a mile from what is now known as David Beckham territory.

The next day after school I went to Janson Road and, sure enough, there was a rough flat track with longish straights and tight bends. There were six or seven lads pedalling around it as fast as they could go. Needless to say I joined them and discovered that they considered themselves to be the Stratford Hammers – all being avid fans of the 'Hammers' of West Ham Speedway and all living in Stratford. Before a few days had gone by I had become one of the gang and we decided to be a team. It wasn't long before we learned of other teams at Beckton, Forest Gate, Poplar and Plaistow (The Black Lion pub team). We set up matches between us and it was huge fun for all.

At the tender age of 14 I then discovered that I had organisational and publicity skills when I became a major mover in setting up the East London Cycle Speedway League, at a meeting held in the back room of The Black Lion pub in Plaistow. I wrote to the *Stratford Gazette* newspaper with all the information and to everyone's astonishment, they then started to publish a weekly Cycle Speedway News column – with yours truly giving them the stories.

As well as our Stratford Hammers, the other major teams in the league were: Beckton Aces, Forest Gate Tigers, Poplar Aces, Black Lion Monarchs and, later, the Warwick Lions of Hackney – organised by Vic White and joining the league as a powerful team.

Without any argument, the best rider by far was Ronnie 'Tiger' Genz who led the Forest Gate team on their track inside the old gun emplacements on Wanstead Flats. He went on to become a terrific speedway rider – first at New Cross and later at Oxford. He was a World Finalist and one of the best riders ever to emerge from cycle speedway.

The Stratford Hammers became a major force in the new sport and rode matches all over England. We were invited at one time to Odsal Stadium, at Bradford, where we raced on a track around the rugby league goal posts at one end before the motor speedway match started. Our West Ham idols were in the match and the late and great Johnnie Hoskins was the promoter. Little did I know then that not only would I get to know the great man but I would be privileged to be able one day to call him a friend.

Anyway, we duly raced our cycle speedway match and beat the best team in Bradford. But it wasn't all over. It was arranged that all of the cycle speedway boys would race one lap of the speedway track during the interval and we noticed that all the local riders were swapping the gears on their back wheels immediately after the cycle speedway match. We wondered why at the time.

The Odsal track in those days was big and narrow, heavily banked in the corners and very spectacular – ideally suited to their star man, leg-trailer Oliver Hart. When we were called to the start line in the interval it seemed absolutely enormous to us. I used to wear a red sweater when I rode my bike so that I was easily seen. All the Bradford boys wore black or dark brown.

As luck would have it, I was one of the first cycle boys to get to the start and was able to pick an inside position. Up went the gate and off I went, pedalling furiously on my low-geared bike. Away in front round the huge first corner with a good lead. Down the back straight and I glanced over my shoulder. Coming up just on the outside was a figure in black, a local lad. With the bigger gear ratio on his bike, his legs were going at half the pace of mine. My lower gear had enabled me to get ahead early on but now the advantage was his.

Round the last bend we raced and by now I was almost done in, my legs feeling like lumps of lard. Another glance over my shoulder made me realise that this black figure had ridden to the top of the banked corner – giving him a good downhill run to the finishing line. I had stayed on the inside, still pedalling as fast as I could manage. Over the line we went, almost together. But I saw him just flash past me a yard before. I was gutted – but I shouldn't have been.

Johnnie Hoskins was the judge. He saw my bright red sweater but not the boy in black alongside me. So I was judged the winner and presented with a plaque to mark the victory. I was a proud boy that day but feeling lucky too! Oh, by the way, West Ham, the motorcycle speedway team that we supported, got soundly beaten by the local Odsal Boomerangs.

After we set up the East London League plenty of other areas followed suit and the sport grew massively in those early post-war years. Teenage youths in those days weren't into drink or drugs and petty crime was not a serious issue. What mattered to us was our racing and finding ways to be even better than we were.

Most of us wanted to eventually become proper speedway riders and, of course, quite a few did. Many successfully, including Pat Clarke who became team partner to Jack Young in the West Ham team. My, how we envied him. Dennis Day, who rode with me at Ipswich, Exeter and Hackney; Buster Brown at Wembley; and Vic White at Long Eaton, plus quite a few more progressed from pedal power to the real thing.

Very few started racing at a young age because National Service was in force and, at aged 18, every boy had to go into the armed forces. So, unlike today, very few started riding speedway at 16. An exception was West Ham-born Reg Fearman, who

That's me next to West Ham speedway star Aub Lawson, who was a regular spectator at our Janson Road cycle speedway track. Other Stratford Hammers are Roy Garnham, Johnny Livings and Dennis 'Twitch' Day.

lived a stone's throw from Custom House Stadium. Aub Lawson and Cliff Watson, stars of the Hammers team, lodged with the Fearman family from 1947 onwards. At the tender age of 15 Reg was able to get on a bike and ride it on a little practice track at the back of the stadium, next to the workshops where engine tuning maestro Alex Moseley was in charge. In later years he tuned engines only for Dennis Day and myself when in semi-retirement. He became a good friend.

On Wednesday mornings I used to bunk off school and go over the back fence by the dog kennels at the stadium and creep through to watch my idols practice. Reg used to be there and one day he let me sit on his bike with the engine running. What a thrill! It was like sitting on the back of a tiger. Very scary.

We were all as jealous as hell when Reg Fearman, tall as he was, signed a contract for the Hammers on his 16th birthday and was put straight into the team. It was what we all dreamed about for ourselves. But none of us had families who could even remotely think about buying a speedway bike. Working class people didn't own cars or even refrigerators and washing machines. Housewives had boilers and mangles to do their weekly wash. Entertainment was the wireless and maybe a night at the speedway or cinema for about half-a-crown (12.5p).

With cycle speedway leagues being formed all over the country it wasn't too long before we were arranging inter-league 'Test' matches and I was very proud to be a regular member of the East London team and, occasionally its captain, as we met teams from Wembley, Norwich, Poole and many others. They were exciting times and we were very successful.

The national *News Chronicle* newspaper put up a huge trophy for an All-England knockout competition and the first winners were none other than our own Stratford Hammers, led by our popular skipper and leading scorer Roy Garnham. It was all heady stuff with few downsides. But I did suffer one dramatic experience.

My parents had gone to the pictures and I was at the Janson Road track, opposite my home, practicing and larking about with the other team members. We were doing stupid things, jumping our bikes over little ramps and trying to knock each other off, just for a laugh. I went over a ramp and landed badly, shooting head-first over the handlebars and landing face-first into the brick rubble – remember, it was a war-time bomb site.

Blood started pouring everywhere and a young girl standing by offered me a tiny handkerchief to use. I took it and, holding it by my face and throat, I ran to my house almost instinctively. When I got there, covered in blood, I looked in the kitchen mirror and was horrified to see what looked like a huge hole in my neck with blood literally pumping out of it.

I opened the back door and called out to the next-door neighbours and Mr. Roberts appeared. As soon as he saw me he swung into action. Grabbing a towel, he literally leapt over the garden fence, wrapped the towel around my neck and half carried me, half dragged me, through the house, then along the street to the main Leytonstone Road. He stopped the first car by risking his own life and piled me into it, while ordering the startled driver to take us to St. Mary's Hospital in West Ham Lane at Stratford Broadway. By now I was drifting in and out of consciousness and I don't

With Stratford Hammers Roy Archie, Duncan Menzies and me, with Roy Garnham in the background.

remember arriving at the hospital.

There is no doubt that Mr. Roberts, with his fast reactions, saved my life. In later years other people were to do the same thing and I've come to believe that somewhere up there is a Guardian Angel looking after me.

What had actually happened was that the skin on my neck was split and the elasticity made it gape open to look like a hole. My whole face was a mess (some say it's never recovered!) and when I came out of hospital late that night I was bandaged completely from my neck to the top of my head, with only small holes for my mouth, nose and eyes.

You can imagine the horror for my mother on returning from the cinema to find her youngest son looking like a zombie out of a horror movie. Needless to say, I was immediately banned from riding my cycle speedway bike and, just as you might expect, I was highly disobedient and carried on (for a while) in secret!

Thinking back to those teenage years, I must have had the cheek of the devil. When I was 17 I wrote to the promoter of Rayleigh Speedway, Frank Arnold, asking for a trial to ride for his team. They were in the Third Division, as opposed to First Division West Ham, so I considered it to be a bit easier to get in.

That sounds innocuous enough . . . until you learn that when I applied I'd never even ridden a motorcycle. What a cheek! Even more amazingly, Frank Arnold wrote back inviting me to a trial.

Now I began to panic. Very quickly I had to learn to ride a bike with an engine in it. One of our club members, Freddie Siggins (who subsequently rode for Long Eaton), had a B.S.A. motorbike and he offered to teach me. The day of the first lesson arrived and I sat on the saddle with Fred on the pillion. He told me what to do and off we went, very steadily at first but gradually speeding up as I got used to it.

We went around a left-hand corner into Janson Road but I was going too fast and ended up colliding into two bicycles, which were leaning on the kerb, and all of us ended up in a heap on the pavement. Fred wasn't too pleased and that was the end of my lesson.

Two days later, on Sunday morning, I was due to have the speedway trial at Rayleigh and Fred took me there on his pillion. We got to the stadium at Rayleigh Weir on the Southend Road and waiting there for me was one of the Rockets' reserve riders, Charlie Mugford, who in later years introduced me to snow ski-ing. He had the track spare bike waiting for me and I had some ex-W.D. gear on, a steel despatch rider's helmet, some D.R. boots and a leather jerkin. I must have looked like an ex-army scarecrow.

Charlie found me a gigantic steel shoe for my left foot and, having started the bike up for me, he let me onto the machine. Before I knew it I was sailing merrily down the back straight. All my thoughts were on what I had observed my heroes doing every Tuesday at Custom House, so I tried to put it into practice. Into the corner with the throttle shut, then halfway round giving it a handful to make it slide. Well, it actually happened and, momentarily, I was in a full power broadside!

Then instinct took over and I shut the throttle off, the bike bucking in the opposite direction as it stopped sliding. Back on went the throttle, then off again, and so it went on. Highly uncomfortable and feeling totally out of control, the bike was sliding then bucking. Amazingly, I stayed on the thing and did maybe three laps or so with this terrible jerking movement.

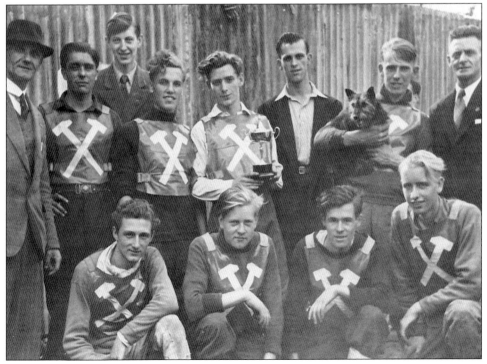

Stratford Hammers 1949: Standing, left to right: I can't name the gentleman in the hat, but the others are Jack Wilson, Duncan Menzies, myself, skipper Roy Garnham, Dennis Day, Johnny Livings and Roy Garnham's father. Front: Ray Willmore, Jimmy Heard (who also went on to race speedway), Eddie Parham and Roy Archie.

Finally I stopped and Charlie took the bike from me and, after a chat, Fred and me set off for home. I was like a jelly with my nerves all jangling from what had been a terrifying experience.

After a few days I had a letter from Frank Arnold inviting me to the Wednesday team practices, telling me that I could use the track spare bike. Wow! I couldn't believe it, my dream seemed to be coming true.

At the *Electrical Times* magazine office in Holborn, where I worked as an office boy, I asked for the time off and, surprisingly, they said OK. (I believe they were curious about a teenage lad becoming a speedway rider.)

The following Wednesday I went to the stadium but rain was falling heavily and practice was cancelled. The same happened a week later and frustration set in. Seven days went by and off I went for the third time. What I didn't know was that during this period Frank Arnold had stopped promoting and a new guy, Roy Dook, had taken over.

Into the pits I went, dressed in all my stupid ex-army gear, and started busying myself around the track spare. Up came this huge man – the new promoter. 'Who are you?'

'Len Silver,' I replied.

'What are you doing here with our spare bike?'

'Mr. Arnold said I could ride it,' I tried to explain.

'Why, haven't you got a bike of your own?'

'No Sir.'

'Well, f*** off then!' he told me in no uncertain terms.

So off home I went with a flea in my ear.

However, life on the cycle speedway went on and just a few weeks after that disappointment my dad loaned me £40 to buy a 350cc AJS vintage 1937 with girder forks. When I got used to it I'd sometimes slide it speedway-style, heavy as it was, round the Janson Road track. I loved it.

My 18th birthday approached and I had to attend a medical prior to my National Service. I went to Wanstead to be examined alongside countless other spotty teenagers. I got past the shock of the doctor grabbing my testicles and saying 'cough', which must have produced the right reaction because I passed the medical. Then I was given the choice of which service to join and what trade I'd like to be in. I chose the Royal Air Force and asked to be a motorcycle despatch rider. Umpteen other youths applied for the same job because it seemed like a great thing to be, swanning about on a motorbike all day. But, because I already had a licence and could ride a bike, I was the only one to be given that job. It made me feel very superior!

My cycle speedway days behind me, I started a new adventure in June 1950 as a recruit in the RAF.

Chapter 3 – National Service
NEAR DEATH IN THE DESERT

SOON after my 18th birthday, and now capable of riding and even sliding a 350cc motorbike, I paid £5 and attended the *Speedway World* magazine training school at the original High Beech track in Epping Forest. The price included lunch in the Kings Oak Hotel next to the track plus the use of a speedway bike – and I rode half-properly for the first time in my life.

Sadly, it ended in disaster.

In my determination to ride flat-out and show what I could do, I managed to crash, smashing the all-chromium school bike to bits. I wasn't very popular and was banned from attending again.

In June I got my call-up papers and after being kitted out with a new airforce blue uniform, my life took on a new era, starting at West Kirby on the Wirral, opposite Liverpool. There I learned to march, handle a rifle, polish my boots and salute anyone with rings on his sleeve.

As an ex-evacuee, I wasn't as shocked by the change to my life as I might have been and, in fact, in some distorted way I quite enjoyed it. All of our squad became great pals and with cigarettes at sixpence a packet in the NAAFI, we all became smokers. We were due to do this training for eight weeks but after only seven I was given two days' leave because my posting was to Egypt, and the sea voyage on the S.S. Empire Fowey started a few days after my leave home.

My first experience of travelling on a big ocean-going troopship was pretty uneventful once I'd got over being violently sick while the ship was still in Southampton harbour! It was almost like a holiday and we all marvelled at the Rock of Gibraltar and the dolphins as they raced and flew alongside the ship as we sailed through the Mediterranean. We dropped anchor just off Port Said and were immediately surrounded by small boats full of dark-skinned locals all trying to sell us leather goods, watches and all sorts of items. It was clear that we had entered a new world.

With our kitbags loaded, we were whisked by a small motor boat into the dock and marched single file to the railway station and onto a train with wooden seats and no glass in the windows. All the time we were surrounded by local kids all shouting out for 'bucksheesh' and youths trying to sell us things. It all seemed very alien.

Soon the long train was steaming out of Port Said and into the desert. Even though we were dressed in our new Middle East shorts and lightweight shirts – still dark Khaki (later to be bleached almost white by the sun), we were wringing wet in the heat and all very uncomfortable.

The train stopped a couple of times *en route* for Ismailia and at each stop someone found that their watch had mysteriously disappeared while a local trader had appeared to sell us something. As I didn't own a watch, I was one of the lucky ones.

At Ismailia I left the train with a few other new recruits and and we were ushered into a big Bedford Q.L. troop-carrying lorry and driven alongside the Suez Canal to the place that was to be my home for the next two years – 324 Wing R.A.F. Deversoir, where the Suez Canal breaks into the Great Bitter Lake.

I was officially 2474983 A.C. Silver, trainee motorcyclist on the M.T. Section of a fighter station with three squadrons of aircraft, 324 Wing. There was already a motorcycle despatch rider, a Scots lad curiously called Jock, on the M.T. Section. I was to be trained by him and the officer in charge of M.T. The laugh was that the officer in charge couldn't actually ride a motorbike! Jock was a great guy and we got on famously.

The big sandy square of the M.T. section had a ring of white painted 50-gallon drums in the middle forming a sort of roundabout. I gained a huge amount of street cred when I slid the 350cc Norton bike round and round the drums, speedway-style. Jock couldn't do it and from that moment he regarded me as his equal – even though I hadn't 'got my knees brown.'

We had two motorcycles on the section – the Norton and a big, old Harley Davidson with a foot clutch, left-hand throttle and a hand gear change on the side of the petrol tank. All back to front to me. In front of the big pan saddle on top of the pear-shaped petrol tank was a large, round speedometer which was calibrated from 0 to 120mph! Underneath it was a brass plate fixed to the tank which carried the message: 'Danger, do not exceed 60mph'.

It was true. The machine was a wobbly death-trap if you rode it over the limit but fun to ride, though, at lower speeds.

We lived in corrugated iron Nissen Huts and by the doorway of each hut was a big earthenware pot which was filled with water each day from a bowser. I was astonished to find out how cool that water was, even though it was in the heat of the desert. It was, of course, because of the scientific principle used by refrigerators, that of cooling being produced when evaporation takes place. The earthenware made the water evaporate and cool – neat, eh?

Apart from the times I had to carry what was called a 'signal' to another camp, travelling up and down the Suez Canal road to Suez, Fayid, Tel-El-Kabir or Port Said in my job as a despatch rider, life was pretty free and easy. The day started at 6am but work ended at 1pm, so most afternoons we were able to swim in the highly salty Great Bitter Lake or in the Suez Canal itself. Sometimes we'd hitch a lift to Ismailia, about 20 miles away, where there was a lovely lagoon with sandy beaches all around. To me it seemed like the Life of Riley and as long as I didn't think about the two years being taken out of my chosen life it was a very agreeable existence.

As a DR I had to carry a big Colt six-shooter revolver when I rode my bike. I felt like Jack the Lad with that big gun strapped to my waist, I can tell you. What 18-year-old wouldn't? Once a month I had to go to the armaments section, where I had to shoot 12 rounds at a small target about 10ft in front of me. During my two years there I suppose I did this over 20 times. Never once did I hit the target and, what's

That's entertainment – playing my ukelele for the RAF troops in the Suez Canal Zone, Egypt, in 1951.

more, the armaments officer who always had a bang at it himself never hit it either! Film scenes of cowboys shooting the flame out on a candle were a far cry from my experience in the Egyptian Desert.

Sometime after my arrival in the Suez Canal Zone, King George VI died and his eldest daughter, then on holiday in Africa, became Queen Elizabeth II. We saw newsreels of the ceremonies at the open-air cinema on our camp and, of course, there was a military parade when we all used the marching skills learned at West Kirby.

Because I knew that I would need money to buy my speedway machine when I'd completed my two years National Service, I arranged for all my pay to be transferred to my mother in England. Pay parade was once a fortnight and the drill was that you lined up and when your turn came you stepped forward and shouted the last three digits of your service number, collected your envelope full of money, saluted and was dismissed. I always called out: '983 Silver', picked up an empty envelope, saluted, and marched off. With literally no money I couldn't go drinking in the NAAFI or smoke like all my pals, but I could go to the open-air cinema three times a week for the change of film on Mondays, Thursdays and Sundays. It was two piastres ('ackers' being the local currency) to get in. However, once inside, if you waited until after the film had ended, you could usually find one or two empty lemonade bottles lying under the seats. These were redeemable in the NAAFI at two ackers each – hey presto! Free cinema plus the odd coin to spend here or there. It was a great discovery for me.

However, as time went by I practiced on my ukulele banjo and also taught myself to play the guitar, albeit banjo fashion. One of my billet mates was a Scot, also called Jock, who played the piano accordion and he and I started to amuse ourselves by making music together. Word got to the Sergeant's Mess and we were instructed to appear next Saturday in their Mess Hall to provide musical entertainment.

I could barely play the cheap guitar (obtained with a loan from the official RAF fund set up for the purpose) and I arrived in the mess alongside Jock with great trepidation. I needn't have worried. By the time we were asked to play, late on in the evening, the whole company – ourselves included 'cos our drinks were free, was as pissed as newts! When Jock started his accordion version of Scottish reels with me, making my fingers bleed trying to keep up with him, the room was rocking and everyone had the time of their lives.

Jock and I were given a pound each and we staggered home to our Nissen Hut feeling like millionaires. The dose was repeated once a fortnight and I even managed to save a little of the money to add to my speedway fund.

My ability to sing George Formby songs meant I became in demand as word spread and I was now and then invited to appear in shows up and down the Canal Zone. The pay was 30 bob for two slots (£1.50) and with this and my Sergeant's Mess money, life was not unpleasant.

I learned that there were two speedway tracks in the Canal Zone – one at the army camp at Tel-El-Kabir and one on the R.A.F. camp at Kabrit. The tiny Norwich speedway star Billy Bales, doing his National Service, was posted to Kabrit and

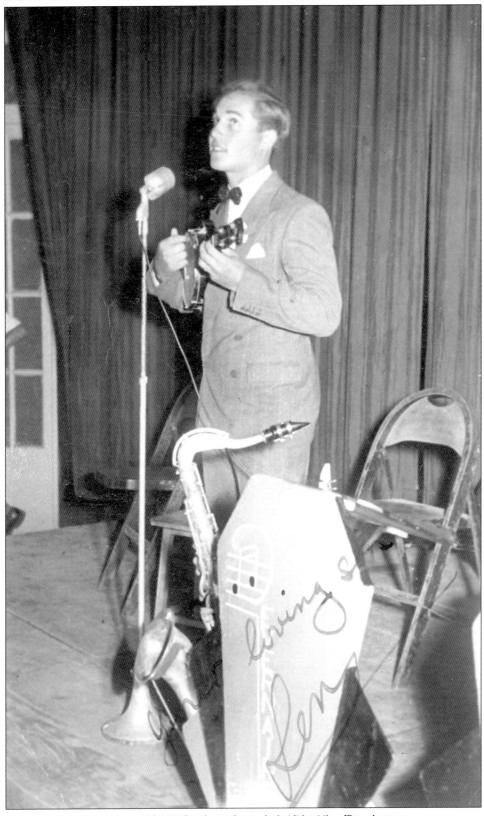

Me and my old George Formby routine again, but it kept the officers happy.

rode on the track there regularly. All of the machines were derived from road bikes and on the couple of occasions that I was able to visit both of the tracks, the speedway I saw didn't differ too much from what went on in England, though the action was not as fast. Billy Bales was allowed to go on leave to Norfolk and brought back with him a proper speedway 500cc JAP engine. With his ability as a professional rider, he beat everyone out of sight anyway. Once he had the JAP engine, then no one else got a look in.

During my second year in Egypt I persuaded the M.T. Officer that we should have a speedway track on our station. My pal and I had acquired two extremely old and rusty motorbikes just before they went for scrap and we stripped them down to the barest of essentials to look like proper speedway bikes. We were allowed to mark out in the sand a 250-yard track near the perimeter fence of the station on the far side of the airfield, which is where we went to race our old bikes. Of course, they weren't very powerful and mine misfired like mad but still we were able to slide around the corners at full throttle, slow as it was.

However, the sand surface very quickly wore away and each corner became a big hollow in the ground. We then devised an idea to bind the sand together with old waste engine oil. There was plenty of that on the M.T. section and our C.O. allowed us to take a barrel over to our track for the purpose. We delivered it late one afternoon, dropping it from the lorry with the intent of spreading it the next day.

Duly we arrived after work to lay the oil, only to discover the barrel had gone missing. There had been no disturbance to the immediate sandy ground and no disturbance to the triple barbed wire perimeter fence but there, on the far side of the fence, were tracks where the barrel had been dragged and rolled off into the sandy distance towards the mud-hut village about half-a-mile away. How the thieves achieved the feat of getting the barrel out of the camp, over the perimeter wire, is still an unsolved mystery to this day. Meanwhile, we had to be content to slide the bikes downhill into each corner and uphill out of it!

It was about this time that the Egyptians got rid of their leader, King Farouk (about whom we sang rude songs involving a hook!), and his lady, Queen Farida. There was huge unrest throughout the country and we were all placed on full military action status. Every airman was issued with a big, heavy 303 rifle which had to be carried everywhere – but not me! As a despatch rider I had the big Colt revolver which I kept strapped in a holster round my waist. Only the officers had such a privilege so you can imagine I was as swanky as hell and all my mates were dead jealous.

However, there was another side to that coin. The local Egyptians, who wanted us out of the Canal Zone, sometimes set traps for troops moving about in the area. One of which was to stretch piano wire across a road, at head height, to chop off the head of any passing motorcyclist! When I was out on the Suez Canal Road, I can tell you my eyes were open wider than they'd ever been and I kept my holster undone in readiness to use my gun if I had to. But I stayed safe and no incidents occurred, other than a lorry or two trying to run me off the road into the canal. Drawing the revolver usually made them steer away and I never got hurt.

The only time I was in real danger was on a trip with Jock and some of the sergeants visiting the Sergeant's Mess at Tel-el-Kabir for a special night out. We went in a small lorry and on the way home, after Jock and I had played the music in the Mess and all of us were pretty drunk, I was sitting in the front with the driver, supposedly as a guard with a gun, but actually playing my ukulele as we drove along the Canal Road in the dark.

We'd only driven a mile or two when one of the sergeants poked his head into the front cab and told the driver, Stan Moran (whom we called 'Stan the Man'), to stop. He said I was distracting him and that we should swap places which, of course, we did and I found myself sitting in the back on the bench seat facing all the sergeants sitting opposite.

The driving cab was to my left and next to me on the cab side was a huge sergeant who must have weighed 18 stone. Off we went again with me strumming my ukulele in the back, swaying about a bit on the bumpy road and looking forward to getting back to camp and bed. Suddenly there was a huge crash. Our lorry had smashed into an unlit vehicle parked half on the road and it virtually split our vehicle in half.

I was thrust heavily into the 18st giant on my left, bounced back and ended virtually upright and intact. Meanwhile, every other passenger was either thrown out of the front or the side, leaving bodies strewn all over the road. Many, including our driver Stan the Man, were seriously hurt. But, as luck would have it, I escaped without a scratch. I didn't even get knocked out of the lorry.

It was, it seems to me, another example of my Guardian Angel at work.

There was another occasion too. It was very nearly time for my service to end and must have been in May 1952. To help out in the M.T. Section I sometimes drove a Bedford QL Troop Carrier on the camp bus run. Its task was to ferry squadron engineers and air crew from the flying side of the station around the airport to the living quarters.

At one point the route crossed the runway at roughly the place at which the planes touched down on landing. There was a controller there in a black and white caravan whose job it was to show a red or a green light to the traffic before they crossed the runway. However, if no planes were flying in the area, the controller showed no light at all. In that case, the driver would simply take a look upwards and if all seemed clear, continue across the runway.

On this fateful May day that is exactly what I did when no light came from the black and white caravan. My heavy old Bedford truck, full of airmen, trundled slowly across when suddenly there was the huge roar of a jet engine. My heart stopped as I realised that an aircraft was about to land on top of us.

I pushed hard on the accelerator to try to get out of the way but the response from the engine was negligible. The shadow of the plane above made my whole body rigid with fear as the lorry rocked sideways. The tarpaulin tilt that covered the passenger seats at the back scorched red as the jet exhaust of the aero engine set fire to it as it screamed only inches above us and then off to our left.

Huge relief came over me as I realised that the jet plane had missed us and I heard the airmen in the back shouting – I think with relief too – as they realised how close we'd come to certain death.

The despatch rider gaining street cred with his sliding skills. These pictures of me were taken at Deversoir in the Suez Canal Zone, by the Great Bitter Lake in Egypt.

Soaking up the sun on the beach at Alexandria in Egypt.

The tilt was still smouldering when I reached the living quarters and standing there before us were two RAF police officers waiting to arrest me. The act of driving across a runway while aircraft were landing is the most serious driving offence in the RAF and I was in deep trouble. Ready to be de-mobbed, I feared that I'd spend the next few months in the glass-house and my speedway dreams would be put on hold even longer.

The next morning I was marched in front of the Commanding Officer who heard the charges and my evidence such as it was. He told me that the pilot of the jet had seen me and had pulled out of the landing at the last minute to circle again. But he was so shaken by the experience that he'd not be allowed to fly again for at least a month. I felt awful.

To my utter astonishment he handed me no punishment because he considered that my belief, that no red light had been shown, was true. I felt my knees go weak as I realised that I wasn't going to military prison. After all these years I still feel strange inside when I recall that experience.

Very soon after that I found myself in a tent at a transit camp halfway round the Great Bitter Lake, waiting to be shipped home. Soon I was on my way, flying in a small troop-carrying plane, noisy as hell. It was heading for first Malta and then RAF Lyneham in Wiltshire. My despatch rider days were behind me.

Formalities over, I travelled, still in uniform and carrying my kit bag, back to London and Stratford railway station. On a bus from there I asked for a tuppeny ticket to The Thatched House in Leytonstone Road, only to discover that it was now fourpence. It was my first experience of inflation as I entered a new life in Civvy Street.

It was July 1952 and I was a civilian.

Chapter 4 – Novice dreams
TWO LAP CHAMPION

THE house at 18, Wingfield Road, Stratford, seemed strangely small when I arrived home from Egypt and I wondered initially what I was going to work at while I tried to get into speedway. Almost miraculously the problem was solved for me.

Just about two days after my return an insurance man from the United Friendly called to collect the Fire Insurance money. Realising, when I opened the door, that I was the prodigal son keen to ride speedway, he began to talk me into working for them. He informed me that, within reason, I could make my own working hours so giving me the time I needed to break into speedway. This was manna from heaven to me and I signed up for the job two days later.

In the meantime I called to see my old cycle speedway pal Dennis 'Twitch' Day. He was quite a bit older than me and had not done National Service because he was a railway engineer, an exempt occupation. Dennis had been training for speedway while I'd been away and was getting rides for Third Division Ipswich.

He introduced me to his mentor, ex-Norwich rider Johnny Davies, who had been making a name for himself at Norwich until a severe accident to the nerves of his arm curtailed his career. During my two years' RAF duty I'd managed to save a little over £200, so I was able to buy Johnny's old machine plus his Chrysler pick-up truck and a new set of leathers from Jack Cooley, a West Ham reserve.

Only a week or so after arriving home, I was ready to go. I had a job giving me spare time, a bike that looked pretty good to me, a vehicle to carry it in and a set of leathers that made me feel that I was a rider already. I couldn't wait to start and very quickly Johnny Davies took me to Rye House, at Hoddesdon next to the River Lea, for a Wednesday practice session. In those days it was a quarter-mile cinder track surrounded by a corrugated iron fence and it all smelled deliciously dirty and oily.

At last I was on the bike and going. It felt tremendously powerful and the slightest turn of the throttle shot the bike forward almost out of my grip. Fairly quickly I got the hang of it and started to move at something approaching racing speed. Sliding the bike wasn't a problem, I could do that, and soon I was broadsiding round the tight bends in real speedway fashion. By the end of the day I was feeling very confident and Johnny was amazed at my progress. My short time on that rusty, old bike at Deversoir in the Egyptian desert had certainly paid off.

The following Wednesday we went to Rye House again and this time I received Johnny's instruction not to shut off until I reached the 'green box'. This was a tin construction, almost like a sentry box, situated outside the safety fence at the very end of the back straight. I did as I was told but as I went into the corner I couldn't handle the speed and landed on my new leathers, ripping a hole in the seat. Not to be deterred, I tried again and again until I could get into the corner at top speed without falling off.

Unbeknown to me, I had been watched by the stadium owner, ex-Australian star rider Dicky Case, who lived in the pub adjacent to the stadium. When the training had finished for the day I was called in to meet him in the back room of the pub. I walked in gingerly, wondering what to expect and found Dicky, then a very plump man, sitting comfortably in a big winged armchair. With a glass of whiskey in one hand and a cigarette in the other, he looked me up and down. I felt like a slave being offered for sale!

'Yer name's Silver, ennit?'

'Yes, Mr. Case.'

'Well, I saw you last week and I saw you today an' I reckon you're ready for a ride. I've fixed up a second-half for you at West Ham next Tuesday.'

With that he waved his hand to dismiss me. With a murmur of almost inaudible thanks, I went outside and climbed alongside Johnny in the Chrysler.

'You lucky bastards!' said Johnny, 'you ain't been riding a fortnight and you've got a race'. I was speechless and filled with excitement, not to say a little scared. The days until the next Tuesday were the longest of my life.

Tuesday duly arrived and I presented myself at the gate to West Ham Stadium so early that nobody had bothered to open it. Eventually I was inside, my bike unloaded and parked in the corner of the pits. The team members started to arrive and I couldn't believe that I was among them, looking out into that vast stadium that I'd frequented so often on the terraces.

The main match went on while I watched and eventually it was over and it was my turn. Someone came over and gave me a plain body colour to put on with a helmet cover to match. I can't remember what colour it was – it didn't matter to me anyway. Soon I was off down the back straight towards the starting line, which unlike today's tracks had a concrete starting area. We lined up and all my bodily functions stopped. I didn't breath or blink and my heart had stopped pounding. Whoosh! Up went the gate, 'bang!' went my clutch and the bike carried me, hanging on for grim death, flat out to the bend.

Now my brain started to react – quick, foot out, lean over the bars and keep the throttle on. Jesus! I was on my own out front and that famous silver sand track, laid by Johnnie Hoskins, seemed enormous. The laps seemed never ending and when the last corner appeared after the yellow flag, I could hardly hold on to the handlebars but no one was going to make me let go or slow up. I sailed past the chequered flag – a winner in my very first professional race. Is that a dream come true or what?

All my old cycle speedway mates from the Stratford Hammers were there and for a short while I was a hero among my peers. When I went to Rye House for practice the next day even Dicky Case came out of the pub to grunt: 'Good on ya kid' in his great Australian drawl.

As luck would have it, the following Tuesday West Ham had a big individual meeting (I think it was the famous Cundy Trophy), so the great John S. Hoskins couldn't give me a ride. However, he fixed me up in a junior race to represent West Ham at the tiny New Cross track they used to call 'The Frying Pan' because it was so small. I wondered how I'd do on the little circuit, although I felt pretty confident.

But it was almost a disaster. When it was time to warm up the bike, it wouldn't start and we still hadn't got it running by the time the race was due. Panic stations, I was almost in tears but we wheeled the bike onto the track more in hope than expectation and with two strong pushers galloping behind me it finally fired up and burst into life. Still mighty cold, though, and not really ready to race. But I had no choice and up to the gate I travelled on the inside position. 'Whang' it went and out I shot, suddenly realising that in the panic I'd forgotten to put my goggles on!

The cold air was in my eyes and I could vaguely see another rider off to my right. My bike felt very sluggish with little power (due to it being too cold) and I knew I'd be doing no good. The rider that I'd seen disappeared and as I entered the back straight big red lights came flashing on to stop the race. 'Thank Goodness,' I thought, 'now I'll get another chance.'

All four back in, and this time my engine was warm and I had my goggles on. But some cinders had got into my eyes from the first outing and as I lined up at the start my eyes were watering like mad and my goggles steamed up. Help! All I could see was a small, clear patch at the bottom of my left eye and this displayed to me only the white concrete kerb round the inner edge. To hell with it – up went the gate and off I went with the bike pulling my arms out of their sockets. I could only see the white line, so I kept next to it – up the straights as well as in the corners. I barely saw the chequered flag and wasn't sure when to stop. I couldn't believe what had happened and I hadn't seen another rider. That was because they were behind me and I'd won yet again!

The fish and chips we ate on the way back to Stratford tasted especially good that night.

Now I was beginning to feel that this speedway lark was made for me and that it was pretty obvious that within the year I'd be World Champion. I totally forgot that I hadn't beaten a single professional rider – only novices. But the dream was nice while it lasted.

The following Tuesday I learned several lessons that have lasted all my life – the first of which was not to 'count your chickens'.

I turned up for my scheduled second-half juniors' race, this time feeling more than confident – cocky even. After all, I was at that moment undefeated. The time came and I lined up on the grippy concrete starting area on gate four. 'Whang' went the gate and I twisted the throttle full on as I dropped the clutch expecting to fly into the lead. Alas I didn't.

Instead, my front wheel shot up in my face and I careered forwards on my back wheel, hanging on like a flag in high wind. At the corner the bike twisted and flung me off sideways, both the bike and me ending in a heap by the fence. Lady Luck looked after me and only my pride was hurt. Even the bike was basically OK but I went home that night sadly disillusioned.

The next day I realised that I was totally skint, not a penny to my name, but I realised I was due £1 for my start money the night before. I got on a 699 trolley bus and went down to the stadium hoping to get the money. (Crikey, I think today – what a bloomin' cheek!')

Johnnie Hoskins had an office in a long corridor under the main grandstand and when I found it I knocked timidly on the door.

'Come in,' said a loud, booming voice and I did so.

'Oh – you're young Silver, the skid kid,' said the great man. 'What are you here for?'

'Just my start money from last night, sir.'

'Great, great, great, I like that, I like a hungry rider.' Johnnie H smiled at me and made me feel I was in a place where I was wanted and welcome. 'I've got your pay – here it is son,' he added, handing me a long, brown envelope. I took it, thanked him and hurried out of the door and down the corridor.

As I left the building I opened the envelope to look at the cheque, expecting to see 'one pound' written on the paper. Instead I saw 'two pounds' – er um, one too many. I studied the enclosed pay sheet. There below the date of the meeting and my name, in the first column it said: 'Start money £1', the next: 'Point money nil', the third column: 'F.O.M £1'.

Mr. Hoskins had made a mistake and paid me too much, so I walked back to his office and knocked and entered for the second time. 'Sorry, sir,' I said, 'You've paid me too much.'

'Oh,' he said, 'How's that?'

'Well, sir, what's this F.O.M £1?'

'Oh that,' he said. 'That's Fall Off Money . . . yours was the best crash we've had at West Ham this year!'

As I said, I learned lessons that day.

Johnny Davies was keen for me to sign for Third Division Ipswich and arranged a second-half ride for me there. The Foxhall Heath track in those days was much bigger than the present one and, in fact, was where the stock car track is now situated. When I saw it I thought that I'd like riding on it and prepared myself for the single race I was due after the main match, feeling very excited.

My turn eventually came and we pushed the bike out for the start. Horror of horrors, it wouldn't fire up. We pushed and pushed but without success. The two-minute warning sounded and still we pushed. The two minutes up, the race got under way without me. I was so gutted to miss my only opportunity that I sat on my bike during the race on the centre green and cried like a baby, just thankful that no-one could actually see the tears.

Another opportunity at Harringay went the same way when my spark plug lead came adrift just as the starting gate rose and I began to learn that speedway has just as many disappointments as successes. By now the season had come to and end and the long winter stretched before me.

But I learned that pre-war star rider Arthur Atkinson and his rather awesome wife, Tippy, had taken over Rayleigh Speedway and were running a winter training school there. It was £5 per session every Wednesday and there was no way that I could afford such a sum. However, my first entrepreneurial tendencies came to the fore and I located another novice, wealthier than me, who, together with a pal of his, would pay me to drive them and their bikes to the track in my Chrysler. They paid me £5 each, so I had enough to practice myself and even after buying petrol there was a couple of quid left over to pay for my methanol and racing oil. A very acceptable solution to my financial situation and I was able to practice the whole winter. By the time spring was in the air I was able to beat every other trainee at Rayleigh. I was surprised that, although it was called a 'school' no-one gave the slightest bit of advice. Least of all Arthur Atkinson, who seemed very disinterested.

Pre-season practice was due at Ipswich and Johnny Davies had arranged for me to be there. Keen as mustard, I arrived bright and early at Foxhall Heath and I was the first rider to be ready to practice on the track that had lain unused all winter.

'Go out and do a start and four laps,' said Group Captain Arthur Franklyn, the rather large and imposing manager who'd stepped right out of a military instruction book and looked like he could swallow you up in a single gulp. He commanded every ounce of respect I could muster and I almost gave him a salute as I wheeled my bike onto the super-smooth track.

Engine running, I arrived at the concrete start line and then I was off at full throttle. After the rather rough and wet wintertime track at Rayleigh, this billiard table like surface was a dream and the bike simply carried me around like an armchair for four very easy laps. When I got back in the pits Johnny came running up to me, very excited: 'You little so and so, you only equalled the track record!' To say I was dumbfounded would be a gross understatement because it had seemed so easy.

'They want you to sign a contact,' said Johnny 'and I think you should.' It was easy for me to agree and I left the stadium to go home as an Ipswich rider.

That was just prior to the 1953 season and I thought I'd made it. How wrong I was. and the future didn't pan out as expected. Now with the wisdom of hindsight and having learned far more about the sport than I knew on that spring day in 1953, signing for Ipswich was not the best career move I ever made.

About a week later I attended the final training school at Rayleigh. As usual I put in as many laps as I possibly could to get my fiver's worth. At about one o'clock, with a couple of hours of training still to go, Arthur Atkinson came up to me. He had a contract in his hand: 'Right, Silver' – the first words he'd said to me all winter – 'I want you to sign this'.

I gulped. 'Well, er, you see I can't. I've already signed for Ipswich.'

'What!' he roared. 'Get out of my stadium right now.'

Suddenly I knew how easy it was to become unpopular – a nasty lesson.

The opening match of the season at Ipswich was a challenge against Second Division Yarmouth on a miserably wet rainy day. I was in the team at reserve. I'd ridden all winter on a track that was often like a bog, so the wet conditions didn't bother me. In my first race I was last out of the gate but passed a couple and I think I got second place.

But Johnny Davies was furious with me: 'What's up with you? All winter you've practiced how to get off a wet gate and you go and screw on full throttle and spin so much you got away last.'

He was so exasperated with me but I listened to his advice. For my next gates my engine was revving so slowly it almost stalled but by the time my rear wheel was off the concrete pad and onto the shale, I had a five-yard lead.

I had a double-figure score that night and I was cock-a-hoop. 'Silver,' I thought, 'you've arrived.'

What an idiot!

All I did after that opening match was fall off the bike. I was a two-lap champion and in race after race I'd drop it on the last lap, mostly out of sheer exhaustion. So much so that Don Clarke, the famous writer on the *Sunday Mirror*, dubbed me the 'India Rubber Man.'

But it wasn't funny. I found out that I was hurting myself and in match after match I raced while feeling pain somewhere or other on my body. Of course the manager, the frightening Group Captain, was not a happy man. 'Now then, Silver' he'd often say before a match, 'what we want are points, not pile-ups!'

I'd shrivel up not knowing what best to do – go fast or slow. Before long I lost my team place and, looking back, I can understand why. But I felt cheated at the time because I knew I could beat the riders that replaced me.

Much later on I learned the reason for my continual falling. It happened for two reasons. The first was that my engine was not actually very fast although it felt fast to me. So I was always over-riding, trying too hard chasing riders with faster motors. Add to that the fact that my arms and wrists were not very strong, although I didn't realise it at the time, and it is clear that my crashes were down to sheer fatigue. The knowledge gained from my own early failings as a rider has been invaluable in deciding the ways in which I have tried to help young riders to progress through my years as a promoter and manager.

It was during my early days at Ipswich that I got to know Alex Moseley. He had been the chief mechanic at West Ham Speedway for countless years and had roots in the very early times of 'dirt-track racing' having been mechanic to the great American 'Sprouts' Elder, a champion of the early 30s.

He was the chief mechanic for Ipswich and many times he would travel with Dennis Day and myself to various tracks all over the country. We used to be fascinated by his stories of the early days and the exploits of the riders whose engines he cared for. My own favourite anecdote, although not to be repeated in the best circles, has kept me chuckling all my life.

It concerned two young Australian riders (well known as practical jokers) who, at the end of the 1930 season, couldn't afford the fare home to Oz. So they both found part-time work with a coal merchant who delivered to houses around countryside Essex. One day while the lorry, driven by their boss, was going through Epping Forest, the boss man pulled up alongside the trees and declaring that he needed to answer a call of nature, jumped down from the cab and disappeared into the forest.

The two young pranksters quietly followed him, carrying a big coal shovel. Creeping up behind him as he squatted to do his 'business', they slid the shovel silently under him and caught the 'business', pulling it away without him noticing what had occurred. Then they watched as their boss turned to see what he'd done – only to find nothing there!

The two then quickly crept back to the lorry and watched the boss searching for the missing substance, feeling down his trouser legs as he made his way back to his cab, with a look of amazement in his eyes. The two never let on and the miracle of the missing item must have puzzled the boss for the rest of his life!

Alex had many stories like that and he kept Dennis and myself amused during many journeys. We were both privileged to have Alex as our engine tuner when he retired and we were his only customers. He looked after our engines out of friendship and we sorely missed him when he passed away. He was one of speedway's great characters and I'm honoured to have known him.

In the colours of my first league team – Ipswich Witches.

Chapter 5 – Ipswich
LUCKY BREAK

I N the spring of 1953, aged 21, I married my teenage sweetheart Vera and with a loan of £100 from my mum, we bought a house at 123 Gurney Road, Stratford for the princely sum of £800. The other £700 we had as a mortgage from the seller – repaid at 32 shillings a week.

We lived in the upstairs flat while the bottom part was occupied by an elderly lady. It was a year when I continued working for the insurance company, United Friendly, and once a week I joined a small team of would-be salesmen knocking on doors in the East End of London trying to sell fire insurance for fourpence halfpenny a week (about 2p in today's money). Although we weren't very successful, it was the finest lesson I ever learned in the art of salesmanship and would prove more than useful to me in later life.

Vera and I first met when she watched me riding cycle speedway at the track in Janson Road. She worked as a blouse machinist, which helped to pay our mortgage and the £1 a week debt to my mum. Her dad was reasonably well-off and was a sort of estate agent specialising in the sale of business premises from his office in Water Lane, just off Maryland Point, Stratford. Well off he might have been but he never lifted a finger to help us in those early married days when, like almost all newly-weds, we needed it most. I didn't like him at all, not because he was miserly towards us financially – I didn't care a jot about that, but because everything he did was totally selfish. The probability was that he disliked me in return, because I couldn't help but display how I felt toward him. He was a miserable individual.

Vera and I were married for just under 12 months when our daughter, Jacqueline, was born. Although at the time the thought of being a father struck fear into my heart, when I first saw my daughter, pretty as a picture in St. Mary's Hospital, Stratford Broadway, the fear melted away like ice in the sun.

As a parent I left a lot to be desired. This was mostly because I was either working or riding speedway, leaving little time for normal family life. Money was very tight too. Vera had to give up work, so we had to live purely on the small amount of money I could produce. Social life was virtually non-existent and usually consisted of visits to Southend, where some of Vera's relatives lived.

What didn't help was the fact that my wife had never wanted me to ride speedway, nor did my mum, so it was a constant source of irritation and didn't help either our married life or, for that matter, my racing career. I made sure that we didn't get into debt but it was a hard period of my life in financial terms.

Needless to say, it didn't help my speedway career to be so hard up and it was impossible for me to invest in a fast motor. Looking back, I sometimes wonder why the Ipswich management, led by the pompous Group Captain Arthur Franklyn, didn't arrange for me to be mounted on good equipment. Their attitude seemed to be that if any of their riders didn't do very well for a week or two, they were dropped in favour of a new incoming rider. It wasn't a successful method then and it still isn't in my view.

An example of the manager's short-sighted view came when, in my first season, we visited Exeter. I went there alone in my Chrysler truck and just outside London *en route* to the West Country my footbrake failed. I only had the handbrake working. With the idiocy of youthful enthusiasm I continued my journey to Exeter, amazingly arriving with my nerves shattered but unscathed in late afternoon. It was pouring with rain and we all expected the match to be cancelled. However, it was decided that we should run and the match, if you could call it that, took place.

The home team came first and second in every race except one and nobody in our Ipswich side emerged with any credit from the mudbath. I scored a third in the first of my two races (that's all reserves were given in those days) and in the second race I was trying to pass one of the home riders when I hit his back wheel and somersaulted over the bars. I was OK but my bike was a little bent.

However, I had performed at least as well as any other member of the Witches team and at least I was actually trying to race – hence my crash.

The next day, Tuesday, we were due to ride at St. Austell, some 70 miles further west along a road that resembled a fairground helter-skelter ride. And, remember, I had no brakes!

Team captain Sid Clark had a new Standard Vanguard pick-up truck and he told me to follow him closely so that if I ran into trouble going downhill, I'd only bash into his rear. He was a brave man and a good friend. It was a nightmare journey up and down the hills but, once again, I arrived at the track in one piece.

After unloading my bike, Sid looked at it and said: 'Crikey, we'd better try to straighten that out.' He proceeded to lay my bike across two railway sleepers and jumped on the engine! Well, it sort of worked after a fashion and I duly got changed into my leathers and started to warm up the engine.

Group Captain Franklyn walked slowly along the riders, who were all warming up their bikes, and stopped when he came to me. He peered at my bike, up and down and side to side. 'Hhrumph, Silver' he growled, 'Your bike's bent . . . you'd better go home.'

He knew about my nightmare journey, he knew why my bike was bent and he knew that I could beat the man to replace me, Geoff Woodger, even if I hadn't got a bike. Yet he sent me home.

My slow drive back to London through the night was undoubtedly the longest and saddest journey I've ever made. The only satisfaction I got from it was that Woodger scored a duck. 'Up you, Group Captain!' I thought to myself. It was a good demonstration of how not to get loyalty from your riders.

My career with Ipswich continued, sometimes in the team and sometimes not, with me still carrying the nickname 'India Rubber Man'.

During those early days in the Ipswich team my mate Dennis Day and I were booked to ride as reserves for the Witches at Southampton, owned and run by the legendary Charlie Knott. He was a promoter of the old school, a showman to his fingertips. He was a short, stout man who always wore a trilby hat and he was respected by everyone, although I didn't know it at the time.

Some tracks had been staging sidecar racing as part of the speedway programme and the Speedway Control Board introduced a ruling that such events had to be staged *after* all normal solo racing was complete.

When Dennis and I arrived at the Bannister Court Stadium, next to the ice rink at Southampton, we installed ourselves in the pits and prepared for the meeting. We were given a programme which we immediately studied to see which races we were due to compete in. As usual, there were two in the main match, Southampton v Ipswich, and one in the second-half. But we were both enraged to see that our second-half race was the very last event in the programme and following three or four events for sidecars. 'That's against the rules,' exclaimed Dennis – and I agreed.

Saucy Cockney that I was, I approached the great Charlie Knott and complained bitterly that our race was after the sidecars and reminded him of the Control Board ruling. He looked me squarely in the eye. 'You're right, young Silver, we'll have to change that situation.'

I felt very satisfied and sticking up for my rights seemed to have been the right thing to do. Then I was shocked to hear him say: 'Yes, we can't have any speedway after the sidecars, I'll cancel *your* race!' With that he turned on his heel and walked away, leaving me dumbfounded.

Dennis was spitting blood when he learned what had happened – angry at Charlie Knott for cancelling our race and furious with me for causing him to scrap it. We had our two team races and went home early. It was a silent journey, both of us feeling very cheated, and maybe a little wiser.

About 10 days later I received the pay cheque for the Southampton match. There was shown two starts in the match (paid £2), two points in the match (another £2). And, to my amazement, one start in the second-half (£1), and three points in the second-half (£3). The old rascal had cancelled our race but had paid us for the start and a win.

We learn from life in many different ways and this time I'd discovered that fair play can show itself in surprising ways. Charlie Knott became a sort of hero of mine and in later years, after he died, I was always pleased to race for his sons who took over the track at Poole after selling Bannister Court for development.

During my first season at Ipswich, in 1953, Dennis Day, who had been a team-mate of mine in the Stratford Hammers cycle speedway team, also rode there. I used to make the 70-mile journey to Suffolk from my home in East London in the big, green Chrysler pick-up truck I'd bought for £70 from Johnny Davies. Dennis had treated himself to a large, black American Packard limousine – a highly luxurious gas-guzzler that the Americans considered their version of a Rolls-Royce. It even had a chromium-plated front grill with a pointed top, not unlike a 'Roller'.

Above: The 1953 Witches. Back row, left to right: Don't know who the man in the suit is but the others are Nobby Stock, Sid Clark, Dick Shepherd, Charlie Mugford. Front: Harold McNaughton, Jimmy Grant, myself and Tich Read. Below: Junior Bainbridge (left) telling me which gate I'd be taking!

I have a sneaking feeling that Dennis bought it because of the huge back seat, ideal for impressing the ladies! Perish the thought.

One day I was tailing him on the way home when, just outside Ipswich and still a long way from Stratford, he broke down. His engine was running OK but he'd obviously broken a half shaft resulting in having no drive to his rear wheels. I gave him a lift home with the promise to help him get the Packard back to Stratford the next day.

So, armed with a very strong tow rope, Den and I travelled up the A12 on Friday morning in my Chrysler. It didn't take too long to get to the Packard, just south of Ipswich, and we hitched it up with the tow rope and started the journey back to Stratford. As we journeyed southward with me driving the Chrysler and Dennis steering the Packard behind me, I got bolder and bolder, faster and faster, sometimes hitting 70mph with Dennis holding on for grim death. I didn't appreciate how difficult it was for him at such speeds but I probably wouldn't have cared anyway!

After a couple of hours we arrived at Gallows Corner, Romford, and then further down the A12 to the Green Man, Leytonstone, and I towed the Packard at a steadier pace down the Leytonstone Road to where Dennis garaged his car. There wasn't enough room for me to tow the car into the yard in front of his garage, so we unhitched the rope and began to push the black limo into the entrance.

Dennis was pushing and steering at the same time while I was at the back heaving with all my might. As we turned into the gateway the off-side rear wheel fell off! It had only been held in place by about two inches of drive shaft because of the break and it could have come off at any time. The thought of what kind of accident could have happened at the silly speeds I'd been driving at haunts me to this day. What if? This could have been a nightmare scenario with both Dennis and myself – and maybe others – kicking up daisies, well and truly brown bread.

Away from the track, some dramatic changes took place. Vera and I took on a small grocer's shop near Maryland Point, which we ran at the same time as my insurance job. It didn't earn much but it helped keep our heads above water.

As well as selling a few groceries, we also sold hot pease pudding and savaloy sausages on Friday and Saturday evenings, mostly to the drinkers from the pub on the corner. When we first moved into the premises we re-decorated the shop parlour, the little room behind the shop itself and I hung some red patterned wallpaper a couple of days before we opened the shop.

Having never cooked pease pudding before, I made enquiries from the previous owner about how best to cook it. He told me to tie the chick peas up in a bag and boil it for as long as possible in water flavoured with bacon bones. So before going to work on the first day of selling the hot pease pudding, I told Vera to make sure that it was perfect by cooking it virtually all day. Off I went leaving her to prepare it.

At about five o'clock I got back home and walked through our tiny shop into the newly-decorated back parlour. As I opened the door I was hit by a cloud of steam emanating from the cooker in the rear kitchen. The whole room was full of hot steam and when I opened the back door to clear it, I had a shock. All of my lovely red wallpaper had rolled off the wall and was draped gracefully over the settee and other furniture. Steam and newly-hung wallpaper obviously didn't go together! We laughed about it for days. The pease pudding, by the way, was delicious.

One day I bumped into Vic Gooden, who had been a rider at Rayleigh and Aldershot. He was in the motor business and was about to open a car showroom together with another ex-rider, Alby Smith, who I knew from my cycle speedway days. Vic invited me to work for him selling cars and I jumped at the chance, knowing that Vic would give me time off to ride speedway. The showroom was in Romford Road, Manor Park and it didn't take long to find out that I had a natural talent for selling cars. I loved it and was able to earn quite a bit more than I had in the insurance game.

The grocer's shop got demolished in a council re-building scheme but Vera and I were given a nice, new council flat just by Plaistow station. Life wasn't too bad and I'd made a regular place in the Ipswich team, although I didn't get that many points. It seemed to me that I wasn't making much progress in my career but I overlooked the fact that each season saw Ipswich elevated into a higher league because tracks were closing down right, left, and centre. There were lots of riders out of work during that time in the mid-to-late 50s. I suppose the fact that I was still employed said something for my modest ability.

I kept hurting myself in various crashes, just as I always had, and then one day in 1957 at Southampton my hand slipped off the handlebar in the first corner (the track there was always bumpy). I fell sideways and my left arm got caught in between the front wheel and the frame – snapping the top of my arm like a raw carrot.

That ended my season but although I didn't know it at the time, it was a blessing in disguise because that injury changed my life completely. I was off racing for several weeks and eventually drew about £300 insurance payment. For the first time in my life I had a chunk of money and no commitment to spend it on. My mum, who had loaned me money in the past (always repaid, of course) coughed up £200 to make it a round 'monkey' (£500).

I gave my notice to Vic and Alby at the car showroom so that I could start up selling cars for myself. They were both very supportive and promised to help me all they could. They were then, and still are, very good mates of mine.

I began buying cars to sell to bigger dealers with showrooms or sites and soon I became acquainted with Bob Howard, who had an open site in Leytonstone Road, Stratford. He had no money and no knowledge of the motor game. Very quickly we became partners and ran Howard's Car Sales on that site very successfully. So successfully that in 1958 I didn't ride speedway at all – I just concentrated on the business. I soon repaid mum the £200 she'd loaned me.

But I missed riding speedway, although Vera was very happy that I wasn't continually hurting myself.

Money was coming in nicely and we spent most of it living something akin to a 'high life', visiting night clubs in London's West End and driving about in big American cars. Oh what fools we were!

It was around this time that the infamous Kray twins ruled the East End

The 1956 Witches – back row, left to right: Tich Read, myself, the infamous Group Captain Arthur Franklyn, Reg Reeves, Bob Sharp and Junior Bainbridge. Not sure who that is kneeling at the front on the left, but Larry Lazarus is on the right, with skipper Bert Edwards aboard the machine.
Below: That's me leading, in what looks my first season at Ipswich, from Les McGillivray of Rayleigh. Les later gave me sterling service at Hackney after I became the promoter there.

underworld and although we had no contact with them or their cronies, we obviously knew all about their vicious reputation. One day I'd been to a car auction, leaving my partner Bob Howard to look after our car site. When I got back he said to me: 'We had some visitors today.'

'Oh, who was that?'

'Well, it was someone involved with the Krays and they were collecting donations to finance a jail escape for one of the brothers!'

I gulped loudly: 'Christ, how much did you give them?'

'Nothing,' said Bob, 'I sent them off with a flea in their ear.'

'Bloody hell, you idiot, we'll have our site wrecked and our cars smashed up. You'll live to regret being so brave,' I told him.

Then Bob got as nervous as I was and for the next month we kept a sharp look-out. But nothing untoward happened and we didn't suffer at all – except to our nervous systems. Obviously the Krays had bigger fish to fry!

In 1959 the Government introduced hire purchase restrictions so tightly that nobody could afford to buy cars and overnight the value of the stock we'd built up became so low that we were virtually bankrupt. However, Bob and myself worked our socks off to get out of trouble, stopped living the high life and instead kept our site open for business every day from 8.30am until 10.30pm in an effort to find whatever buyers there were out there. All our staff were sacked and we did all the cleaning and other jobs ourselves. So we managed to weather the storm of that year.

Then a strange quirk of fate affected my life yet again. I sold a car to a guy who'd tried to take up speedway but failed. I took his speedway bike in part-exchange. Now I just couldn't resist having a ride on it, so I secretly went to Rye House where Mike Broadbank had built a training track on the site where the kart track is now situated. I gave Mike a fiver to let me use the track on my own that afternoon and there I was, broadsiding a bike again at full throttle. It felt good and I just knew I had to get back racing again. But how to break the news to Vera?

Fate stepped in and helped me again in the most bizarre way. During the winter of 1959-60 my dad told me about a tip that he'd had for a horse due to run in the first big classic race of the 1960 flat racing season. Now I'm not a gambling man but for some weird reason I put £10 each-way on this horse. Lord knows why I did it, because it was totally out of character.

Having placed the bet several weeks before the race was due, I then promptly forgot all about it. Time passed and on the day of the race I went ten-pin bowling at the new facility at Stamford Hill. When I came out, for some reason I can't remember, I had to get a bus as I didn't have a car with me. On the top deck of the bus a guy in the seat in front of me was reading a newspaper and I could see the headline about the big race which I'd forgotten all about. I asked him which horse had won and he told me. Wow! It was the horse that I'd bet on and it had won at 14/1. With the each-way bet, I won almost £200 – a huge sum of money in those days.

I got home and told Vera about my big win and unashamedly bribed her to agree

Happier days in 1960 – back row, left to right: Vic Gooden, Birger Forsberg, Peter Moore, Jack Unstead, Jimmy Squibb, Colin Gooddy, Maurice Littlechild. Front: Ray Cresp and myself, with skipper Les McGillivray on the bike.

to me riding speedway again if I gave her the winnings. To my amazement, she agreed and I started to prepare myself for another assault on the sport I loved.

My pal Dennis Day called round to see me to talk about us both riding together again and with Vic Gooden, my ex-boss in the car sales business, taking over Ipswich Speedway, we both signed a contract to ride in what was then a First Division club.

I was a regular reserve team member of the Witches side that included two riders who in later years rode for me at Hackney – Les McGillivray (an ex-cycle speedway friend) and Australian Jackie Biggs (who later met his untimely end in a track accident in Australia). Vic Gooden's co-promoter was Maurice Littlechild, who later opened King's Lynn, and for the first time ever I was riding for a good management team. Vic helped me a lot with good advice and I kept my place even when I didn't score. By the end of the 1960 season I'd improved quite a lot compared to the form I'd shown in my previous years under Group Captain Franklyn.

The new Provincial League had been formed that year, spearheaded by Mike Parker, an ex-midget car driver, together with my old schoolboy mate Reg Fearman and ex-rider Bill Bridgett (whose nephew, Alan, is now recognised as one of the best track curators in the country).

Another long-standing friend, Exeter promoter Wally Mawdsley, joined veteran Falcons' rider Pete Lansdale to open Rayleigh in the new league and speedway in general started to look a lot healthier now that a second division had been formed in addition to the ailing National League (Division One).

Chapter 6 – Exeter
FLYING FALCONS

AS the 1961 season began I was still in the Ipswich squad but didn't score as well as I should have done. Dennis Day was at about the same level as me and both of us feared for our place. After several weeks of the season had gone by Wally Mawdsley appeared one night at Ipswich to sign up Dennis on loan for Exeter. Dennis had a thumping night and rode out of his skin to score 10 points while I managed about three or four.

So Vic Gooden said to Wally: 'Sorry, you can't have Dennis but you can have Len instead.'

But when Wally first asked me to go to Exeter, I flatly refused. There was no way I wanted to drive a round trip of almost 400 miles every week. However, he invited me to go there for a one-off open individual meeting and I agreed. On the day I suffered a couple of crashes, plus an engine failure, and only got four points. But I managed to ride round the outside of Pete Lansdale to beat him in one race, which impressed both him and Wally.

It didn't take them long to persuade me to join them even though the local press published their opinion that I 'wasn't worth considering!'

They were almost proved right when, in my first appearance as a Falcon at Rayleigh towards the end of April 1961, I clipped a back wheel, high-sided it and broke my collarbone. Three weeks later I was back in action even though I had to ride through the pain barrier. Slowly I began to weigh up the banked Exeter track and in a match against Sheffield in June, I grabbed my first ever 12-point maximum.

On the way home with my team-mate Dennis Day, who also joined Exeter after me, I remarked that it must have been a fluke. But another maximum followed seven days later – this time against Middlesbrough – and by the end of the season I really felt that I'd at last found my niche.

Good promoters and supportive fans were very instrumental to my success in 1961 and what followed was the most successful period of my riding days.

That was in 1962. My car sales business was doing well and I had taken a showroom in Romford Road, Manor Park. It had a flat upstairs where Vera and I lived with daughter Jackie. We were fairly comfortable, financially, so I was able to invest in very good equipment.

Dennis was working for me on the car sales side and he was also able to do small jobs on my bike. He was particularly good with clutches and mine worked like a dream. Although I started the season with some engine problems they were soon sorted out and I recorded my first maximum at Plymouth on Good Friday.

With my great friend Dennis Day after we'd both moved from Ipswich to Exeter.

But it was a sad day because my very good friend and team-mate Jack Unstead had been killed while riding for Ipswich a few days earlier, on Friday, April 13. It brought home to me the dangers that riders face and I've never, ever forgotten it.

It was an honour for me to win the Jack Unstead Memorial Trophy later that year but my drive home to London was fairly quiet because Dennis, my travelling companion, had bust a couple of ribs in the same meeting.

Things seemed to get better and better for me and my confidence was on a high when I qualified for the Provincial League Riders' Championship Final at Belle Vue in 1962. I really felt I could win it but it was a meeting that demonstrated to me that speedway promoters in those days were a pretty mean bunch.

The old Hyde Road stadium in Manchester was packed to capacity on that September Saturday night, with somewhere in the region of 20,000 people having come from all over Britain to support their team's top rider. There were 27 riders in the pits and it took 24 heats to decide the night's top four.

The qualifiers for the final with 11 points each were: Guy Allott (Sheffield), Brian Craven (Newcastle), Wayne Briggs (Edinburgh) and myself. I'd dropped my only point to New Zealander Briggs in Heat 4.

At the first attempt to run the final, Craven held a slight lead over myself when Allott fell in the first corner while in third place and the race was re-started with all four back in.

Briggs led from the gate in the rerun and I was close behind. He made the mistake of sticking fairly close to the line but I followed the dirt nearer to the fence, riding the big sweeping bends in the same way that I always rode my home track at Exeter. My extra speed carried me past Wayne after a couple of laps or so and I went on to win the race and the biggest event of my career. I felt like a World Champion even

Trying to keep my white boots clean in this tussle with a couple of hungry Wolves, Rick France and Maury Mattingley, at Monmore Green. The green-and-white jerseys also made the Falcons stand out.

INSIDE AND OUT: Trying different race lines in this exciting battle with Sheffield's Ron Bagley at Owlerton.

My finest moment as a rider: Receiving that nice-looking trophy from Ron Cliffe after winning the Provincial League Riders' Final at Belle Vue. Shame I didn't get to keep it.
Below: On the tractor with Wayne Briggs and Brian Craven.

CUP WINNERS: When Exeter defeated Stoke in the 1962 KO Cup Final it capped a memorable year for me. Above: About to push off for a race against Potters' Jimmy Heard and Ron Sharp.

Above: Using the banking to get the better of Ken Vale.

Left: Pensive moments before a race in Falcons' most important match of '62.

though, of course, I wasn't.

With Briggs, Craven and myself on board, the old tractor took us for a celebration lap with me holding the huge silver trophy that had been presented to me as winner. Thousands of people jumped over the safety fence and surrounded the tractor which had to finally come to a halt. Right alongside the tractor appeared ex-rider Dent Oliver, then manager of Belle Vue. 'I'll look after that trophy for you Len,' he called and I gratefully handed him the immense cup, which enabled me to climb off the tractor and slowly make my way to the dressing room while signing autographs.

I was obviously very happy to have won but I felt that the £30 top prize was a bit on the mean side considering the huge attendance. Then I learned that £25 had been added by Ron Cliffe, a top Sheffield sponsor, which made it feel better. Not that money was my motive but it was still nice.

After a shower and having packed away my gear, I made my way to the speedway office to collect my huge trophy which I thought might look good on display in my car showroom. I entered to find Dent Oliver in there. 'I've come to pick up my trophy,' I said.

'No you don't,' said Dent. 'That trophy belongs to Belle Vue. We won it in 1937.'

'Oh, what do I get then?'

'This one,' replied Dent, before handing me a tiny plaque mounted on a bit of black plastic and measuring less than six inches long. It must have cost all of £2. I was devastated.

On the way home, with Dennis Day – who'd helped me in the pits that night – doing the driving, I threw the plaque out of the window. We both laughed about it.

The '62 season was almost over and I managed to retain the Silver Sash Match Race Championship title by beating Stoke's Pete Jarman at the County Ground, which meant I kept it throughout the winter months. To complete my best season in the sport as a rider, the team I was proud to captain, Exeter Falcons, emphatically won the Knockout Cup Final against Stoke.

The Potters included the fast-starting Colin Pratt, who was to become a life-long friend. Yes, 1962 was a memorable year.

I was 30-years-old and new doors were about to open . . .

Above: Our 1962 KO Cup-winning team – standing, left to right: Dave Stevens (PL secretary), Dennis Day, Francis Cann, Howdy Byford, Wally Mawdsley. Front: Alan Cowland, Pete Lansdale, myself and Eric Howe.
Below: Enjoying myself with the Falcons.

Chapter 7 – Rider to Promoter
MAKE IT A DATE, FRIDAY AT EIGHT

ALTHOUGH the 1963 season wasn't quite as successful for me as the one before, my team performances remained about the same and I was one of the leading scorers in the Provincial League.

Injuries to my knees, caused by looping at the gate, halted my progress in the PL Riders' Championship so I wasn't able to defend my title, won that year by Newcastle's Ivan Mauger.

However, I did win many friends with an off-track stunt that almost ended my life. The Exeter management had engaged the great Stanley Lindbergh who performed a high-diving act in which he finally dropped, all in flames, from a 100ft tower into a round tank containing just six feet of water.

I had blown up an engine during the preceding match against Newcastle and had no bike to ride for the second-half of the programme. So for a bit of fun I stripped off my racing leathers, keeping on only a pair of trunks and my white boots.

To everyone's amazement I climbed up the tower to a tiny platform half-way up, where I proceeded to copy Stanley Lindbergh by taking off my boots and ceremoniously dropping them to the ground. Everyone cheered loudly.

Now I'd intended to then climb down the tower ladder to safety but my nerves gave way. It seemed very high up and the vertical ladder impossible to get onto. I looked down at the extremely small tank a long way below me. There was no other way down for me, so I jumped, whizzing downward like a World War Two bomb, hitting the water hard. My feet smashed into the bottom of the tank and my knees came sharply up to hit my chin, knocking me out! I woke up being dragged from the tank and hearing a tumultuous cheer from the crowd.

Later I learned that because I'd jumped, rather than stepped off, the platform, I'd landed almost on the support wall of the tank instead of the centre of the water. Almost certain death would have resulted had I jumped just a few inches further out.

Once again my Guardian Angel had looked after me.

The 1963 season saw Mike Parker reopen Hackney Wick, which was very near to where I lived – over the showroom at Manor Park. It quickly became known as 'Agony Wick' because the track was so rough but I rode there a couple of times for Exeter with some good scores.

Sometime in about mid-summer I learned that Charlton Greyhound Stadium was up for rent and I fancied the idea of becoming a promoter. Wally Mawdsley, my boss at Exeter, quickly became interested and we decided to do something in partnership. We met the owners and half agreed a deal but it never materialised.

As the weeks went by we kept being given the run-around until we finally realised

Above left: Me and my Exeter team-mate Howdy Byford entertaining the crowd at Stoke.
Above right: The advertisement I placed on the back cover of the 1962 Speedway Digest.
Below: Leading on the heavily banked Exeter track from Eric Hockaday and Pete Jarman.

Two views of me racing for Exeter at Hackney in 1963, shortly before joining the Hawks as rider/co-promoter. Alan Cowland is my race partner in both shots, although I'm afraid I can't identify the home riders.

that it probably wasn't going to happen. Nonetheless we went on trying and started to put a team together in time for the 1964 season. We even attended that winter's promoters' conference with the idea of entering a Charlton team into the Provincial League.

But that was the 'Winter of Discontent'. The senior National League (First Division) had shrunk to just seven tracks and the then Speedway Control Board ordered the Provincial League champions, Wolverhampton, to elevate.

However, the astute Mike Parker, promoter at Wolves, flatly refused. In response, the Board threatened to take away his licence. But they had under-estimated the man and his power. He got his fellow promoters in the Provincial League to agree to run outside of the control of the SCB. All of the PL riders were warned by the SCB that if they rode on unlicensed tracks they would lose their own licences and lots of second division riders were very nervous about it.

Exeter were due to stage the first 'black' match in the middle of March, so I took it upon myself, as captain, to personally telephone every rider due to appear that day and persuade them to ride against the SCB's wishes. It turned out to be a miserable, cold and wet day but the stadium was packed with fans and every Exeter rider appeared, as did most of the Cradley Heath opposition.

The unlicensed league had got underway and in spite of more dire threats from the Control Board, the return match at Cradley Heath the next Saturday took place. But not before I had negotiated a better pay rate for all the riders with the promoters before the match started.

Mike Parker had opened a new Provincial League track at Somerton Park, Newport and I rode in one of the first meetings. And with a little luck on my side, I managed to win the Newport Open Championship. After the meeting Parker came over to me: 'I see you're not having any luck getting Charlton off the ground and, what's more, you won't get it. I've been negotiating for it myself but neither of us is going to get it, so it's not going to happen.'

I was shocked. I had no idea that Parker had been involved.

'If you want to be a speedway promoter, why don't you buy half of my business at Hackney?' he added.

This sudden offer hit me like a bombshell and for once in my life I was almost lost for words. But not for very long.

'How much will it cost me?'

'A grand,' Mike replied, 'and we can start the partnership right away.'

Within a week I'd sent Mike a cheque for a thousand pounds and I was his partner in the speedway track nearest my home.

Now I was in a silly situation – scoring heavily as captain of Exeter but owning half of rival club Hackney. Of course, it was obvious that I had to ride for my own team and after some delay I rode my last race in Exeter colours on Whit Monday in the Westward TV individual championship. There was, sadly, no triumphal exit for me. Instead, while contesting my last race where a win would have given me the title, I hit the steel fence while trying to pass the other three in the first bend and ended up very bruised, sore and with a badly buckled bike.

That was the end of my Exeter career and I became a member of the Hackney Hawks under the captaincy of Colin Pratt, who subsequently became a life-long friend. It was a natural move on my part to become involved in the management side of the business and all other aspects of promoting.

I wanted to get rid of all the holes in the Waterden Road track but my knowledge about such things was zilch and my efforts weren't very successful. But the learning process had begun and the track became a bit of an obsession with me – an obsession that stayed with me for the rest of my life.

Unhappily, my track work came to an abrupt halt because I suffered a bad racing accident, flying over the fence in the first bend and landing myself in hospital with a badly broken wrist, a cracked neck bone and a damaged shoulder. It laid me low for a while but when I was on the mend I decided that the management side of the business was what I should concentrate on. My new life as a fully-fledged promoter had begun.

It didn't take long for me to learn that promoting is a very risky business and by the end of the season Hackney had lost £3,000 and I had to send Mike Parker, my partner, £1,500. It was a huge sum of money in 1964 and I wasn't surprised that he wanted to 'cut its throat' and close down.

But I was determined to keep it open to run in the soon to be born British League. I agreed to buy Mike's half share for just £300 and with that I became sole promoter of Hackney – the start of 20 years' immense pleasure.

As I mentioned before, my idol was the great Johnnie Hoskins – the showman supreme. I decided to model myself on him. I went out and bought a trilby hat which I wore on the first day I presented myself as a promoter in front of the Hackney crowd. As an ex-rider I automatically had the goodwill of the Hawks' fans, so when I introduced the meeting using the centre green microphone I got a big cheer and in response I waved my hat, just as I'd seen Johnnie Hoskins do on countless occasions. I even copied his style of speech, albeit with a Cockney accent, and I thought that I was doing great.

Two weeks went by and my friend, Dave Stevens, who was the Hackney announcer and a 'black' referee at the time, came to me. 'What on earth are you doing waving that hat about and talking with a booming voice?'

'It's what Johnnie Hoskins would have done,' I said.

'Well, you're not Johnnie Hoskins, you're Len Silver and you'd be better off being a Len Silver than a second-hand Johnnie Hoskins.'

His words of wisdom hit home and I instinctively knew he was right. At that moment Len Silver, the promoter, was born!

That was in 1964 while Mike Parker was still my partner and our attendance figures were not very good. I began a series of events to try and persuade more people to come. In those days before sex discrimination laws came into force, girls were not allowed to ride speedway. However, we were running in the 'black' Provincial League with no Speedway Control Board to answer to – so I devised a girls' race.

Enjoying a yarn with my hero – the late, great Johnnie Hoskins. I'm so proud to have known him.

I can't remember how I found her but a pretty little 18-year-old called Mary Mansfield presented herself as a would-be rider. For about a month I trained her to ride a bike using the Hackney track every morning from seven o'clock until eight. She was an able pupil and eventually got to slide the bike, albeit not at full throttle.

Maury Mattingley, a good speedway rider who also manufactured frames (I was one of his customers during my racing days) telephoned me to say that his wife, Rosita, could ride a motorbike and it didn't take long to set up a match-race challenge between the two ladies.

I was astounded by the interest shown by the press and on the day of the race the *London Evening News* published half-a-page on our unique female match-race in all their editions. More than 500 extra people came to see the race – a huge success in percentage terms and highly satisfactory for me. Mary Mansfield, by the way, won the race and she turned out to be a great show-girl, playing to the crowd and extracting every possible cheer. I'd learned a good lesson in promoting.

It was during this period that I became known as Leapin' Len and it came about because I had started to generate enthusiasm from the crowd by leading them in war-cries. Over the public address system I'd start them off: '2-4-6-8, Who do we appreciate? H-A-C-K-N-E-Y – Hackney!' I'd shout louder than anyone. (Sadly, such war-cries are out of fashion these days.)

Then, as a follow-up to these cries, while the race was in progress I'd be on the centre green showing obvious excitement. If a Hackney rider passed his opponent I'd jump up and down waving my arms in the air in obvious joy. My plan was to let

My first season at Hackney, in 1964, and my last as a rider before I joined the promoting ranks.
Left to right: Roy Trigg, John Poyser, Brian Davies, Alec Ford (team manager), Dennis Day, Les McGillivray and myself, with skipper Colin Pratt on his JAP.

my own enthusiasm generate the same from the fans on the terraces, and I believe that it had that effect.

In an attempt to repeat the success of the girls' race I arranged with my good friend Allen Briggs, who ran stock cars at Walthamstow, to bring a stock car for a race against a speedway bike at Hackney. I announced the event as 'Man against Machine' and everyone wondered what it was all about. But I hit a snag. None of my riders would enter the race! So the event that I'd advertised looked like a non-starter.

However, I'd have none of that. If nobody else would do it, I'd do it myself! It was about three months after my accident so I was more or less OK although I hadn't ridden a bike. The day came and the stock car, driven by Allen, lined up on the back straight with me at the normal starting gate. Off we both went, flat stick. I could hear the roar of his four-litre engine as I kept my throttle wide open for four laps. Down came the chequered flag and it was declared a dead-heat. Honours were even and the crowd had their fun.

At the time I joined Mike Parker as a co-promoter, Hackney were running on Wednesday evenings and this seemed to me to be a poor choice. Very soon after I'd transferred from Exeter to Hackney I had talks with our landlords and agreed to run on Fridays instead. Fred Whitehead, one of the stadium directors and himself an ex-speedway promoter, told me that in pre-war days the Hackney slogan had been: 'Make it a Date – Friday at Eight!' I seized upon it eagerly and resurrected the slogan for it to become the nationally recognised Hackney motto. From then on, no-one was in any doubt what day we ran and at what time – an essential ingredient to successful promoting.

During this time I continued my business as a car dealer, retailing mostly from the showroom in Romford Road. It was an area, between Manor Park and Ilford, with car showrooms in abundance, where the public could choose from a huge range of vehicles, in very close proximity to each other. And most of us did very well.

It was necessary to stock as many cars as possible to ensure that any would-be buyer who wandered onto the premises had the biggest chance of finding a suitable vehicle. For the more modest dealers such as myself, this meant stocking more vehicles than could be paid for out of the capital available, and we had several ways of achieving this goal.

One of the most interesting aspects of the business was the 'cheque swapping game'. Myself and three other small dealers, including old friends Vic Gooden and Alby Smith, would meet a couple of times a week as necessary. Each of us would have been told by our respective bank managers how much money we would need to pay into the bank that day in order to meet payment of cheques we'd issued previously. So, for example, I might need, say, £3,000.

What would then happen is that Vic would give me a cheque for that amount. I, in turn, would give one of the other dealers a similar amount and that dealer would pass a £3,000 cheque to the fourth member, who would then issue a cheque to Vic. Each of us then had £3,000 to pay into our bank and those cheques would take at least three days to clear, effectively giving each of us £3,000 worth of capital for three days.

After the three days we'd all meet and repeat the same exercise but in the other direction, which meant we'd 'have' the money for six days at least. Of course, we actually varied the amounts slightly so that it wasn't obvious to the banks and it was a good wheeze so long as we could trust one another not to bounce any of the cheques! Fortunately, the people I dealt with were honourable men and we didn't ever let each other down. I'm sure the banks knew what we were doing but didn't care.

The motor business in those days had a very poor reputation in general, although, frankly, it was largely undeserved. I had serious dealings with quite a large circle of traders, all of whom I could trust implicitly and within our circle your word was your bond. A handshake was as good as a written contract.

Of course, there some villains in the game, some of whom I knew quite well even though I wouldn't have dreamed of dealing with them. One of them, who lived in the same East End street as the Kray twins, was known to have defrauded a finance company of about £25,000 – a huge sum at that time. He achieved it by submitting bogus hire purchase documents on vehicles he didn't own but which he knew for certain were not registered as being on HP, so they couldn't be checked. The vehicles he used, in particular their registered numbers, were for buses operating in Blackpool! He put them all 'on the strap' and promptly vanished with the money.

To my knowledge, he was never caught, although many of us knew who he was. No police ever came asking questions as they regarded finance companies as 'fair game' and didn't seem to care. They were bizarre times.

I learned a lot during my first season as a promoter – mostly the hard way by losing my money. It made me become very prudent as I tried to keep my costs to the bare minimum. Any rider signing for Hackney was always aware that he would probably have been paid more by other promoters. But I made up for it in other ways.

For example, by opening before the other tracks and closing later than them at the end of each season, it gave my riders two or three more meetings in which to earn their pay.

I made absolutely sure that my star men had the easiest route to the scratch race final (what was then the climax of the second-half of the programme, a small individual tournament between the riders of both teams).

I also made it my policy to pay everyone their money within a week of the meeting – and I never failed in that even when times were particularly hard. Then I had to subsidise the speedway income with money from my motor sales.

The Hackney track, after I had altered it to make it smooth and heavily banked, became famous for its excellent racing and the vast majority of riders from all over the world loved racing there. It was my pride and joy and I spent countless hours in preparation, grading and re-grading day after day. I loved doing it and there is no doubt that because of the quality of racing it produced, Hackney followers became very loyal in spite of little silverware won by the Hawks.

The riders who wore the famous chequered body colour of the Hackney Hawks all became great personal friends and throughout my 20 years at The Wick none of them ever screwed me for money. They all knew that I paid

Leapin' Len gets 'em going at The Wick.

Charles Foot (left), who once tried to insult me, pictured with Reg Fearman and myself.

the most I could afford and, looking back, I'm quite humbled by that thought.

For the most part I got on well with the other promoters, although one I admired greatly, the late Charlie Foot of Poole, once called me a 'guttersnipe'. It was his term of ridicule for a Cockney because I'd signed up a promising junior ahead of him. Far from being insulted, I thought it was hilarious.

There were some I didn't really hit it off with, one of whom was John Berry, promoting at Ipswich. From the time of our first senior meetings with the Witches in the early 70s, he seemed to introduce an atmosphere of unfriendliness in his pits, where visiting riders were deliberately harassed by his staff. I didn't care much for that and our mutual dislike of each other certainly filtered into the crowd and matches between our two clubs were almost always 'needle' affairs.

When I visited his Foxhall Heath track with my team I only had to step out onto the shale to provoke the jeers and boos of the Ipswich crowd. Maybe some of the older supporters on the terraces had been there years earlier to see me race for their team? Anyway, I lapped it up!

But I didn't like John and in later years that dislike was intensified when he wrote disgraceful words about my marital status in his speedway programme for which I have never forgiven him.

At the close of my first season as a promoter at Hackney I organised a big firework display, something which my hero Hoskins had always done. It was a good show and the crowd loved it but it was mightily expensive, so I decided that I should do something else to spice up a final meeting instead of spending money I couldn't afford on fireworks. I hit on a plan which ultimately became a popular feature of season-ending meetings at Hackney.

I placed alongside the start-line area a small amount of petrol and some matches. Then I cleaned and pressed some old trousers which I wore over very tight-fitting swimming trunks. At the end of racing all the Hackney riders were called to the starting line where they spoke over the public address system to say their farewells to the crowd. At the end of the last speech it was pre-planned that they would grab me and strip off my trousers, which were then burned with the petrol, before covering me in flour which I'd also placed at the start line in readiness.

It was a hilarious piece of slapstick, knock-about fun in which I ended up trouserless and covered in white flour.

Hackney favourite Bengt Jansson leading the traditional end-of-season fun and games as I once again find myself trouserless and caked in flour and water.

The fans, particularly the kids, loved it to bits – and it cost nothing! We did it every year and each time we tried to make it more hilarious, with the riders chasing me all over the centre green as I tried to escape from my uncomfortable fate.

But one year I had a huge fright. As usual they chased and caught me, stripped of my shoes and trousers and made a bonfire of them. Then, unexpectedly, they doused me in water from a bucket that had previously held petrol, causing the water to stink of petrol. I thought that they had unwittingly doused me in fuel!

So when they then picked me up to hold me over the burning flames, you can imagine my panic. On that occasion I struggled and kicked more intensely than ever before because I really believed that I'd be going up in flames! Of course, I didn't but it certainly put real fear into my heart.

On another season-ending jolly one of my riders, Geoff Maloney, who also worked part-time for a chimney sweep, smothered me in black soot instead of flour. My God it was awful – it got in my mouth and my eyes and I couldn't breath properly. I was staggering helplessly all over the place, unable to see. Needless to say the crowd loved it. The more uncomfortable I was, the better they liked it.

I suffered for my showmanship.

Chapter 8 – The sport expands
SPREADING THE WORD

WHEN I first took over from Mike Parker as sole promoter at Hackney after buying his shares in 1965, I realised that a huge amount of publicity work and local promotion needed to be done if the track was to make progress.

The first action I took was to use a big, red Commer van, that I'd taken in part exchange for a car at my Manor Park showroom, and turn it into a publicity vehicle. Both sides were covered in posters advertising Hackney Speedway and I had it fitted with a loudspeaker system – a bit like those used by politicians during election campaigns.

On Friday afternoon I would drive around the local area with BBC radio music blaring out of the loudspeakers. Every couple of minutes I'd interrupt the music and over the speakers I'd announce: 'This music comes to you courtesy of Hackney Wick Speedway. Exciting dirt-track action takes place tonight at eight when the Hackney Hawks take on (insert opponents) in a league match. You'll enjoy 20 heats of non-stop action with thrills and spills to excite you and your children. Don't forget it's Hackney Wick Stadium every Friday. Make it a Date – Friday at Eight!'

People always seemed to take notice but every now and then a member of the Metropolitan Police would stop me and make me disconnect the equipment because I didn't have a licence to broadcast. Needless to say, I'd move along a mile or so and start up again.

Then I started fly posting (now considered highly illegal but, although illegal even then, almost acceptable in the East End of London in the late 60s). I would go out at night all along the Mile End Road and all over the East End slapping up colourful advertising posters on every place that I could. It became a source of annoyance that soon after I put them up, they would disappear. I always wondered why until about six weeks or so after the first posting I got a phone call. It was from a guy (whose name I can't remember) who made it clear that he was one of about six men who,

The main grandstand and home straight at Hackney Stadium in 1969.
Below: It looks as if the fly posting has worked.

Bringing some Christmas cheer to the boys on the children's ward at Homerton Hospital in 1966. Hawks rider Gary Everett, team manager Maurice Morley and myself paid them a visit, which proved another good PR exercise.

between them, controlled the fly posting all over London.

'You either work through me, mate, or your signs get covered as soon as you put them up,' he told me.

I was dumbfounded, not realising that a sort of mafia controlling London's illegal poster advertising even existed.

My first reaction was to tell him to get stuffed but I realised that, in fact, he held all the aces and I either had to stop the poster campaign or do it through him. Reluctantly, I agreed that we should pay him to do it and started working with him straight away.

I came to realise very quickly that it actually wasn't a bad idea. Hackney posters could be seen all over the place and it was almost impossible to miss them. He did a great job and I never regretted having to endure his threats.

Another problem I had in the 60s was the lack of public transport to get to the stadium. Hackney Wick is a little hidden corner of the great metropolis, tucked away at the edge of Hackney Marshes. Not everybody had cars in those days, so a bus service was almost essential. I spoke to a couple of local coach companies but either they weren't interested or their fees were such as to make the idea prohibitive.

Not to be thwarted, though, I bought three old coaches myself and set up a company called Essex Coachways Ltd, to run the service transporting fans to the stadium, mostly from pick-ups at Stratford Broadway. It was quite successful and a guy I met ran it for me and also picked up a few school contracts to help pay the costs. Unfortunately, he dropped dead soon afterwards and I was left to cope with the business on my own, knowing nothing about it.

I then linked up with another coach operator, called Smith, who took over the running. However, he used the link mostly for his own ends and it wasn't long before he placed me in an impossible situation in which I was forced to sell my half share of the business to him. It was either that or for me to get nothing, because the company would go belly up. I took about three grand for my share and, lo and behold, almost immediately afterwards Essex Coachways started to prosper as if by magic!

A little later the bus service was operated by my long-standing friend Peter Sampson, an ex-rider, who'd started a travel and coach company, and he operated it very successfully. In later years he went into the Zoo business and acquired Paradise Wildlife Park in Broxbourne, Hertfordshire, where the Speedway Museum is now situated. So my first few years at Hackney were certainly eventful.

Chapter 9 – Rayleigh

RE-LAUNCHING THE ROCKETS

THE new British Speedway League was founded in 1965 following a ruling by Sir Hartley Shawcross, the Solicitor General, which took control of the sport away from the original Speedway Control Board Ltd and handed it to the promoters, and it became a thriving and successful endeavour.

The public obviously approved of the set-up – an amalgamation of the old National League and Provincial League – and from 1965 to 1967 I enjoyed running Hackney as a member of the new British Speedway Promoters' Association (BSPA). It was not part of my plan to be an empire-builder but, as events turned out, that was exactly what I became.

At a gathering of promoters, my friend and former Ipswich team manager Maurice Littlechild, who had opened the track at King's Lynn a couple of years earlier, suggested to me that we should join together to open speedway at the Tilehurst Stadium in Reading. Within minutes he'd pulled Reg Fearman, Ron Wilson and Danny Dunton into the plan and the five of us all thought it a good idea.

Simultaneously other promoters were suggesting the formation of a British League Second Division, so the five of us agreed to help get the new league going at the start of 1968. Within days we'd formed a company called Allied Presentations Ltd and had moved to open tracks that had fallen by the wayside a few years earlier.

My role was to reopen Rayleigh, which was still running stock cars at the time even though speedway hadn't been seen at the Essex raceway since the Rockets were withdrawn from the PL in 1963. It was there that I met Peter Thorogood, an avid Rayleigh Rockets fan, and recruited him onto my track staff. It was to begin a life-long association and friendship and we worked together in various guises and at numerous tracks over the years.

At about this time I received a phone call out of the blue from New Zealand. 'Hello, is that Mr. Silver?'

'Yes, who is this?'

'My name is Graeme Smith and I live in New Zealand. But I'm coming to England to ride speedway for you. I reckon I can do you a big favour and score plenty of points.'

'Oh, do you? Well, when you get here, give me a ring' and I put the phone down and promptly forgot all about the call, which I thought came from a nutcase. However, a couple of weeks or so later the phone rang again. 'Hello, Mr. Silver, it's Graeme Smith here and I'm in Weymouth.'

I was very surprised: 'What are you doing in Weymouth?'

Happy days: On the centre green with Reg Fearman (far right – Maury Littlechild and Danny Dunton are partly hidden behind him) at Reading's Tilehurst Stadium after Second Division speedway opened there in 1968.

'Well, I arrived two days ago and I know Barry Briggs. He's running a speedway school at Weymouth this Sunday and he'll let me ride one of his bikes.'

'OK,' I replied, now half convinced that he wasn't a nut. 'I'll come down to Weymouth and see you in action.'

Sunday morning turned out to be a wet and cold late winter's day and I set off in my Volvo, windscreen wipers on the go the whole way there. It was about 11.00am when I arrived, the rain by now just fine mist. I walked out onto the track to find the surface, as expected, very wet and muddy. A voice behind me said: 'Mr. Silver, I'm Graeme.' I turned and found standing there a slim young man in his late teens dressed in a pale blue corduroy suit.

'Hello, son, call me Len. No-one calls me Mr. Silver. Are you getting ready to ride?'

'Yes, Barry said I can ride his bike and it's being warmed up in the pits now.'

'Well, you'd better go and get changed then,' and he duly disappeared towards the dressing room.

A few riders were in action and it didn't surprise me that they were all having

*Popular Dingle Brown at Rayleigh in 1968 – the season
we reopened speedway at The Weir.*

difficulty handling the wet track. Soon Graeme appeared pushing the Jawa machine onto the track. He had on his corduroy suit, a pair of boots obviously too big for him and a crash helmet he'd borrowed. I gasped: 'Are you going to ride dressed like that?'

'Sure, I'll be OK,' and with that he got someone to push him off and started the machine. He toured slowly for a lap and let it rip. Flat out in the mud and although a bit wobbly in the conditions, he could obviously handle a bike.

'No,' I thought, 'he's no nutcase.'

After a few laps he came back into the pits. I heard myself saying: 'You'll do, son, give back the boots and helmet, and get into my car. I'm taking you home.'

I made the story known at the time and dubbed him 'The Corduroy Kid'.

He turned out to be an ace discovery and rode for me in the ensuing years at Rayleigh, Hackney and Sunderland.

While at Weymouth that day I also saw another youngster called Laurie Etheridge, who impressed me with the courageous way he rode in those awful track conditions. I signed him up too. So my damp trip to the south-west was very fruitful indeed.

I had by this time more or less given up on the motor trade to concentrate on promoting. I sold my Manor Park showroom and moved with Vera, my wife, and daughter Jackie, then aged 12 and a horse-riding enthusiast, to a nice semi-detached at Rise Park, on the edge of Romford. My son Andrew was born and spent his early years in that house with Graeme Smith living with us as part of our family.

The young Kiwi was a member of my Rayleigh Rockets team and as Andrew got older he would take him for rides on the handlebars of his speedway bike. It scared me and Vera to death – but my son loved it to bits.

One day Jackie arrived home from school with one of her mates who came from a broken home. My daughter had befriended her and asked if she could stay with us for a while. We both agreed and she shared a room with Jackie. Her name was Hazal and little did I know at that time what an enormous influence she was to become in my life. Then she was just a 14-year-old girl, who immediately started to care for my son and she fitted into our home in the most natural way.

My marriage to Vera certainly wasn't one that was made in heaven and, after 15 years, cracks were beginning to show. My workaholic life did nothing to enhance our relationship and Vera got no excitement or enjoyment out of my occupation, so it wasn't surprising that she sought these in other ways and she started modest

My young son Andrew just before being taken for a ride around Rayleigh with 'The Corduroy Kid', Graeme Smith.

gambling to give her life some spice. But we bumped along together without too much disharmony. Like many marriages, I suppose, each of us facing the fact that we had different interests but also a family to care for.

The house in Cree Way, Romford was ideally situated for our Saturday trips to Rayleigh Speedway but quite the opposite for my daily run to get to my office at Hackney Stadium. Not that it was very far, it was just the horrendous traffic that filtered into London via the Southend Arterial and it often took me an hour to do a

LIFT OFF: The relaunch of the Rayleigh Rockets gave me a lot of satisfaction. Here (above) is our 1969 line-up – left to right: Mike Gardner, Dingle Brown, Dennis Mannion, Roger Wright, Terry Stone and Laurie Etheridge, with myself and skipper Geoff Maloney on the bike. Below: A year on, the 1970 Rockets are – left to right: Charlie Mugford, Barry Lee, Gary Moore, Laurie Etheridge, Laurie Guilfoyle, Geoff Maloney, Tony Hall, (not sure about this one!), Dingle Brown, Terry Stone and myself.

25-minute drive. I made up my mind to move closer to Hackney as soon as money and opportunity allowed.

Much as I loved running Hackney Speedway every Friday, I also really enjoyed the Saturday involvement at Rayleigh. The stadium there had a rather special atmosphere, mostly created by the announcer, Maurice Jardine, who had a happy knack of using every announcement to help create enjoyment. One of his ploys was to start a chant whenever my rider Dingle Brown appeared. Dingle was a good-looking young man that all the females in the stadium loved to bits. He was also quite a handy rider, so he had plenty going for him.

As he would leave the pits to ride almost a full lap to the starting gate, Maurice Jardine would start chanting 'Din-gle', 'Din-gle' and the crowd would pick it up on it *en masse* – I'm sure their chanting could be heard at the end of Southend Pier. It was magic.

As it turned out, Dingle became a life-long friend and at one point we even did a bit of business together, selling a few cars. He was always fun to be with and we had a lot of laughs. Years later he became a speedway promoter at Wimbledon and Mildenhall and, like myself, looked back on a riding career that was very unkind to him. He suffered a seriously broken thigh at Exeter and a broken back at King's Lynn. It didn't dampen his enthusiasm, though.

One afternoon in September 1968 we were busy at Rayleigh watering the track in preparation for that evening's racing. Helping me was Charlie Mugford, an ex-rider and, as it happens, the very man who got me onto a speedway bike for the first time 20 years earlier. He casually turned to me and said: 'I've just booked up for my holiday.'

'Cripes, you're a bit late, ain't you?'

'Oh no, we go ski-ing,' he said.

'Bloody hell, that sounds like a great thing to do,' I said, intrigued.

'Yeah, we've been going away for four years and it's great. Hey, why don't you come with us?'

I was taken aback. 'Can I really?' I said.

'Sure,' said Charlie. 'We rent this apartment in Alpbach and there's plenty of room. We're going in January – it would be great if you came with us.'

That conversation probably had more influence in my life than any other and when January 1969 arrived my daughter, Jackie, then 14, came with me and Charlie and Jean Mugford to Austria for our first ski-ing experience. Vera didn't want to come and she stayed at home to look after two-year-old Andrew.

We all drove to the Austrian village of Alpbach in my VW estate car and as we crossed Germany towards Munich on the autobahn, it started snowing heavily. The journey took all day and we finally arrived in the pretty village, 3,000ft above sea level, at about 9pm. Our apartment was spacious and very alpine with everything built in pinewood to give it a very local atmosphere. Deep snow was everywhere and Jackie and I were very excited about getting on our skis the next day.

It was Sunday morning and the sun shone as Charlie took us both to the ski rental shop. There we were kitted out with strong, leather lace-up boots and skis almost two metres long – the fashion in those days. It was intended that we were to attend the local ski school but their activities didn't start until Monday, so Charlie took my daughter and me to the centre of the village where there was a field with a very gentle slope covered in deep, white snow.

He showed us how to shape our skis into a snowplough, to enable us to slow down or stop, and left us to practice while he joined some friends to ski on the upper slopes. We both started to slide down the field, making our own tracks in the deep snow. At first we kept falling over at the bottom but after a few goes we got the hang of stopping with the snowplough, heels out, toes in, and our runs to the bottom became much quicker. Mind you, the walk back up to the top made us pant a bit and neither of us enjoyed that.

We practiced for most of the day and while doing so watched with envy at the people above us using a T-bar drag lift facility to get to the top of the nursery slope there. The idea of not having to walk up seemed very appealing and it must have been at about four o'clock that I suggested to Jackie that we might spread our wings a bit and use the steeper slope above us, with the drag lift to get us to the top.

By now the sun had dipped below the peaks and it became immediately very cold. However, as I'd been working really hard all day I was actually very hot and I'd put my hat in my pocket and had my anorak fully open. In that state we both lined up to get on the lift, not even realising that we needed a ticket and certainly having no idea how to use it. The rather elderly attendant asked for our tickets in a heavy German accent and we had no idea what he was saying. Getting somewhat frustrated by our inability to respond, he allowed us to step into position ready for the T-bar to pull us up the slope. In our ignorance, when the bar came round as we stood side by side, we both tried to sit on it – and landed on our backsides on the ground. A couple more efforts with the same result gradually taught us that we had to remain with our weight on our feet, so that the bar could just pull, rather than carry, us up the hill.

But by this time my body had cooled down dramatically and my hatless head was beginning to feel painful in the ice-cold air. As we were pulled up the slope, which now seemed far steeper than it had when we were looking at it from the lower field, I became colder and colder and my forehead was so painful I began to feel quite faint.

We arrived at the top and instantly fell in a heap as we disengaged ourselves from the T-bar. I laid there feeling quite ill and very sorry for myself and watched with some amazement as Jackie got to her feet and headed face-forward down what looked like the North Face of the Eiger. At what seemed like about 200mph she hurtled down and ended up crashing alarmingly at the bottom. Through watery eyes I could just make out what had happened and it only served to make me feel more poorly than before, especially as I wondered how on earth I'd get down the slope.

Over to my left I could just about make out a white wooden fence and, with my mind not functioning normally, I thought: 'If only I can get to that fence, I'll be safe.' Somehow I half crawled and slid down and across what felt like a cliff-face to arrive at the fence, which I clung on to as tightly as I could. 'God help me now and save me from certain death.' This thought was, of course, a slight exaggeration of

Only Charlie Mugford and me didn't have on our blue-and-yellow bobble hats for this chilly early season visit to our Essex rivals Romford in 1971. The riders – left to right: Allan Emmett, Hugh Saunders, Bob Young, Terry Stone, Dingle Brown and Alan Jackson, with Geoff Maloney aboard his two-valve Jawa.

the situation but it was a scary experience at the time.

Unbeknown to me, Charlie Mugford had arrived to see how we were getting on. He summed up the situation quickly and came to my rescue, half carrying me down to the bottom where I discovered Jackie none the worse for her experience. Charlie wrapped me in his own anorak to warm me up and as I thawed out, the faintness and nausea faded away and I quickly got back to normal. How we laughed about it over dinner that evening and how I've laughed about it with Jackie many times since.

The next day, Monday, I enlisted into the ski school and we had Ruth, a German girl in her 20s, as our instructor. She was absolutely brilliant and within four or five days we could snowplough, stem turn, kick turn and sideslip and be able to tackle a large part of the ski-ing area. Both Jackie and myself were totally hooked, although I had to admit that she managed to master the technique far more readily than me. Much as I loved it, I didn't find it easy but I had already made up my mind that ski-ing was an activity to be enjoyed as often as possible. I had my 37th birthday while on that holiday in Alpbach.

Above: The main entrance at Crewe Speedway, where we opened to a huge crowd in 1969.
Left: Colin Tucker – the man who built the massive, new 420-yard track around a cricket field.
Below: One of the early Kings teams in '69 – left to right: Geoff Curtis, Ian Bottomley, Dave Parry (on bike), Pete Seaton, Glyn Blackburn, Pete Saunders, Rob Jackson.

Chapter 10 – Crewe & Sunderland
ALLIED FORCES

AT the start of 1969 our company Allied Presentations Ltd had opened a big, banked track on railway property in Crewe. The whole place had been built from old railway sleepers supplied at five shillings each from our landlords.

We had employed a young New Zealand rider called Colin Tucker, who was also a carpenter by trade, to do the construction work. He rode for me in my first season at Rayleigh before joining the new 'Kings' in '69.

Almost single-handed, he built the safety fence on the outside of the huge track (which circled a cricket pitch), the perimeter fence and turnstile buildings. It was a superb achievement and when we opened for the first ever Monday night's racing with our team called the Crewe Kings facing my own outfit, the Rayleigh Rockets, the stadium was so packed with people we never ever knew just how many there were. But we took enough money that night to almost pay for the comparatively modest cost of the building work.

My co-director Maurice Littlechild was in charge of Crewe and every Monday I would drive up with him and his teenage nephew Buster Chapman (later to become the owner of King's Lynn Speedway) from his home near Epping Forest to help him run the meeting. At the end of which we'd break all speed records doing the 190-mile journey home in just over two hours! We were always on the look-out for blue flashing lights.

In 1971 I sold our house in Romford and moved to Eagle Lane, Snaresbrook, which was only about 10-15 minutes' drive from Hackney, cutting my daily travelling time dramatically.

My son Andrew was then four-years-old and we bought him his first motorbike. It was a small Italjet machine which worked only with a throttle and brakes – no gears, no clutch – so it was very simple for a small boy to ride. He loved it and would ride it all the time in the garden and sometimes even inside the home, riding it through the kitchen into the lounge and back into the other end of the kitchen to complete a small circuit. Vera wasn't very happy!

Being much nearer to Hackney Stadium it was easier for me to bring home some hot supper after our Friday night meetings and it was my habit to stop off on the way home at the pie and mash shop at Harrow Green, on Leytonstone Road, to buy pies, mash and liqueur plus some stewed eels which were still hot when I reached our home in Eagle Lane. None of us thought about our waistlines as we tucked into traditional East End fare that I'd loved since a child living in Old Ford Road, Bow, before the war.

The house had cost £20,000 but I'd earned a good profit on the Romford property so the mortgage only amounted to £15,000. It was a very good investment, perfectly positioned just behind the Eagle Hotel in the best part of Snaresbrook, and its value was about to rise dramatically as property inflation started its relentless rise. It was as true then as it is today – that bricks and mortar are probably the best investment anyone can make.

Soon after moving in to Eagle Lane in 1971, Allied Presentations acquired the speedway rights at Sunderland, where the sport hadn't been staged since a premature closure in 1964. The track was a mere 300 miles from where I lived! As it was the sixth track in our little Allied empire, it meant one of the five of us had to be responsible for two venues – and it was workaholic Joe Muggins who drew the short straw.

Sunderland Stars ran on Sunday afternoons, so I had a hectic four-day stint: Hackney on Friday, Rayleigh on Saturday, Sunderland on Sunday and Crewe on Monday. Thinking about it now, the North-Eastern track was the most bizarre in many ways.

Three of the Sunderland riders – the father-and-son combination of George and John Barclay, plus Graeme Smith – came from my neck of the woods. On Sunday mornings at about eight o'clock, we'd set off with the three speedway bikes on a trailer behind my car and the four of us crammed inside. Off we'd go up the A11, then the A14 and join the Great North Road at Huntingdon, eating up the miles before stopping near Doncaster for a quick café lunch. We'd finally arrive at East Boldon, just outside Sunderland, where the stadium stood, just after one o'clock.

While the riders sorted out their bikes I would start to water the track and generally prepare for the meeting. One or two of the extremely friendly locals, including the late George English whose son, George jnr, went on to promote the sport at Newcastle, used to help me and at 3pm we'd start racing.

The official position of 'clerk of the course', whose responsibility it was to ensure that the meeting ran smoothly and that everything was in accordance to the rule book, was a job I couldn't find anyone to take on. The speedway rules didn't allow a promoter to hold a clerk of the course licence, so I wasn't allowed to do it myself. So, tongue in cheek, I took a chance and applied for a licence to the Speedway Control Board in the name of Nel Revlis (my own name spelt backwards). To my utter amazement, the licence was duly issued and no-one ever queried it. The very idea makes me laugh like a drain even today!

After running the meeting, I'd climb aboard the tractor and grade the track ready for the following meeting, while the riders got changed. I'd collect up all the official paperwork from the referee and off southwards we'd all go, leaving East Boldon by about six o'clock.

Once in the car, George Barclay would drive while I sat in the back working out the riders' pay and writing out the pay sheets and cheques. Then I'd write the programme notes and do the programme lay-out ready for the printer, write up the riders' booking forms for their meetings due to come, and check the fixture list for any changes that needed to be made.

STAR-GAZING: The Sunderland team in 1972. Left to right: Jack Millen, Brian Whaley, Graeme Smith, (team manager), George Barclay, Dave Gatenby and Pete Wrathall, with skipper Russ Dent on the bike.

Right: 'Gentleman' George Barclay, who accompanied me on the weekly 600-mile round trip to the North-East.

I'd then take over the driving while George wrote his section of the following week's programme – the column headed 'Captain's Corner.' We'd stop for a greasy supper about half-way home and finally arrive back in Eagle Lane by midnight – the whole operation wrapped up completely in one single but very busy day.

My fellow directors in Allied Presentations really had no idea what I did or how I did it. All they knew was that Sunderland ran smoothly, although it was never a big money-spinner After two years of the 600-mile round trip every Sunday we pulled out of the track and sold the operation for £1,500 to Elizabeth Taylor and her son, Ken, who were already running speedway at Berwick.

'Crazy' Jack after joining Sunderland from Crewe. I've never seen anyone tougher, on and off the track.

Chapter 11 – Jack Millen
CRAZY JACK

JACK Millen was one of the riders who appeared in my Sunderland Stars team. He was the toughest man I ever knew and I loved him to bits. He came over from New Zealand to ride for Crewe in 1971 and I picked him up at Tilbury Dock when he first arrived.

As he had nowhere to live and I had no room at my home, I let him lodge for several days in my office at Hackney before he headed for lodgings in Crewe. To me it was the least I could do for a man so far from home but, to Jack, it was as if I'd given him a luxury flat to live in. Ever afterwards he'd do anything for me without question and relish the task.

As I said, he was tough, both on and off the track. One day, while riding in his normal head down, ass-up style, he crashed and broke his ankle. Naturally, I expected him to be sidelined for several weeks. But I soon learned how formidable and determined this wholehearted character really was.

His left leg was encased in a plaster cast from his foot right up to his knee. Most riders would have been out for weeks but Jack just had a huge steel shoe made to go over the plaster and he simply carried on racing. It was amazing – he never even eased off!

Any rider in a race with Jack knew they faced a fearless opponent. They were very well aware he'd take the craziest chances to beat them. That's why I dubbed him 'Crazy Jack Millen' – and the name stuck.

One cold winter's day Jack was doing some work for us at Crewe Stadium and I decided to drive up there to see how he was getting on, as well as taking him some wages. As I left home in the morning it was bitter with sleet driving almost horizontal in the wind. Up the M1 I went with the heater in the car and the windscreen wipers both going at full pelt. The further north I travelled, the windier it got and when I finally arrived at the stadium, next to the railway lines behind the Kings Arms Pub (hence the team's nickname), I didn't want to get out of the car.

The stadium gates were open, so I knew Jack was there, and I pulled on my big overcoat and hat as I made my way to the old cricket pavilion where our offices and changing rooms were located. I expected to find Jack huddled over a fire somewhere in the building but the place was empty.

Pulling up my coat collar, I ventured out onto the track, the sleet stinging my face and the icy cold wind making my nose tingle. I could see no sign of Jack around the speedway pits or the pavilion area, so I crossed the track onto the wet cricket pitch. Vision was very limited and it was like walking in a dense freezing fog.

As I crossed the pitch I could barely make out a figure ahead of me but as I got closer I could see someone busily wielding a shovel. At last I was close enough and

Chatting with Jack Millen in the pits at West Ham in 1972, just weeks before the famous old Custom House track where I'd first watched speedway was sadly closed for redevelopment.

there I finally saw it was Crazy Jack – dressed in shorts, a singlet, and flip-flops on his bare feet – shovelling red shale as fast as he could go.

'Christ, Jack, what are you doing? You'll catch pneumonia, you silly bastard.'

'No mate, not me. I'm getting myself fit for the season!'

THAT was Crazy Jack.

He suffered so many injuries on the track but just got on with it. Nothing, it seemed, could keep this iron man down for long.

Until the awful early hours of Saturday, April 29, 1978, when this great crowd-pleaser (who was riding for Berwick by then) was killed after his Jag collided with an articulated lorry on the A1 at Grantshouse. Jack's car burst into flames and a young lad travelling with him also died in the accident.

I cried for a week.

Chapter 12 – Breaking up
LIFE CHANGES

IN the early 70s I continued making every effort to make Hackney pay its way and be successful. The team was young and exciting but tragedy struck in the summer of 1971, when Graham Miles, whose contract I had acquired from the great Johnnie Hoskins (who then promoted at Canterbury), ran into the fence and hit a gate post head-first. He crushed his vertebrae and lost the use of his legs.

The heartbreak of that incident was all the more hurtful when Hackney fans recognised that, in Graham, the team had a highly courageous and talented youngster who would undoubtedly have lifted the Hawks to great success.

The boy himself was not bitter about the dreadful accident and went on to lead an almost normal life, albeit wheelchair-bound, earning a living, first as a motor mechanic and later on in showbusiness. It was certainly a case of mind over matter and Graham Miles is a shining example to us all.

I was always trying to think up ways of entertaining the crowd and one day I set up what I thought was going to be a great wheeze. Daughter Jackie had a boyfriend whose general features and build were quite similar to mine. One Friday I dressed him in my white jacket and Hackney tie while I put on women's clothes using my old white racing boots which, from a distance, looked like those worn by 'Essex Girls' at the time.

Then 'he' interviewed me over the public address system. I spoke for 'him' and he spoke as the girl. No-one twigged I was the 'girl' or who Jackie's boyfriend really was. Out came our captain Barry Thomas on his machine and I, as the girl, was to have a ride round the track with him as a prize for winning the raffle. I climbed onto the front of the bike, engine revving, with Barry sat behind. I let out the clutch, only to turn the bike over because of Barry's weight on the back. I fell on my knees, grazing the skin in the process and drew lots of blood. The crowd gasped in horror but still didn't realise that the 'victim' of this prank wasn't actually a girl. I was gobsmacked that our little subterfuge hadn't been found out.

Once again I got on the bike, bloody knees and all, this time whispering to Barry not to put any weight on the back wheel. Now I let the clutch bang home, engine at full throttle and, as planned, 'Thommo' fell off the back as I roared off.

Even at that point the crowd still thought I was a girl and reckoned that I had totally got out of control and was hanging on to a monster of a machine with my life hanging by a thread! Naturally, I roared around the track, sliding at full throttle to complete the lap back to the start line, where Jackie's boyfriend had been jumping up and down to imitate me.

I got off the now silent machine, removed my big blonde wig and bowed to the fans who were roaring with delight – finally realising it was all a huge hoax.

It was during these years that Hackney enjoyed the services of the great Swedish rider Bengt 'Banger' Jansson and the finest Polish rider ever, Zenon Plech. They not only both served Hackney with distinction but became great personal friends of mine – a privilege I enjoy to this day, long after they have both retired from racing.

Zenon lived with me for a long period and at one time I had intended to legally adopt him to get him out of the then Russian-controlled Poland for good. But he had family commitments in Gdansk and wouldn't let me do it for fear of repercussions from the ruling communist regime.

Although the passage of time means that various incidents in my life become mixed up, date-wise, and my memory doesn't always get things in their chronological order, one date is stamped inside my head for ever. It was November 16, 1974 , the day my daughter married Dave 'Tiger' Beech, one of my Rayleigh riders – a likeable young man with a powerful sense of humour.

We had the wedding reception at home in Eagle Lane and the hugely successful day only brought home to me that my daughter's married happiness, about to begin, only highlighted the fact that Vera and I had drifted further and further apart. In reality we were both overdue for a change – and it happened with a bang.

Jackie's friend Hazal, who had become part of our family, had grown into a highly attractive 20-year-old and I secretly admired her, although at that stage I didn't have the guts to do anything about it. I didn't realise that she had secretly come to love me. Jackie's wedding changed all that and we then began a love affair which in one way or another was to last the rest of our lives.

It wasn't long before our affair became widely known and I left Vera to live with Hazal – initially in a caravan in the newly-built Reading Speedway stadium at Smallmead, from where we commuted to Hackney and Rye House each week.

Vera and I had a mutually agreeable 'quickie' divorce in which she became the sole owner of the big house in Eagle Lane while I retained the various speedway enterprises I was involved in. It was an arrangement which suited us both and we had no acrimony between us. Although our marriage had not been as successful as it might have been, we always remained friends until she died in August 2009.

The building of the new purpose-built Reading Stadium in the winter of 1974-75 had caused the split of Allied Presentations Ltd. Not all of the consortium wanted to be involved in the highly risky and expensive business of constructing a new stadium on a council rubbish tip.

Dear Maury Littlechild had died prematurely of cancer in the summer of 1972, otherwise different decisions may have been taken. Maury was an outstanding entrepreneur and despite his interests at King's Lynn and Crewe, he would undoubtedly have wanted to be involved in this exciting new enterprise.

Although I was involved in promoting Speedway at many nationwide venues as a partner in Allied Presentations, the income from this source was actually quite modest. It was mostly a labour of love with the odd share-out between the five of us amounting to a few hundred quid about three or four times a year. We'd all meet at

Toddington Service Station, on the M1 just north of Watford, where we'd have a bite to eat in the restaurant and report to each other the financial state of the tracks that we were directly involved in. Each of us would bring five envelopes to the table containing a 20 per cent share of whatever profit had been earned since our previous get-together. Overall it didn't amount to a great deal and none of us were getting rich out of that enterprise. But it was huge fun and a very exciting time of my life.

As it was, Ron Wilson and Danny Dunton pulled out to concentrate on their main businesses running Leicester and Peterborough respectively, leaving Reg Fearman and myself to find new partners to join us at Reading.

The unlucky Graham Miles shortly before his career-ending crash.

Frank Higley, a timber merchant and plant hire businessman, and Bill Dore, a dog-racing enthusiast who owned a big building business in Wiltshire, were the chosen two and we set about creating the new stadium that would become home to the 'Racers' following their eviction from Tilehurst at the end of their 1973 championship-winning season (the Reading riders were reallocated to other BL tracks for the 1974 season).

Each of the old directors of Allied inherited the tracks they had been running for the company and in the mutually agreed deal both Reg and I ended up with the newly-acquired Rye House, at Hoddesdon in Hertfordshire.

Rayleigh had been sold by the stadium owners for industrial re-development and at the end of 1973 I transferred the Rockets team, lock, stock and barrel, to the little stadium next to the River Lea for the start of the 1974 season.

But Reg was a 'sleeping partner' and I wanted none of that, so I insisted that he sold his 50 per cent interest and persuaded my long-standing friend and ex-Hackney team captain, Colin Pratt, to buy his shares. The price was £3,000 and I had to do a lot of talking to get 'Pratty' to part with his money. But part with it he did and we began a very successful partnership at Rye House, where he did all the track and team work while I handled the administration and acted as front man.

Hazal and I also both did jobs at the new Reading Stadium. Reg actually controlled the speedway activity, Bill Dore promoted the dogs, Frank Higley took charge of stadium development and upkeep while I ran the bars and catering. Hazal handled the tote operation for the greyhound racing.

It was a busy time and the whole enterprise was extremely successful – partially due to our employing top Radio One disc jockey 'Diddy' David Hamilton whose Monday afternoon national broadcast radio show always ended with him saying: 'See you all at Reading Speedway tonight . . . .' It was great publicity.

Daughter Jackie, Dave Beech and their baby son David junior.
Below: How Rayleigh Rockets' fans will remember 'Tiger' in 1972.

Above: Here's to happiness . . . Hazal and me after our wedding.
Below: Mum with my son Andrew (right) and his friend Troy Pratt (Colin's son).

All smiles . . . Hazal has been so good for many in different ways.

When we finished laying the actual race track I insisted on being the first ever person to slide a speedway bike on it, and this duly happened not long before our opening meeting, against Hull, in April 1975. Shades of my past re-emerged as I slid to the ground on the slick surface after only a couple of laps. The spill left me nursing a sore backside but at least I was still the first to actually ride the new Reading track!

Soon after Smallmead opened I borrowed some money from Lloyds Bank and bought a very old lathe and plaster bungalow at Three Mile Cross, just outside Reading. Andrew came to live with me and Hazal. He was eight-years old at the time and we arranged for him to start racing in schoolboy scrambling events, which he loved.

But our life at Reading was not as happy as it should have been. My schoolboy pal Reg Fearman was proving difficult to work with and we didn't always see eye to eye. I decided to sell my shares in Allied Presentations Ltd and a price of £30,000 was agreed, which was probably about half of its true value, but I was happy to be away.

Hazal and I went house-hunting back in the areas we had lived in most of our lives and finally settled on a bungalow in an acre of ground, covered in fruit trees, just around the corner from Colin Pratt. It was in Takeley, very near Stansted Airport. Young Troy Pratt, Colin's son, is the same age as Andrew and they were great pals, so it made sense for us to live nearby.

Soon after the move, Hazal and I were married on July 8, 1979 in the local registrar's office at Bishops Stortford. We both entered a period of complete happiness.

In the weeks leading up to our marriage ceremony both Hazal and I went on diets so that we'd look our best on the day. I don't know why we did that because we planned an extremely quiet affair with only my mother to actually join us – my dad had passed away following cancer in 1970, while my brother Ron had died of a heart attack in his 50s some years after emigrating to Canada.

Nonetheless Hazal and I both prepared ourselves as if a massive audience would be there, Hazal looking stunning in a turquoise outfit and I still have on my bedroom wall a photograph of the two of us taken that day. It is one of my most precious possessions and I take joy every time I look at it.

The wedding marked the start of 10 years of a happy life together sharing everything that we did and loving every minute of it. During that 10-year period Hazal developed as a person from a typical fun-loving 20-year-old into an astute business woman with an uncanny perception of people's characters and an immense ability as an administrator. Her input into my business affairs had a profound effect on our finances and I came to rely on her to an ever increasing degree. The fact that we worked together on every facet of life made us extremely close. She didn't mind the long hours and heavy travelling schedule that went with a life in speedway, and for me, her company made the long journeys seem much shorter.

Hazal loved our joint involvement with speedway and readily put up with having various riders constantly in our home. At one time we had Keith White and his wife living in a caravan in the garden, with Polish stars Zenon Plech and Roman Jankowski sharing a bedroom in the bungalow.

However, life was not always a bed of roses and it was a struggle to make ends meet with Hackney, as always, proving difficult financially. I decided to step back into the motor trade and set up a business selling Ford Cortinas. With the land we had there was room to park quite a number of vehicles and our garage was big enough to use as a workshop. Of course, we didn't have planning permission to use our premises commercially but I didn't worry too much about that.

I ran a simple two-line advert in the local paper saying: 'Ford Cortinas, drive away for only £200 deposit' plus our phone number. The response was truly astonishing and on Saturday afternoons our one-acre garden was like a main road showroom with loads of people coming to inspect our stock. We sold at least five cars every week to earn enough money to prop up the speedway and give ourselves a good living as well. It went on for almost four years before the local council came down on us like a ton of bricks. Our residential property couldn't be used for commercial purposes, a fact of which I'd always been aware. Still, we'd got away with it for a long time and it helped to keep our heads above water.

When Hazal and I moved from Reading to Takeley I sold our old bungalow in Three Mile Cross to my daughter, just for the money I'd borrowed from the bank. That was about £7,000, although I'd paid £10,000 when I bought it. The difference of £3,000 was a sort of belated wedding present.

Jackie was keen to live somewhere in our area and, shrewd judge that she is, she managed to sell the bungalow for £14,000 so that she finished up with a very acceptable nest-egg of £7,000 which she used to buy a house very near us in

Takeley. Her husband, Dave, then came to work for me in the new car sales business, so it worked out fine for all of us.

One day while buying some cars in Warren Street at the top of Tottenham Court Road, one of my business associates told me that he'd just purchased some impressive fire extinguishers. They were supposedly instantly active, would work on every type of fire and were non-toxic. He suggested that they'd be ideal for use at speedway stadia and within the pits area, and I agreed.

The firm selling them was not far away so I paid a visit to find out all about them. Sure enough, the extinguisher did everything claimed – it was a hand-held canister with an easy-to-use trigger. I was very impressed and thought I could probably sell plenty of them around the tracks. The wholesale price was £4 each and because they retailed at £8, it represented quite a good profit margin.

I had further thoughts – this extinguisher was so effective and at such a good price, I reckoned I could easily sell them on the open market. Net result was that I bought about 1,000 of them, all boxed up and ready to transport.

Knowing that the son of one of my neighbours in Takeley was out of work, I thought I'd offer him a job to sell the extinguishers, door-to-door, with £3 per unit going to him and £1 back to me. It seemed like an exciting project. Soon I had a meeting with the young man, Ian, and we agreed that he'd go on the road as a salesman. Because he'd never sold anything in his life, I said I'd go out with him for a day or two and show him how to sell them.

Out we went, just locally in Bishops Stortford. On the first day I had hit upon a great idea to impress potential buyers. Out came one of my old sports jackets, cleaned and ironed to look smart, which I wore. In the pocket was a small container containing lighter fuel and in another pocket was a cigarette lighter.

When we entered a premises to try and sell, very early on in the conversation I would pull out the lighter fuel, pour some on my left sleeve and promptly set light to my left arm! The eyes of the onlookers went really wide as they witnessed this lunatic act.

Then, just as quickly, I grabbed one of the extinguishers and with one squeeze of the trigger . . . 'pooof!' – and the flames went out. An impressive act, to say the least, and unloading the extinguishers at £8 a time was like taking candy from a baby. Ian was astonished at what he'd seen me do but I hoped he'd learned a good lesson.

The next day I loaded a Cortina with fire extinguishers and gave it to him. 'Off you go and come back for more when you've sold that lot.'

Ian disappeared in the Cortina and I looked forward to filling his car up again in a few days time. Alas, I didn't see him for four weeks and when he returned he looked a bit sheepish.

'How many have you sold?' Deathly silence. 'Well, *how* many?'

He opened the boot of the car. It was crammed full of extinguishers.

'None,' he said softly. He went off, leaving my car and the extinguishers, to look for a job that didn't involve selling anything. I was able to dispose of the stock around various speedway tracks but they all wanted a discount, so I didn't earn anything. But I can laugh about it now!

Chapter 13 – Weymouth
EDDIE SAVED MY LIFE

IN 1977 I was offered the opportunity to promote speedway at Weymouth. The National League (Second Division) track was then owned by Harry Davis, the father of England international John Davis, who owned a successful nearby caravan park. The deal was that I would rent the stadium from him for a year or two with the ultimate aim of acquiring the freehold for £65,000 as soon as I could raise the money. It seemed an exciting project and I duly took over in time for the 1977 season.

An ex-rider of some distinction named Eddie Lack, who had worked for me in the car business from time to time and also at Reading Stadium, agreed to live in a caravan on the Radipole Lane stadium site and look after matters there, manage the team, and also start working on stadium improvements for me.

Eddie had been a good friend for many years and both Hazal and I thought the world of him. Mostly because when we first got together and arrived at Reading to live, he had given us both tremendous help and support – in fact, the only person to do so at that time. He was to prove to be a friend of the very best kind.

Weymouth's home meetings ran on Tuesdays and Hazal and myself would drive down through Dorset to arrive in early afternoon, in good time to help Eddie get everything ready for the night's racing.

One afternoon the water bowser wouldn't start, so I got out our big Fordson tractor and drove it onto the centre green area, where the lorry was parked, and hitched up a tow rope so that I could get it started with Eddie in the driver's seat of the bowser.

I'd never used a big tractor in such a way before and, in my ignorance, I hitched the tow rope *above* the axle line of the tractor wheels. What a dramatic effect that would have!

As soon as I tried to tow the heavy water bowser, instead of moving forwards as I had expected it to, the front of the tractor started to lift off the ground and turn the whole unit over backwards . . . with me in the driver's seat. I quickly realised that it was about to crush me even though it seemed to be happening in slow motion. I remember thinking to myself: 'Christ, this thing's going to kill me – I pray to God that it won't hurt!'

But unbeknown to me, as it started to crush the cab, Eddie had seen what was happening, jumped out of the bowser and grabbed a length of scaffold tube that, as luck would have it, had been laying nearby.

He quickly shoved the tube below the overturned tractor and put the other end on his shoulder, relieving the full weight of the tractor from me. The effort and strength needed to achieve what he did was certainly more than any human could normally muster and it was an absolute miracle that Eddie succeeded.

Eddie Lack in his racing days with Edinburgh.

In fact, he kept the main weight off of me for nearly half-an-hour until the fire brigade arrived to get me out. I was covered in hot oil that had run all over me from the upturned diesel engine and my shoulder and back, both of which were squeezed by the collapsed cab, were causing me excruciating pain.

One of the firemen quickly inserted an air-bag under the tractor and as they filled it, the weight came off me and Eddie's shoulder. He collapsed with exhaustion and I was nearly in tears with relief.

An ambulance took me to the local hospital, where I was cleaned up and X-rayed. Amazingly, I had no broken bones, just a lot of heavy bruising around my left elbow, shoulder and back. Later on I discovered that I'd damaged a nerve in my elbow, which caused me to lose the use of two fingers in my left hand for several months.

But at the time I didn't care a jot about any of that. I just wanted to get back to the stadium to see how Eddie was and thank him for saving my life. Fortunately he was OK, although his shoulder was heavily bruised.

I realised, yet again, that my Guardian Angel had stepped in to give him the strength to save me. It was a humbling thought.

Eddie would come to my rescue again during my brief time at Weymouth, although he didn't know anything about it at the time.

With all the driving I did to and from speedway venues up and down the country, it was no surprise that I often got nicked for speeding. Usually on empty roads in the early hours of the morning when the police had nothing better to do. In the 'totting up' process I did, from time to time, lose my licence as the points were added up. I always felt that the system was totally unfair. No allowance was ever made for the fact that in the middle of the night a bit of extra speed on, what were in those days, empty roads, constituted no danger to anyone. Nor was any allowance made for the fact that I used a car constantly in the course of my business.

However, since I had lost my licence Hazal had to drive me about. One night on the way home from Weymouth, she started to feel really ill and was not able to continue driving. It was about one o'clock in the morning, so we had no choice but to change seats and for me to drive the rest of the way.

Our route used to take us through the centre of London to Aldgate, along the Mile End Road to Stratford, up the M11 and home. On this night we arrived at the traffic lights at Aldgate and stopped on the red. A Hillman Minx pulled up alongside us and inside were four big fellows. One of them wound down his window as we sat waiting for the lights to turn green and started to gesticulate at us.

'My God!' said Hazal, 'what are those yobs up to?' and the lights changed. I put my toe down and the powerful Mercedes left the Hillman Minx well behind. The Mile End Road was virtually empty and I sped quickly past the London Hospital, only to find red lights at the crossroads by the Blind Beggar Pub. As I waited there, up came the Hillman Minx again. This time all four of the men inside, all in their shirtsleeves, were waving their arms at us and shouting words I couldn't hear as my windows were shut tight.

'For God's sake lose them,' pleaded Hazal, 'they're up to no good.' This time, when the lights changed, I really booted it and left the people in the Hillman to wonder where I'd gone. The same thing happened at the crossroads by Mile End tube station and Hazal was by now terrified, certain that the yobs intended somehow to stop us and perhaps rob us.

Once again I zoomed off at full speed, intent now to get rid of them for good. But when I got to the Bow Town Hall lights they changed to red and I slowed down. As I did a police Black Maria skidded up alongside and pulled in front of me, making me brake really hard to avoid smashing into it. A whole army of policemen jumped out of the Black Maria, pulled my door open and yanked me out of the driver's seat. I was terrified.

Then the Hillman Minx drew up and the four troublemakers inside got out. They were policemen! I was furious at that, as I'd been racing at speeds of 80-90mph because of them.

One copper produced a breathaliser kit and made me blow into it. I certainly hadn't had a drink – I was a virtual teetotaller anyway – so I had nothing to fear in that direction. He confirmed that I wasn't drunk. Suddenly it struck me that not only had I far exceeded the speed limit, but I was also driving without a licence – something I'd completely forgotten!

My mind worked overtime. How could I get out of this? I thought: 'The best method of defence is attack,' so I started to raise Cain about the actions of the four policemen in the Hillman and how my wife was in fear of her life. The strategy worked and their attitude changed dramatically: 'OK, sir,' said the leader, 'we're sorry you've been inconvenienced, please drive home safely.'

I nearly collapsed with relief as I got back behind the wheel of the Merc.

'Oh, by the way sir, what's your name?'

'Eddie Lack,' I lied, as I put her into gear and pulled away quietly before any more questions were asked.

Looking back at those years, I chuckle when I remember certain minor incidents. Of course, having no driving licence put me in an impossible situation. I had to travel by road from my home in rural Takeley both to Hackney and Rye House, let alone Weymouth and any away tracks I felt I needed to visit with one or other of my teams. Public transport wasn't an option and I couldn't afford a chauffeur. Hazal drove me about whenever she could but that wasn't always possible.

So I hit upon a plan – technically illegal, but very necessary in the circumstances.

I applied for, and received, a provisional motorcycle licence and bought myself a 250cc bike for about 40 quid. I then used the bike, duly fitted with L-plates, to travel between home and my track.

Since a lot of the local 'plod' knew me through having visited the speedway, I wore a full-face helmet with darkened goggles and a mouth scarf so that I wasn't recognised! I always used the back roads but I lost a lot of weight from sweating with apprehension. Fortunately, I never got caught but I was very thankful to get my car licence back after three months.

By the end of 1978 I had organised the money to buy the freehold of Weymouth – partly with an agreement from my landlords at Hackney to run greyhound racing there too and partially with a bank loan. I visited Harry Davis to cement the promised deal only to discover that he'd entered into another agreement for the Allied Presentations Company at Reading to take over. I was dismayed. All the plans I'd laid based on the words of Harry 18 months earlier had been for nothing. It was yet another harsh lesson I had to learn.

Meanwhile, at Rye House, my partner Colin Pratt decided during the 1979-80 close season that he wanted to sell out, which came as a complete surprise to me at the time. We got on so well together and had built such a successful National League team that had just pushed Mildenhall all the way in the race for the title, missing out by just a single point. We gained some consolation by comfortably beating Berwick in the KO Cup Final and the future looked bright, so I couldn't understand Colin's reasons for quitting and he never did enlighten me.

I took out another bank loan and purchased his 50 per cent stake for £30,000 – 10 times more than he'd originally paid for it only five years earlier. So he didn't do too badly out of the deal and that's when I became the sole promoter of the Rockets.

One of my longest-serving riders, Channel Islander Hughie Saunders, who had ridden for me since signing for Rayleigh in 1971, replaced Pratty as team manager and track man, so I was still well served in that direction. Hughie was highly reliable and well respected and after he hung up his leathers at the end of 1979, he took over as team manager the following year and we won the NL championship for the first time, pipping Newcastle by one point.

I came close to celebrating a league double in 1980, but Hackney finished three points behind Reading in the senior division.

Every year it became tougher and tougher to earn a living from promoting speedway and I found myself having to work harder at selling cars in order to subsidise both Hackney and Rye House.

Chapter 14 – National Service Part 2
ENGLAND RULE

IN the early 70s England did not feature at international level because it was considered by the BSPA that we did not have enough riders of the quality required to compete successfully in world class events. Instead, it was the practice to include the best Commonwealth riders, notably Kiwis Barry Briggs and Ivan Mauger, to spearhead a team labelled 'Great Britain'.

Team managers were chosen on a match-by-match basis and it was usually the staging promoter who was selected to do the job. That has enabled many people to claim that at one time or another they managed a British team. Others were selected to manage the team in overseas events, such as tours to Australia, simply based on who was available to do it or, quite often, the man who was keenest to have a freebie trip abroad.

However, in 1973, it was decided to change the system by appointing a single permanent manager which obviously made much more sense if we hoped to gain some success in an era largely dominated by Sweden.

To this end the promoters appointed Dent Oliver, the former Belle Vue and England rider who went on to successfully manage the Aces. It was an excellent choice, as he was a man of great experience, had been a rider of distinction and was held in high esteem by everyone in the sport.

At the same time it was proposed to put together a young England side at senior level and I was given the job of looking after the youngsters. I don't remember too much about the actual matches I was involved in as manager, except for a disastrous trip to Poland in May '73 when both sets of riders – a senior British team headed by Mauger and my under-23 side – plus various other British promoters all went in a specially chartered aircraft to what was then a country behind the Iron Curtain and ruled very harshly by Communist USSR.

The two British teams each rode against Poland in a series of three Test matches at different tracks and we were soundly beaten in all but one of them, returning home with our tails between our legs. The huge Polish tracks were so different compared to those in the UK that the results were no real surprise.

In the final under-23 match, at Gniezno, Belle Vue's Chris Pusey, one of Britain's gutsiest riders and our leading scorer on this tour, had broken his collarbone in a frightening three-man pile-up which held up the meeting for nearly an hour. They took him by ambulance to the local hospital where they slapped tight bandages around his arm and shoulder. They then insisted that he stayed in overnight which would have meant him missing our flight home that was due that evening.

Pusey flatly refused and despite being in absolute agony, he discharged himself

Above: The GB Under-23 team I managed at Gniezno in Poland. Back row, left to right: John Titman, Doug Wyer, Bobby Beaton, Alan Wilkinson and Chris Pusey (who was off to hospital soon after this was taken).
Front: Graham Plant, Barry Thomas, Peter Collins.
Below: Trying to keep Thommo's spirits up on the same Polish trip.

from the hospital and made the journey to the airport to join us on the plane. When he boarded, quite a while after everyone else because he was late getting to the airport, it was to the loud cheers of all the riders, promoters and various press men who had made the trip into Eastern Europe.

It was a journey made sadder because it had been undertaken just after the unexpected and untimely death of the senior manager, Dent Oliver, whose role at the third Test in Gorzow a few weeks later was fulfilled by Reg Fearman. All the members of the BSPA management committee were on the trip and during the flight home they had an emergency meeting and decided to offer me the position of senior manager. After pondering on their offer, I replied that I would accept the position but only on the understanding that the team I was in charge of would be known to all as England and not Great Britain.

I didn't want to manage a side that included Mauger, Briggs or Ronnie Moore – not that I had anything against those riders. Indeed, I had great relationships with them all but I thought it was time for us to stand on our own two feet as a single nation.

It came as something of a surprise to me that the management committee agreed to my terms and the appointment was duly confirmed at the next general council meeting of senior league promoters.

The England job thrust me into the public eye within the world of speedway racing and, I have to admit, I milked it for all it was worth at the time. I used the extra publicity I received to help promote my club at Hackney.

I purchased a red nylon jacket on which I sewed a strip of red, white and blue ribbon and, as I remember, a small union jack flag. This became my 'uniform' that I wore at every England match.

I always made a point of being alongside my riders on parade before the start of every match, standing prominently on whatever vehicle was being used so that the public not only knew that I was in charge, but also that I was totally immersed with my riders and had huge confidence in them before a wheel had been turned. This had the undoubted effect of stimulating more enthusiastic public support for the team and there is little doubt in my mind that, in turn, this greatly boosted the riders' performances.

My first task was to steer the England team through the 1973 Daily Mirror International Tournament in which teams from all over Europe, plus Australia and New Zealand, competed for a place in the final due to be staged at the Empire Stadium, Wembley. The competition was intense but *en route* to the final my new England team took on and defeated Sweden, Denmark, USSR, Poland, Australia and New Zealand. The other team to make the final were hot favourites Sweden, who were still considered at that time to be the most powerful speedway nation.

We duly took our place at Wembley on a track that I had installed and prepared and fought a titanic battle against opponents who neither gave, nor asked for, any quarter. After the scheduled 13 heats the scores were tied at 39 points apiece and the atmosphere in the stadium was electric when it was announced that there would be a match-race between one rider from each team to decide the final outcome.

Each manager had to decide who to select for the extra race and my heart was pounding as I realised the consequences for my career as England manager if I picked the wrong man. We all knew that the strongest element in the Swedish side was their ability to make very fast starts. It was the major reason for their international success. At the same time none of my young English riders were well known for fast starting. Their strength was their tenacity and gritty determination which enabled them to battle past their opponents in race after race.

But this race was different. The Swedes had selected the great Anders Michanek, who was like streaked lighting from a standing start, and we all knew that to pass him would be virtually impossible.

The whole stadium went silent as everyone waited for my decision. Who would it be? I finally made my mind up and walked over to the young Peter Collins, the new 19-year-old sensation from Belle Vue who had been with us in Poland on the under-23 tour but still in his first full season of international racing.

'Peter,' I said, 'we're all relying on you. If ever you're going to make a good start in your life, now is the time.'

He was as cool as a cucumber. 'Don't worry, boss, it's in the bag.'

Such confidence from him was almost alarming and like every person in that vast stadium, my heart stopped beating as they lined up at the starting gate – the white tapes stretched across the track lightly fluttering in the evening breeze as both riders revved up their powerful Jawa engines, holding in the clutch levers tightly, waiting for them to rise.

Whooosh! . . . up the tapes went and Peter, on the inside starting position, shot out in front of the great Swede, swooping around the first corner at full throttle as Anders took a wider line, getting ready to gain extra speed in order to pass Peter in the back straight. He was a hair's breadth from being successful as he gained on our man in readiness to enter the pits corner.

Flinging caution to the wind, the flying Swede dived under Peter on the entry to the corner but it was an ill-advised move and PC was thrown sideways off his machine, ending up in a heap by the pits gate.

A huge roar came from the 35,000 crowd, whistling and booing its disapproval at the robust actions of the tall, slender Swede.

Meanwhile I was only concerned for Peter and was highly relieved to find him cussing and blinding about what had happened – and very concerned that he might have been at fault in some way. Physically, he was OK so I knew that if referee Arthur Humphrey made the right decision, then he would be fit to go in the re-run.

Now the stadium went eerily silent once again as they awaited the decision of the official in charge. Then it erupted into a cacophony of sheer joy as the words came booming out of the public address system: 'The rider in white is excluded for dangerous riding.' With 'Mich' thrown out, it meant that Peter only had to cruise around unopposed in the re-run to clinch victory for England.

It was a famous moment in speedway's history and I still get a lump in my throat now whenever I think about it.

For me it was a blessing, because that single race, all on its own, had established

A proud moment for me with my England team before we beat Sweden at Sheffield early on in the 1973 Daily Mirror International Tournament. Standing, left to right: Martin Ashby, Eric Boocock, Reg Wilson, myself, Terry Betts, John Louis. Kneeling: Doug Wyer and Peter Collins, with skipper Ray Wilson on the bike.
Below: PC and Ray Wilson after our victory over Sweden in that dramatic Wembley final.

England as a world force and myself as a credible leader.

The riders in the England team that evening were: Ray Wilson, Terry Betts, Malcolm Simmons, Peter Collins, Martin Ashby, John Louis and Eric Boocock.

Throughout the whole series I had made it my business to really get to know all of the English team members personally. Some, of course, I already knew very well but I felt it essential that each of them should regard me as their friend and biggest supporter.

It was at this time during my period in charge of the team that the England captain, Leicester's Ray Wilson, started to refer to me as 'Youth' and he would always welcome me with that title. I never did learn where that idea came from and he never enlightened me. He was, in any case, a great skipper and supported me in every move I made. We had a good relationship all the time I had the job. When England returned to Wembley in September of that year and won the final of the World Team Cup, I was very happy to begin a period of huge success at world level for both Ray and myself. He had top-scored for the victorious GB team in Poland with a maximum in 1971 and was in the side, along with Terry Betts and John Louis, again when Mauger led Britain to success in Germany in 1972.

But the 1973 triumph in front of the ITV cameras at Wembley was the first time an all-English team had won the sport's premier team trophy. 'World Cup Willie' led a team that also included the King's Lynn pair of Betts and Simmons, plus the unbeaten Collins, with Dave Jessup at reserve.

Having put together a successful team in '73, much to the surprise of many of my fellow promoters – one or two of whom were not enamoured of my flamboyant style when I was with the team, I knew by the end of the season that every single rider was capable of improved performances the following year, if only because they had achieved success when few people expected them to. Remember that in previous seasons they had ridden alongside the superstars of New Zealand and the top Aussies. So I looked forward to the 1974 season with huge confidence.

Little did I know then just how confident I should have been. It was a season of incredible, unprecedented success for the England team. We rode at almost every track in the country in Test match series, drawing huge audiences as the public began to realise that they had a national team to follow that was achieving results.

The record book shows that we met Sweden in a five-match series and beat them 5-0. We then took on Poland in seven matches and thrashed them 7-0. Along came the Soviet Union for five matches and we sent them packing – 5-0.

Then we had the audacity to return to our previous 'graveyard' in Poland, on the enormous track in Chorzow, and win the 1974 World Team Cup. Our super team at Katowice that day was Malcolm Simmons, Dave Jessup, Peter Collins and John 'Tiger' Louis, with Ray Wilson in reserve. It rounded off an unforgettable season in my managerial career and even silenced some of my critics.

The success story continued in 1975 and in fact, if anything, my young Lions were even better. We had a home and away Test match series against the powerful Swedish national team with five matches in each country. To everyone's astonishment we beat them 10-0, which naturally included five matches in the Land

HISTORY-MAKERS: Above: The first all-English team to win the World Team Cup. With me in the pits at Wembley before the meeting in 1973 are (clockwise): Ray Wilson, Malcolm Simmons, Terry Betts, Dave Jessup and Peter Collins. Below: I'm pouring the champagne for the boys while Nelson Mills-Baldwin, chairman of the Speedway Control Board, looks on. Bettsy had broken his arm between the final and our visit to the RAC's HQ.

of the Lakes and that set of matches provided stories worth telling.

My England team were not the regular members that I was used to working with. So as not to disrupt the domestic calendar of league matches in England, every match in Sweden saw us track a different line-up. We flew riders in and out of the country to put together a patchwork quilt team in order to fulfil our commitment to the Swedish speedway authorities. Only Martin Ashby of Swindon was an ever-present and he (and we) were fortunate that he was using a new four-valve engine designed and built by Australian rider Neil Street. The motor – a Jawa conversion – proved a huge success and Martin top scored in the series on that power unit.

It turned out to be the engine that revolutionised the sport because everyone wanted four-valve engines when they saw what it had done for Martin and it wasn't long before the Czech factory producing the Jawa engines marketed a four-valve version which everyone clamoured to buy.

However, it wasn't just the engine used by Martin Ashby that won us the Test series in Sweden. It was the sheer determination of my riders. A great example of this was in a match at, I think, Eskilstuna. To the astonishment of my fellow promoters in England I had selected a young teenager from Belle Vue called Chris Morton, who had ridden for Ellesmere Port in the Second Division just 18 months earlier. Anyone with half a brain and a little knowledge about the game could have seen that he had a special talent even though he had been riding for five minutes, so to speak – and that's why I picked him for the Test team.

Anyway, during this particular match we were finding it tough going until young 'Mort' came out in a reserves' race. Last away from the start, a trait he would never manage to shake off, he held his throttle wide open for the four laps, passing the other riders with what seemed comparative ease. Myself and all the other team members watched with excitement and awe. Here in our midst was a new wonder kid and as he entered the pits after the race he was swamped as we rushed around to congratulate him. His race win had helped pull back the small deficit that we had and put us back in with a chance.

Chris had placed an ace in my managerial hand and I immediately entered him into the next race in place of one of the less successful riders, I can't remember who. Wow! He did it again and the whole place was a hub of excitement once more.

Studying the programme of events so that I could review what races had still to come and the strengths and weaknesses of both sets of riders, it was obvious to me that if I placed Chris in the very next race, which had looked like a weak one for England, we might just have a chance of sneaking a slim victory. But that meant three consecutive races for the little lad from Manchester, so I telephoned the Swedish referee and asked him to allow extra time between races to give Chris a chance to recover. His response astonished me: 'The decision to use your rider in three consecutive races is yours and you must bear the responsibility if he is tired – the race will start immediately.'

With that he sounded the two-minute buzzer. To say that I was livid would be the understatement of the century and I ran back into the English section of the pits and quickly told my riders what the referee had said. They were as incensed as I was and from that minute the Swedes had no chance. They rode their hearts out from the start to the finish in every race, performing incredible feats and all of them trying to emulate the success enjoyed by young Chris.

While he was the inexperienced young rider who inspired us all, it was finally a gutsy team performance that made the Swedish referee regret his decision. It also taught me a wonderful lesson in sports psychology, which I have used on odd occasions since that memorable match.

But that was not the highlight of England's international success that year. We went back to Poland, a country where we had been humbled more than once, for another Test series. The opening defeat at Bydgoszcz – without Peter Collins – was England's first defeat in more than two years under my charge but we had the last laugh by fighting back to win the series 3-1. An outstanding performance, because the Poles on their own huge raceways were something else, I can tell you.

We were full of confidence when we went to northern Germany and the vast track at Norden bidding to complete a unique hat-trick of World Team Cup Final wins. Defeat was not in our vocabulary and there was never any doubt that we would retain our title, which we did with comparative comfort. My team that day was Peter Collins, Malcolm Simmons, Martin Ashby, John Louis and Dave Jessup.

However, the other significant thing for me at Norden that day was the fact that top Polish rider Zenon Plech agreed to come back to England with me to race just the last few matches of the season for Hackney. The story of how we made it happen still brings a smile to my face.

Thrilling action from the 1975 World Team Cup Final at Norden, with John Louis looking for the gap between Russian Vladimir Gordeev and Zenon Plech (inside). Zenon arrived with the Polish party but he left with me.

Chapter 15 – Zenon Plech

ILLEGAL IMMIGRANT IN MY BOOT

IN 1975, after a season-long negotiation with his Polish club Stal Gorzow, I finally got their permission to sign Zenon Plech for the Hawks and it was agreed that he should join us for a handful of matches at the tail-end of the season, with a view to him joining up for a full season in 1976.

Zenon had first burst onto the international scene as the Polish wonderkid in 1973, aged 20, but it had been impossible for any British promoter to secure his release from Poland, and its strict iron curtain regime.

Poland's youngest ever national champion and World Finalist, he was one of the most exciting riders ever to appear for me and worth going to great lengths to sign, which is exactly what I did!

I had a sign language chat with him on the day of the World Team Cup Final at Norden in which I suggested that he travelled in my car to England with me after the meeting. He had his Polish passport but did not have a visa allowing him entry into Britain. Nonetheless he agreed to come with me and after we'd supped on some big German sausages we'd bought from a sausage stall in the stadium, we set off for Ostend and Dover.

During the long drive west we didn't speak much – I knew no Polish and he knew even less English – but we enjoyed a chocolate bar between us and, without language, we seemed to enjoy each other's company.

At Ostend and onto the ferry, I began thinking about how we were going to get past Dover's port immigration with Zenon possessing no entry visa. I started to think of the consequences which I hadn't given much thought to previously. When we docked in Dover harbour and went to the car deck to disembark, I began to get very nervous. Then I had a silly thought: if Zenon doesn't show his passport, they won't know he hasn't got a visa!

'Quick,' I said to him as I opened the boot of the car. 'Get in there . . .'

His eyes were wide open with astonishment but after some gesticulating he climbed in and I shut the lid.

Now I held my breath as I joined the car queue to exit the dock, praying that I wouldn't be searched. I held out my blue British passport as I approached the window. Customs Officers were standing to one side and I was certain they'd guess that I had an illegal immigrant with me. I'm sure I stopped breathing but the man behind the window glanced at my passport, looked me straight in the eye and waved me on. I didn't start breathing again until I was going up the hill towards the A2 road leading from Dover to London.

At the top I pulled into a lay-by and quickly opened the boot. There was Zenon.

Zenon Plech, one of the most popular riders ever to wear the Hackney racejacket, pictured before his debut at Waterden Road towards the end of the 1975 season. But don't tell customs!

Above: Interviewing Zenon Plech at the Hackney end-of-season dinner-dance in 1976.
Below: Zenon at the same function with Barry Thomas and Trevor Hedge.

Above: The Hawks on the night Zenon joined us for the first time at the end of 1975. Back row, left to right: Dave Erskine (team manager), Dave Kennett, Mike Broadbank, Zenon, Dave Morton and myself. Front: Laurie Etheridge, Barry Thomas (on bike), Ted Hubbard and Steve Lomas.
Below: The 1976 team – left to right: Trevor Hedge, Zenon Plech, Keith White, Barry Thomas, Steve Lomas, Dave Morton and Dave Kennett.

Who's the cheerful looking Hackney fan wearing the Zenon Plech rosette? Hope he paid to get in!
My one month ban by the Control Board couldn't stop me from cheering on the Hawks from the main stand.

All curled-up but laughing like a hyena. We kept grinning all the way home.

He rode in only four BL matches for Hackney at the end of '75 but still made a great impression on our supporters, who loved his hair-raising, 100 per cent style, which was in stark contrast to his very personable, smiling off-track demeanour.

The following year, Zenon was able to appear for the Hawks in virtually every match and he was the darling of the crowd.

It was in mid-May that Hackney visited Swindon for a league match, the result of which was in doubt all the way through. Almost every race was a hard-fought, neck and neck affair and my boys were doing me proud.

We were three points down going into the crucial final Heat 13. When Barry Thomas fell and the Robins' pair of Geoff Bouchard and Bob Kilby hit the front, it looked all over for us. But never-say-die Zenon had other ideas and in the last corner, he dived inside Kilby to snatch second place on the line. A pulsating end to a great race and, despite the disappointing 40-37 defeat, we'd given our all.

Then, to my utter astonishment, the announcement was made: 'Zenon Plech has been excluded for unfair riding!'

To say that I was gobsmacked would be the understatement of the century. It had been a hard, but fair, race for four laps, neither rider got into difficulties or even momentary problems. The decision of referee Martin Palmer, a local West Country man, was totally diabolical and clearly biased towards Swindon. I lifted the pits phone to talk to him but he wouldn't discuss it.

'Oh,' I thought, 'we'll see about that. You're going to discuss it whether you like it or not.'

I raced to the back of the grandstand, where there were stairs leading up to the referee's box, perched on the roof of the stand. Running up the stairs and along a narrow gangplank, I opened the rear door of the box. There, perched high on a stool, was the cropped-haired Martin Palmer. His eyes wide open with fear as he saw me entering the box.

'So you don't want to discuss it, eh? Well discuss this!'

With that I took a swing at Palmer's jaw but my aim wasn't too good and I missed the target as he ducked away. My punch landed on his shoulder instead.

The referee tumbled off his stool, still staring at me like a startled rabbit. He looked so pathetic that I started to see the funny side of it and actually laughed as I left the box and headed back to the pits on the third/fourth bend.

My riders, especially Zenon, thought it was terrific and for just a few short moments I was their hero. The referee wouldn't change his mind, though.

We eventually lost the match, 42-35, but it didn't end there as far as I was concerned. I was subsequently charged with 'ungentlemanly conduct' by the Speedway Control Board and suspended from any participation in speedway for one month. It didn't bother me at all. In fact, I milked it for all the publicity I could. Buying myself a blue and white scarf, a Hackney bobble hat and rattle, I marched around the dog track at Waterden Road with the cheers of the crowd ringing in my ears. I joined the fans on the terraces, where I stood to watch the meeting.

They all thought it was hilarious. So did I.

Chapter 16 - National Service Part 3
ENGLAND SCAPEGOAT

SADLY, my long success story with England did not continue in 1976. With the same set of riders that had retained the World Team Cup in Germany the year before, we were knocked out of the competition in the UK qualifying round when Australia beat us at Ipswich.

The result was a great disappointment to everyone, especially with the final due to be held in England again – at London's White City – later in the season.

It was a chance for my critics to stick the knife in, which they did, and I was relieved of my position. I was sacked by my BSPA colleagues on the pretext that, as I'd thumped a referee during Hackney's match at Swindon that season and been banned for a month by the Control Board (see previous chapter), I was not the sort of person who should be in the public eye as England manager.

My previous successes in the job were quickly forgotten and I found myself back in my normal routine. I felt a bit relieved at the time because the commitment of managing the national team – an unpaid, honorary role – had brought me an extraordinary workload. I thought that whoever was appointed after me would discover that the job was not all fun.

It had never occurred to me that I would ever be offered the job back, or, for that matter, that I would event want it but the chance came my way five years later, in 1981, when I was approaching my 50th birthday. I have to admit that my memory of the five years after I lost the job in 1976 is hazy, to say the least, but I believe England regained the World Team Cup under John Berry's management in 1977 and the next time we won it was when Ian Thomas and Eric Boocock were appointed together as joint-managers in 1980.

However, for whatever the reason, the BSPA asked me to take on the job again in 1981. I was a little reluctant, believing that I was on a hiding to nothing. If I was lucky enough to rekindle past glories I would get no thanks and if I didn't, my band of critics would have a field day. Nonetheless I could not resist the challenge – my personal ego wanted me to prove to everyone that I should not have been sacked five years earlier.

During that five-year gap two nations had emerged as major forces on the world stage. Denmark, led by Ole Olsen and Hans Nielsen, were probably the top dogs, man for man, and close behind were the Yanks who had fast-emerging star riders such as Bruce Penhall, Dennis Sigalos, Bobby Schwartz and the Moran brothers.

England had some outstanding performers as well, one of the main ones being Michael Lee who had taken the individual world title in Sweden the year before.

It was announced that England would meet both Denmark and the USA in Test

We looked strong enough before the World Team Cup UK round at Ipswich in 1976, by my team of (clockwise)
Peter Collins, Malcolm Simmons, Martin Ashby (reserve), Dave Jessup and John Louis couldn't live with the
inspired Australians on a day that shocked British speedway.

match series and I must admit I privately felt that it would take a superhuman effort to beat either of these teams.

But any inner doubts I had were not transmitted to the public, as I again donned my little nylon jacket. I should have had more self-belief in the riders, for we defeated Denmark 2-1 in a three-match rubber and repeated the dose by giving the USA a 4-1 drubbing. Given the respective strengths of those two opponents, the results we achieved were quite remarkable and I felt that my English boys were in the hunt for even more glory.

We had to go to Olching, a large track near Munich in West Germany, for the final of the World Team Cup but disaster struck the English team just a couple of days before the event.

First of all, the outstanding Peter Collins broke his leg so was unable to take part. Then I also lost the services of World Champion Michael Lee who was, at that time, in the midst of his crisis period involving the use of cannabis and he, too, was unavailable.

In the final, England ran a close second to Denmark with what could only be described as our 'second' team. It was a result I was actually proud of, given all the mitigating circumstances, so I was very surprised to find myself condemned out of hand for losing by the British press and even more surprised to find that, at the next promoters' meeting, the condemnation continued.

The build-up to my resignation as England team manager in 1981 is quite a story in itself. My Hackney team had caused me a lot of heartache that year. Our long-time captain Barry Thomas asked to drop a division to ride for Crayford in the NL and one of my Polish riders, Roman Jankowski, wasn't allowed to leave his club Unia Leszno to come back to England. It was a difficult time.

Hackney and Rye House kept me going flat out, work-wise, yet I couldn't resist saying 'yes' when the BSPA asked me to build the track in Wembley Stadium for the individual World Final, due to be staged six days after the team final in Olching.

It was quite a big job with lots of inbuilt difficulties – doing the work in between dog meetings and without disrupting the well-oiled Wembley Stadium machine. I was pleased to do it, though, not least because the money I earned – £3,000 per meeting – went a long way to making ends meet at Hackney.

Unlike previous occasions when I'd performed the same task, for the 1976 Inter-Continental Final and the 1978 Golden Jubilee World Final won by Ole Olsen, the stadium owners gave me three weeks for completion in 1981. It was because the Football Association had agreed that their annual Charity Shield soccer match, which was played one week before the speedway World Final, could take place on a slightly narrower pitch than normal, allowing the speedway track to remain in place. This meant I could lay the track before the annual football curtain-raiser and simply add final touches during the week between the two events.

My good friend Peter Thorogood helped me to lay the track and on the Friday at the end of the three-week period we both left Wembley with the track laid and ready for the practice six days later. That night I was, of course, at Hackney Stadium to run our normal home meeting and immediately after the last race I set off in my car towards Dover, to catch the midnight ferry on my way to Olching.

I was planning to drive all night and arrive there in time for the World Team Cup Final practice session due on Saturday afternoon – the meeting proper being on the Sunday. With Olching situated not too far from an alpine glacier, I'd decided to take in three days ski-ing. After three hectic weeks at Wembley and the WTC final, it was an ideal opportunity to grab a relaxing holiday. My good ski-ing pal, Czech citizen Alder, came with me, with our skis mounted on the roof rack of my car. We left Hackney Stadium on the Friday night in good spirits, both looking forward to the racing at Olching and then on to our favourite pastime. Little did we know what was in store.

We arrived at Dover at around 11.30pm and as luck would have it, we found a huge queue of traffic stretching out of the dock and way up the hill above the cliffs. We had forgotten it was a Bank Holiday! The queue moved at a snail's pace and, of course, it meant that we missed our midnight ferry by a proverbial mile.

It was a factor that we hadn't considered and by the time we'd finally got lined up on the dockside to await the next ferry, we were at least four hours behind schedule and beginning to panic. Having worked hard at Wembley since 7am and then promoted all evening at Hackney, I was feeling pretty exhausted and as we waited in line at the dock I dozed off to sleep. After maybe half-an-hour I woke to find that all the vehicles around us had been loaded onto the ferry ship, just to our right, and standing nearby was a dock steward.

Winding down my window, I called out to him: 'Why haven't you loaded me?'

'Oh,' he said, 'you're on standby.'

'No I'm not, I've got a proper ticket and I need to be on the boat.'

'No, you've got to wait – there may not be room.'

'Sod that,' I replied, 'I'm getting on.'

With that, I drove off to my right towards the loading ramp with the steward waving his arms wildly at me. At the ramp I slowly eased my car down and onto the ferry and it was obvious that I was one of the last vehicles to make it. It was a huge relief to be on board and about to set sail for Ostend.

Alder and me left the car and made our way up to the passenger decks expecting the big vessel to start moving out of the dock – but nothing happened. After about 20 minutes a steward appeared with a policeman alongside him.

'That's him,' he said, pointing towards me, and the copper grabbed me and led me through the lounge area to a small room off to one side. A bemused Alder followed me in. Once inside the room I was asked why I had ignored the directions of the steward and I explained what had happened.

'Well,' said the officer, 'I must warn you that you will be reported for dangerous driving and may be prosecuted!'

'Listen,' I heard myself saying, 'I may have ignored the steward but I certainly didn't do any dangerous driving. How could I? It was only 20 yards to the ramp and I couldn't have moved at more than 15 mph.'

'You've been warned,' came the reply and off he went, leaving me exasperated. Still, the most important thing was that we were on the boat, and soon after it set

The England team that defeated Denmark in the Test at Hackney in 1981. Left to right: Sean Willmott, Kevin Smith, Michael Lee, Kenny Carter, Les Collins. Front: Chris Morton, skipper Dave Jessup (on bike) and Gordon Kennett.

sail. We were on our way at last, albeit many hours behind schedule.

The drive across Belgium and Germany was a blur. It was, as far as was possible, flat out all the way and we finally arrived, thoroughly exhausted, at Olching Speedway in bright sunshine . . . only to discover that the practice session had just ended. While I was upset at having missed the session, I knew, both as a manager and ex-rider, that my presence there wasn't of vital importance. As long as all my riders had tested the track and were all fit – which they were, I saw no problem in me having missed practice.

A good night's sleep had me feeling back on top form and I spent Sunday morning helping my riders to prepare and getting them all in the mood to produce the goods. But without Peter Collins and Michael Lee, our top two riders, England were far from favourites. The most powerful outfit that day, the clear favourites, were the Danes, led by Ole Olsen and well supported by the fast-emerging Hans Nielsen, Erik Gundersen and Tommy Knudsen.

But the strength of their team, with my own Hackney skipper Finn Thomsen also adding his wealth of experience, didn't faze us and, inspired by the brilliant Chris Morton, we put up a tremendous fight. A fall and an engine failure had cost us vital points but when the battle was finally over, Denmark had beaten us by seven points, with Germany close behind us in third place and the Russians last. I felt that we'd done ourselves proud and said so to the English press men who were present.

The writers from *Speedway Star*, the sport's number one magazine, didn't think so, though, and in the following week's edition I was condemned out of hand, saying

With the team that put up such a heroic fight on the big, flat Olching track in 1981. Left to right: Gordon Kennett, Dave Jessup, Kenny Carter, Chris Morton and John Davis.

that I 'showed no remorse' for my failure! It was a ludicrous judgement but their remarks hurt and I'm still sore about it to this very day.

The reaction of my colleagues also caused me dismay. I'd managed England to a historic three consecutive World Team Cup victories, beaten most of our rivals out of sight in the Test arena and, apart from that shock defeat by the Aussies in the qualifier at Ipswich in May 1976, my international record over a five-year period – 1973-76 and 1981 – was virtually unblemished.

It wasn't as if losing in the final to the Danes was without precedent either. They had beaten England by a larger winning margin in 1978, when John Berry had a full strength team to pick from, and in 1979 England had again failed to reach the WTC final after being eliminated in the first qualifying round.

All this history, though, was forgotten by the various British officials from the ACU and the promoters' association, who were all basking in the German sunshine on a free jolly-up, with no responsibility, and staying in the best hotel at someone else's expense. To a man, they condemned me for arriving late for the official practice without any conception of my hectic workload and travel problems. They'd all arrived in comfort by plane and been taken by taxi to their hotel the day before.

I thought to myself: 'What a load of wasted space this lot are,' and promptly forgot their unfair criticism.

However, with the meeting over and my responsibilities complete, Alder and I set off for Kaprun in the Austrian Alps to ski on the Kitzsteinhorn and the big delta-shaped glacier there, putting all thoughts of speedway out of our minds.

But not before I'd phoned home to my wife Hazal and asked her to go to Wembley just to see if my track was OK after the Charity Shield soccer match. We'd skied all day on Monday and in the late afternoon I phoned home to speak to Hazal. As soon as she heard my voice she blurted out: 'You'd better get your arse back here smartish, they've dug great holes in your track!'

I was gobsmacked and after a few more words I rushed back to pack my bags, throw everything in the car and with Alder wondering what on earth was going on, started to drive as fast as possible back to Ostend. It was the nightmare journey outwards all over again, only this time in the opposite direction, and we arrived at the docks early on Tuesday morning. The four-and-a-half hour crossing seemed to last forever but once we reached Dover I set off directly towards Wembley and the Empire Stadium, wondering what horrors I'd find there.

Dropping off Alder in London so that he could catch his train back to Wales where he lived, I finally got to the huge national arena in mid-afternoon. I walked up through the entrance tunnel, past the big dressing rooms and out, over the dog track and onto the centre. I looked in horror at where, in clear contravention of our agreement, the four corners of the soccer pitch had been laid over the top of my track. There were four huge holes dug out by a bulldozer biting into the banking of the speedway track, so that the turf of the football pitch could be laid flat.

I learned later that the manager of one of the Charity Shield teams – I think it was Tottenham Hotspur – had flatly refused to use the previously agreed narrower pitch and that it was on his instructions that a bulldozer was brought in to destroy my track. No apology or explanation to me was ever forthcoming, not even from the stadium manager who had clearly allowed it to happen.

My feelings towards these selfish individuals couldn't be put into words. But it was no good me sitting and crying about it. The official practice for the final was due on the Thursday, so I had no time to spare. Already having had only a couple of hours sleep on the ferry, I started immediately on the repair work, staying in the stadium all night and using the headlights of my car to make my vision of the circuit a little easier. Thank goodness for a clear sky and a bright moon!

I managed to get the rough work done by the early hours of Wednesday morning and went to sleep in my car until 8.00am. When I resumed work early that morning I was being helped by Peter Thorogood who, reliable as ever, arrived soon after I started. We packed the shale and graded over and over for hours. The track had to be without a bump or a hole and only by continuously working the shale, round and round the track for hour after hour on the tractor and grader, could we achieve what we wanted.

By late on the Wednesday Pete and I were both satisfied with what we'd done and left the stadium for home at about 6.00pm. I was grateful to get back home to Takeley for a long sleep in my own bed. It felt like heaven.

The next day's practice session went off without a hitch and life seemed to be good again after what had been a week of complete hassle and stress. We had a good meeting at Hackney Speedway on the Friday and it was back to Wembley again on Saturday morning to make the final preparations for the sport's biggest night.

Pete and I spent all day re-grading, packing and watering, all of which were completed just as the turnstiles opened to let in the early arrivals for what turned out to be the last ever World Final staged beneath the famous Twin Towers.

I was due to spend the evening enjoying the racing from a super vantage point in Wembley's Royal Box, so when I'd finished working I took my decent clothes with me into the famous Wembley dressing room, where so many illustrious sportsmen had prepared for many hugely important occasions. The big bath was already full of steaming water and such was its size it was almost like a small swimming pool. I stripped off and slid down into the relaxing water, washing off the day's grime.

Just as I was about to get out, I was astonished to see the great American rider Bruce Penhall, the idol of thousands and such a handsome figure, walking towards the big bath, obviously intending to enjoy a pre-match soak in the hot water. He was, of course, completely naked and I remember thinking what thousands of girl fans would have given to be in my place at that moment! Instead, I just called out: 'Jump in, Bruce, the water's lovely!' It was a magic moment.

Soon I was dressed in my best suit and tie and ready to join Hazal and the other promoters in the Royal Box. Before doing so I had a last, slow walk of inspection around the inside of the track as the stadium filled up fast with eager fans all wearing their favourite colours and chanting slogans and good-natured banter. Some of them saw me on my walk and called across to me: 'Hope that bloody track's all right or you're for the high jump!' It was all good-natured fun and I gave them a welcome wave.

By now I'd gone past the starting gate area and reached the first corner, where I stopped, frozen and horrified, as I saw that the track was far too wet. How had that happened? Both Pete and myself had been very careful and I knew we hadn't over-watered during our earlier preparation.

Then I looked more closely and noticed that the seepage was coming from a split pipe on the inside of the dog track and was spreading slowly around the top edge of the speedway track and then creeping down the whole area. I rushed to find a stop cock and, luckily, there was one only a few yards away, which I turned frantically. Thankfully it worked and my heart stopped thumping as the water stopped flowing.

But the damage was done and I was terrified that when the four riders roared into that vital first corner in Heat 1, all of them would go down like a pack of cards. As the racing was about to begin, I went down the other end to the pits gate, where the four riders for the first race were lined up ready to be pushed off. Each one was warned by me that the first bend was very wet. They nodded to indicate that they understood but I had the feeling that they hadn't really taken in what I'd said.

I hurried to my seat in the Royal Box to watch the first race from there. My heart was in my mouth and I was trembling from the fear of a first bend disaster as the four riders – Edward Jancarz, Tommy Knudsen, Ole Olsen and Larry Ross – revved their throttles on the start line. On the edge of my seat, I gripped it tightly as the gate went up and the four riders held their throttles wide open and roared, flat stick, into the wet shale of the first bend, neck and neck, pushing and shoving, weaving around the corner – as if the surface was in perfect condition.

Above: Overseeing track watering before another big Wembley occasion.
Below: With Peter Thorogood, who gave me great help in preparing the Wembley track.

AGAINST ALL ODDS: My England team after they had clinched a 4-1 series victory over the USA at Cradley Heath in May 1981. With me standing (left to right) are: Michael Lee, Phil Collins, John Lewsey (Mirror Group Newspapers), Alan Grahame, Gordon Kennett. Front: Ian Cartwright, Dave Jessup (skipper), Les Collins, Chris Morton. We went on to defeat the Danes later that summer but the international year ended acrimoniously for me.

I almost collapsed with relief!

The track turned out to be as perfect as any track could be and that 1981 final is recognised by all knowledgeable speedway pundits as being one of the finest ever seen. The track record was broken several times and fell eventually to Erik Gundersen, while 92,000 fans enjoyed racing of the highest calibre with the man who had shared the big bath with me, Bruce Penhall, claiming the ultimate victory.

I felt very proud that night.

After the meeting all the promoters, riders and officials, together with their families, enjoyed a banquet upstairs in the stadium restaurant. I was sitting quietly with Hazal and some friends waiting for dinner to be served when I had a tap on my shoulder. It was Charles Ochiltree, the highly respected promoter of Coventry, one of the most astute and knowledgeable men in the business. He was the master of subtlety and understatement: 'Were you satisfied with your track?' he asked. I had no reply, realising immediately that he was giving me the highest praise he could and it left me speechless.

On the way home I thought: 'My goodness, only Charles Ochiltree was big enough to acknowledge the work that Pete and I had done, everyone else took it for granted.' But his thoughts were enough for me and I went to bed a happy man that night.

The epic surrounding the two big World Championship events of 1981 was not yet over, though. Some time afterwards I received a police summons to appear at Canterbury Court to face a charge of dangerous driving in Dover Dock. Since I knew that I hadn't driven dangerously, I decided to defend the case myself and not employ a legal mouthpiece.

On the day of the hearing I arrived at court and before the case I was confronted by the police prosecution officer. He was compelled by law to show me the prosecution evidence before it came in front of the beak. I was aghast when I read what was to be told to the court. A pack of lies from beginning to end, with one witness even prepared to swear that I'd carried him, spread-eagled on my bonnet, as I'd driven down the entry ramp at 50 miles an hour!

The prosecuting officer, a very fair-minded man as it turned out, in realising how disturbed I was about the evidence, advised me that dangerous driving was a criminal offence and that, therefore, I could choose to be tried by jury. So when I faced the bench, led by a rather stout and grim-looking woman of about 60, I asked if I could be tried by jury.

'Why?' she asked very sternly and obviously annoyed at my request.

'Because Ma'am,' I said, 'I'm not likely to have justice here today.'

She almost choked with rage as she glowered at me, clearly frustrated because she could do nothing about it and the case was set aside for jury trial at a later date.

Almost a year later I was back in the Canterbury Court facing 12 good men and true. I was legally represented this time and as the lies presented by the prosecution became obvious, the jury found me 'not guilty.' However, the judge had the last laugh – he turned down my barrister's request for costs, even though I'd won the case, and I ended up over £1,000 out of pocket. So much for British justice.

By then I was no longer England manager. At the BSPA's inquest into the defeat at Olching, I sat at that meeting seething inside, knowing how unfair their criticism was. I thought: 'What a load of tossers you lot are,' but, instead, I said out loud: 'I think you had better appoint another person to take on the job as I'm clearly not up to it.'

My sarcasm was lost on them and they appointed two men – John Berry and Eric Boocock – to take over my role in 1982. That was so that each one could blame the other if England didn't win.

Nobody since has equalled my winning record.

I never did the job again after 1981, a sweet and sour year, and nor would I.

Chapter 17 – Dark days
TRAGEDY

IN 1979 one of the worst tragedies speedway has ever suffered happened at Hackney. I shall live with the horrible memory of it all my life and now, every time I think about it, my throat tightens and tears come into my eyes. I refer, as any speedway supporter will know, to the untimely death of our own Vic Harding and the awful career-ending injuries sustained by Eastbourne's Steve Weatherley.

Between the outer greyhound circuit and the speedway track were the lamp standards designed, in pre-war days, to hold the lights for both dog racing and the bikes. In the corners there was a large area between the two tracks so that the metal lamp posts could be positioned about three metres behind the speedway fence. But as there was much less room between the dog track and the speedway oval along the straights, the posts there had to be closer to the wire mesh speedway fence.

Two or three years earlier I had raised the height of the fence on the straights to about seven or eight feet – well above the 4ft 6ins minimum height requirement laid down in the rule book – to avoid any rider hitting a post without protection.

The fateful day was Friday, June 8 and we were staging a four team tournament featuring ourselves, Eastbourne, Wimbledon and Canterbury. Our leading rider, Bo Petersen, was involved in a crash in one of the earlier races and reserve Vic Harding came in to take his place for the rest of the meeting. Every Hackney rider had performed absolute miracles in race after race and when Vic went out in his final ride, he only needed a third place to clinch victory for the Hawks.

We had a very big crowd in the stadium that night and as the race started there was huge excitement as they sensed the victory about to be theirs. The tapes rose and all four riders roared into the bend in line abreast, no-one giving way and so they raced neck and neck for two laps.

Then with Vic sandwiched between Steve Weatherley (on his outside) and Wimbledon's Roger Johns on the inside, he and Weatherley locked handlebars on the exit of the third/fourth pits bend. They careered like that down the home straight, then suddenly twisted together, the sudden action flinging Vic into the air, over the high fence and onto the dog track.

But his head had hit the lamp post before he fell to the ground. Weatherley smashed headlong, together with the two bikes, into the bottom of the fence.

Deadly silence fell on the stadium as everyone realised the severity of the accident The St. John Ambulance staff quickly got the two injured riders off the track and to hospital but the crowd stayed put. Not a soul moved and no noise came from anywhere. Eventually I had to take the microphone and I heard myself saying in a

The popular Vic Harding. His death at Hackney in June 1979 hit me badly.

The 1979 Hawks before tragedy struck. Left to right: Vic Harding, Bobby McNeil, Keith White, Barry Thomas (on bike), Bo Petersen, Sean Willmott and Finn Thomsen. The loss of Vic affected us all.

strange and strangled voice: 'I'm sorry everyone, there'll be no more racing tonight.'

Still people didn't move immediately but after a while the stadium slowly emptied. However, a few were still on the premises until after midnight, just waiting there in the forlorn hope of good news.

Alas they waited in vain.

The newspapers reported the following morning that Vic, almost 27, had died as a result of his head injuries and that Steve, who would be 27 later that year, had broken his back and was likely to be left paralysed. Indeed, sadly, he was.

All of the team, the fans and anyone involved with Hackney Speedway were, like myself, totally devastated. I couldn't face organising another meeting and I cancelled the following Friday's event. As it happened Vic's funeral was arranged for that day and his cremation took place in Upminster.

I never got over it and as regularly as possible I've staged an event in Vic's memory. There were some good things at Hackney in 1979, notably the return of the popular Zenon Plech after an absence of two seasons, and skipper Barry Thomas' 10-year testimonial, but they were all overshadowed by Vic's death.

Unfortunately, it wasn't the first fatal crash I had witnessed in my 20 years of promoting at Hackney and nor would it be the last. On January 8, 1972 Hackney's then No.1 Garry Middleton and myself were running a training school when Alan Clegg crashed and died from his injuries. I must admit, I knew nothing about young Alan, a 22-year-old from Beckenham in Kent, but that didn't make his death at my track of any less significance.

With Vic Harding's sister, Beverley, at one of our annual meetings to honour the memory of her brother.

And then, on July 16, 1982, Reading's American rider Denny Pyeatt lost his life after being catapulted over the wire mesh fence on the entrance to the third bend and colliding, head-first, with a steel lamp post.

It was particularly distressing, because after what had happened to poor Vic a few years earlier, as a further safety measure I had stacked rubber tyres from the base of the lamp posts to a height level with the top of the safety fence.

Why I did not pile them even higher still is a question that still haunts me to this day.

There was some talk at the time that the larger, wide, USA-made Carlisle tyre, which was new to British speedway and provided extra grip compared to other tyres on the market at the time, had been a contributory factor in Denny's crash. He certainly did seem to 'collect' some sudden and unexpected drive after colliding with another rider's wheel at the end of the back straight.

Even so, I can't hide how badly I felt as the extent of Denny's injuries became clear as soon as we rushed to his aid on the other side of the fence. One of Reading's Swedish riders – it might have been Jan Andersson – turned to me and asked: 'Why didn't you pile the tyres higher?'

I was dumbstruck, unable to give him a satisfactory reply. Truth is, I had no answer. I had protected the lamp post in question, and others, with tyres piled 8ft high but it still wasn't enough to prevent Denny's death. I couldn't believe it, I'd never seen a rider propelled that high over a fence before, and I felt very guilty afterwards. No matter which riders are killed while racing at your track, or the circumstances that caused the fatal crashes, the staging promoter always feels a deep sense of partial responsibility and, yes, guilt too. I know I certainly did.

The death of 24-year-old Denny Pyeatt at Hackney in the summer of 1982, just three years after the loss of my own rider Vic Harding, had left me gutted and definitely contributed to my decision to sell Hackney Speedway at the end of 1983.

Chapter 18 – beginnings and endings
PERSONAL TURMOIL

WITH Zenon Plech living at home, my son Andrew started to become keener to take up speedway. Up until then he had grown to love moto-cross – or scrambling as it was called then.

He was quite good at that and took part in schoolboy events most Sundays, watched by Hazal and myself. But watching and helping Zenon to prepare his bikes in our garage saw him swing towards my favourite sport.

He asked if he could ride at the Hackney Saturday training school and, of course, I said 'yes' but I deliberately didn't help him very much. I wanted to make sure that he was keen enough to do things on his own and most weeks he would have to take a bus to Bishops Stortford railway station, catch a train to Stratford and walk about two miles to the stadium. It was a tough journey for a boy of 12 or 13 but he did it without grumbling.

I knew then that he had it in him to make the grade. In his earlier years he had been a mascot at both Hackney and Rye House while riding a miniature speedway bike constructed by my old mate Don Smith. Don was a famous trials rider and won the European Championship on the Isle of Man several times. The island even had his picture in action, wearing a cloth cap and with a fag in his mouth, on their postage stamp – as if he was royalty!

He was a great guy and a good friend. The bike he made for Andrew was an exact replica of a proper speedway bike – all chrome-plated. He only charged me £200 for it even though it must have cost him a good deal more. Don rode speedway for a while at West Ham in the mid-60s and later in life got seriously involved in schoolboy BMX cycling events. He even had a Ford Cortina estate car with the number plate 'BMX IT'. A great character but, sadly, no longer with us.

On the bike Don built for him, my son would race against fellow mascots and future stars, Troy Pratt and Andy Galvin – all young kids together – before the meetings, so he started to get used to what speedway life was like at a young age.

In 1983, when he was 16 and old enough to own a speedway racing licence, Andrew started to race professionally by riding in second-half events at Rye House. I did him no favours – he had to beat the team reserves several times before I put him in the team proper. It was tougher for him but none of the other riders were ever able to suggest that he got his team place through favouritism. He well and truly earned it and straight away started to earn good points as race partner to our skipper Bobby Garrad, who was so good at nursing the younger riders.

Unhappily, after racing for only about five or six weeks, Andrew had a nasty crash at Canterbury, where a rider fell immediately in front of him, and he broke his thigh.

Two views of young Andrew with the moto-cross bike and (left) with my former Exeter team-mate, Howdy 'The Champ' Byford.

Above: Andrew getting to grips with a proper speedway
bike at Hackney and (inset) riding the scaled-down
machine at the age of 12.
Left: On his moto-cross bike.
Below: Helping out Bo Petersen in the Hackney pits.

He spent 12 weeks in traction in Canterbury Hospital and didn't ride again that year. It didn't put him off speedway, though, and that winter I sent him to race in Australia, partly to help him recover in the sunshine and also to get him racing again without any pressure. The plan worked even better than I'd hoped and at age 17 he became one of the top scorers in the Rye House team.

However, a great deal had happened in my personal life during this period. My track at Hackney had been steadily losing money and by 1983 my bank overdraft stood at over £60,000 with little sign of me being able to turn things around. Fortunately, I had a good bank manager in David Carpenter, who wasn't as tough as many other managers might have been. In all my business life he was undoubtedly the most helpful bank manager I ever had. In fact, we became quite good friends, often enjoying a social lunch together when he would tell me all about his personal difficulties with the seniors at Lloyds Bank.

My landlord at Hackney Stadium was George Walker, ex-boxer and manager of his heavyweight boxing champion brother Billy Walker. Frankly, I didn't like the man and he certainly didn't keep his word to me when, at the end of 1982, he promised to reduce my crippling rent. In addition to a set charge of £400 per meeting for water and electricity, which was way over the top, they also kept 15 per cent of the speedway gate receipts, plus all bar and refreshment takings. Then, just one week before the start of the 1983 campaign, they told me my rent would be increased to 17.5 per cent of the gate. This came as a bitter blow, long after I'd committed myself to running Hackney in the British League again for that season.

That was only one of the factors that led me to pull out of the East End promotion. The main reason was the end of my 10 years of happy married life with Hazal. We had enjoyed living together in Takeley and running our two speedway tracks. Unlike my first wife Vera, she involved herself deeply in my business affairs. Like me, she is a workaholic and enjoyed the day-to-day involvement and the long hours of work that went with it. We were a good team and she became ever more important as the years went by.

But in 1982 we made a decision to end our marriage – not because we'd fallen out or had stopped loving each other. It was for a very personal reason which would be wrong of me to make public. I was very unhappy at the time. Indeed, it would be true to say that at no other time in my life did I have that awful feeling of devastation, constantly, day after day.

Hazal, knowing how I felt and not wanting me to remain in the state I was in, suggested that I should spend as much of the coming winter as possible on the alpine slopes. She knew that my passion for ski-ing had probably overtaken my love of speedway and suggested that a whole winter out of England, in the beautiful snow-covered mountains, would be the best recovery therapy I could get. As usual, she had grasped the fundamental requirement and was exactly right in her diagnosis.

I took her advice and became a rep' for the Ski Club of Great Britain and took myself off, first to Courchevel in France and then to Niederau in Austria, acting as a sort of mountain guide or ski leader to members of the club. I loved the life and its therapeutic effect allowed me to get back to something like my normal cheery

*Above: Andrew at 16 and in his first season
for Rye House. Left: My son and Steve Naylor.
Below: Andrew (second left) battling for a team place with
fellow youngsters Dale Rook, Peter Johns and Andy Fines.*

self, even though there was a remaining sadness deep inside.

Towards the end of that winter Hazal married Steve Naylor, one of my riders at Rye House, and a year later they were both blessed with the arrival of their daughter Vicky. They lived in the town of Steve's birthplace, at Maidstone, Kent, in a modern semi on a new estate on the edge of town.

It was then time for me to sell my Hackney promotion and at first I entered into a contract with a coach operator from Buckinghamshire called Chris Shears, to buy the whole lot – lock, stock and barrel. But at the last minute he reneged on the deal and, instead, became a partner in Ipswich Speedway.

I didn't have much choice but to sell off the assets individually. After contact from my solicitor, Sheras paid a five-figure out-of-court settlement for breaching our agreement. I sold my First Division racing licence to Oxford, together with the contracts of Jens Rasmussen and Marvyn Cox. In later years, Chris and I both laughed at what happened – there was no bitterness on either part.

My other Hackney riders were sold elsewhere and the physical items in Hackney Stadium, such as plant and machinery, went to Terry Russell whose National League interests at Crayford in Kent were about to suffer an enforced closure due to stadium redevelopment. The timing worked out well for him – he simply moved his homeless Kestrels team to Hackney and ensured speedway's continuation there in 1984, with the renamed Hackney Kestrels competing at NL level.

All in all I didn't do too badly out of it financially. I was able to pay off my big bank overdraft with still a little money left over with which I bought a big house in Hoddesdon, only about half-a-mile from Rye House Stadium. This after I'd sold the bungalow in Takeley for a good profit. I went to live in Hoddesdon, having converted the house into three apartments. One was for my mother, who was then a widow aged almost 80, and one for my son Andrew. He also had a big workshop in the garden of the house.

Part of the deal with Oxford was that I should be the new-look Cheetahs' team manager for one season and help them to get established in the senior league. In the summer of 1984 I travelled a lot with their team, spearheaded by Hans Nielsen and Simon Wigg, who would both go on to become world champions at speedway and long-track in the seasons ahead.

My operation with the Rockets at Rye House continued throughout 1984 and 1985

Doing a deal with Chris Shears in 1983 – or so I thought. We later became friends.

before I sold the promoting rights to Ronnie Russell – Terry's brother – for £30,000 – the same amount I'd earlier paid to Colin Pratt for just 50 per cent of the shares. I didn't come out of that deal too well but by then I was in a position where I really had to sell. I'd started a new life in the ski-ing industry.

They were quite turbulent years and my life had shifted so dramatically that it was hard to keep up with all the changes.

Above: Hackney Hawks 1983 – my final year at The Wick. Next to me are: Jens Rasmussen, Finn Thomsen, Martin Hagon, Bo Petersen and John Titman, with Toni Kasper and Sean Willmott at the front.
Below: The 1983 Rye House Rockets – Hughie Saunders (team manager), Chris Chaplin, Steve Bryenton, Bob Garrad, Peter Johns, Kerry Gray and Steve Naylor, with Andrew at the front.

Chapter 19 – an (alpine) fresh start
SKI-ING

AS I explained earlier, my passion for ski-ing began in 1969 when my daughter Jackie and I joined Charlie and Jean Mugford for a two-week holiday in Alpbach in Austria. I was hooked immediately and couldn't wait for the following year's trip back to the same resort.

Then I found out that one of my partners in Allied Presentations, Ron Wilson, was also a keen skier. So for the next two winters I skied with him and his wife Freda at Seefeld, another Austrian resort where we stayed in the rather posh King George V Hotel. I thought it was far too swanky.

By now I was so smitten with ski-ing that I began having more than one winter holiday in the snow. In fact, in 1973, My whole family, including my mother and first wife Vera, stayed for five weeks in Davos, Switzerland, a huge resort covering three different mountains. The journey was quite an experience.

For reasons I cannot now imagine, I decided to pull a big trailer behind my Mercedes in which we had all our luggage plus large quantities of food. Squashed into the car were myself, Vera, Andrew, Jackie, David Beech (her then fiancé) and my mother. The accommodation we had booked was a big apartment over the top of a farmhouse situated near the top of the Bergen ski-lift and at the end of Bergensway. I had picked it out from a map of the town as an ideal ski-ing spot with the ability to put on our skis right at the front door.

We had completed about half of our journey when disaster struck. It was in the early hours of the morning and a tyre stripped on one of the trailer wheels. We seemed to be in the middle of nowhere. It was pitch black and we couldn't do anything except wait until daylight. The whole wheel had broken up and was totally useless.

Now I had to find a garage that could help us. So, leaving David to watch over the trailer, I set off to find one. It took me over an hour to locate a small establishment in a village somewhere south of Paris and using the best sign language I could, I persuaded the proprietor to bring out his breakdown truck to get our trailer back to his premises.

He followed me to where it was parked and, on arrival, we couldn't see David. On closer inspection, we found him fast asleep under the trailer cover where he'd gone to escape the cold. But he was still frozen stiff because it had been a bitterly cold night.

Anyway, the breakdown truck lifted the trailer clear of the ground and set off for the garage a few miles away, with me and the family following in the car. The huge weight of the trailer was making the front wheels of the truck almost lift off the ground and the whole lot was swaying dangerously from side to side. Luckily the roads were empty and we arrived at the garage just about in one piece. We were there for about eight hours while the mechanic fitted a new pair of wheels and tyres on the trailer, although we had phoned the lady who owned the farmhouse to tell her we'd be late.

Finally, off we set to complete our journey, aware that we'd now be arriving at night instead of late morning, as planned. Soon it started snowing and that slowed us down even more, but we kept going and eventually arrived in Davos at around midnight. I had the town map and went to where Bergensway was marked but it wasn't there! Driving up and down the main street several times, I finally gave up hope of finding the road to our apartment without help. Meanwhile the snow was falling thick and fast. I pulled up opposite a big hotel facing Davos Dorf railway station, where I went to find the night porter and ask him to call up a taxi. He did as I asked and after about 20 minutes one arrived. I asked the driver to take the family to the farmhouse and then come back to show us the way. Everyone except David and me piled into the big taxi and it disappeared quickly into the falling snow.

Then we both decided to put the snow chains on the Mercedes even though neither of us had any idea how to fit them. But we jacked up the back wheels and got them on after a fashion. Just as we were finishing the job, with David lying on his back under the axle, the car fell off the jack, trapping David in the cold and wet snow underneath. It was panic stations for a bit until I realised that, although he was trapped and uncomfortable, he was, thank God, unhurt. Soon I got the jack back in place and he crawled out covered in snow and grease. He was not a happy bunny.

Now the taxi returned and I indicated that I would follow him, which I did, pulling the big trailer and with snow chains on my back wheels. Then I understood why I had not been able to find Bergensway. As I followed, the taxi suddenly veered left and disappeared into a short tunnel under the railway lines – the entrance to Bergensway! I drove through the tunnel, following his lights. The road had a high snow wall on either side and, as I followed, he suddenly turned sharp left and I went round the bend after him – only to discover that I was facing a steep hill covered deep in snow, up which I had to pull the trailer.

All the odds were against the Merc making it and, sure enough, having managed to get some of the way I was starting to spin the wheels. Luckily there was a flat space in front of a small chalet to the right and with a little persuasion I just managed to pull off the lane and onto the parking space. The taxi was up ahead and Dave and I walked up the hill to discover the farmhouse about 300 yards farther up the lane. Snow was still howling down and my mother and all the family were going berserk at me. 'Where have you brought us? We're on top of a mountain and stranded. We'll never survive!'

I shrank. Then Dave and me went back to the trailer to get all the baggage and it took us both over an hour to unload it all and cart it uphill through the deep snow to the farmhouse. By this time we were both utterly exhausted, miserable and because of his earlier escapades in the cold, Dave was physically ill. Everyone was condemning me for my utter stupidity in booking such an outlandish place and I had to agree. Finally, we all got to bed and each of us quickly drifted into deep slumber.

It was no surprise that we all slept in late and didn't get out of bed until about 10.00am. Now we looked in wonderment out of the windows. The sun was shining on the fresh powder snow all around us and multi-coloured skiers were sailing past the farmhouse in what was a chocolate box picture. The town was just below us, only a short ski away and, far from being outlandish, the farmhouse was actually in a perfect position. Over breakfast, all was forgiven and we were soon out there in the snow enjoying ourselves. We've had many a laugh over the affair since.

Unlike myself, both Jackie and Andrew were natural skiers and each of them left me well behind in the ability stakes. But rough and ready skier that I was, I was able to tackle even the most difficult runs, albeit without much grace.

As the winter seasons went by and we spent holidays in most of the major alpine resorts, my ski-ing slowly improved, although I got to the plateau that many holiday skiers reach in which, although able to tackle most things, that extra polish that is reserved for the 'experts' continued to prove very elusive.

On one holiday in Cervinia (Italy) I met a Czech who had fled his homeland during the Russian onslaught on his country. He was a potter by trade and had a small business on the coast of North Wales. He was also an excellent skier, having learned as a small child in his local mountains. His name was Alder and we became great pals that year as we skied in the Italian resort under the picturesque and magnificent Matterhorn, crossing at 12,000 feet on the Plateau Rosa into Switzerland and the famous ski area of Zermatt.

Our friendship continued after that memorable holiday and we skied together on many occasions afterwards, including that fateful trip to Germany in 1981 which is covered earlier in the book. He was a great sportsman and played tennis almost every day and was very fit. so it came as a huge shock when he suffered a stroke and lost the use of his left arm and leg in 1982. Of course, Alder could no longer ski and although we kept in touch over the years, our friendship no longer included our ski-ing experience together. It was very sad.

I became a member of the Ski Club of Great Britain and in 1982 joined a special pre-season training session organised by them in Val D'Isere, one of the foremost resorts in the world. Most of the instructors were Scottish except one who was, like myself, a Cockney. We got on well together and I elected to become one of his eight trainees. It quickly became obvious that this young man – probably half my age (I was then 50) – was an expert skier and worth listening to.

He was able to point out a few small but important technical deficiencies to help me improve and it is true to say that, for me, he was like an evangelist, making me 'see the light' and in that fortnight's training I was able to turn the corner in so far as my ability on the snow was concerned. Ever since, I have used the simple but effective methods he taught me to help others to improve, spreading the 'good word' like an evangelist myself!

In the early 80s I had been in the habit of organising ski trips for groups of my friends, including the Dugard family of Eastbourne Speedway fame and Alf Hagon, a great grass-tracker of the 60s who also rode speedway. The trips would be booked with a small company called Ski Bonne Neige, run by a vintage car dealer, Mike Carter, who had started his small ski-ing company having rented two chalets in Courchevel 1550 – a very popular French resort.

After my divorce from Hazal and having spent a large part of the 1984-85 season in the Alps, I was keen to repeat the exercise, only for a longer period during the winter. A large part of the summer was spent trying to persuade Mike Carter to give me a job working for him and the Ski Club of Great Britain, together, guiding his guests and Ski Club members around the slopes of Courchevel. But he didn't seem much enamoured with the idea, although the Ski Club were very keen since they'd never at that time been able to get a rep' into that resort.

The summer passed with only my Rye House Speedway to run. Having sold up all my Hackney interests, I was keener than ever to spend the winter on the slopes. By October I'd realised that my chances of working as a guide were now pretty remote until, out of the blue, I had a phone call from Mike Carter.

'How do you fancy becoming a ski tour operator?' I immediately jumped to the conclusion that he wanted to sell me his business and was quite cautious.

'Well,' I replied, 'I might do, but you'd have to tell me a lot more.'

'Well,' he said, 'there's a company called Ski 3V and they've gone bust but they have some chalet contracts and a few other assets they want to sell. It might be a way into the business for you.'

Now I was excited and listened intently as he suggested that, if I went ahead, I could share his office, share advertising costs and generally work together. I'd heard enough and within a week I'd paid £12,500 for the assets of Ski 3V and suddenly I'd become a tour operator!

Then it hit me that I actually knew nothing at all about the business except that I could ski and I realised that skills in that direction wouldn't help me much in the market place. Still, with Mike to help me, I thought it wouldn't be too bad. At least I'd get to ski all winter – my dream!

Mike's office was near the Oval cricket ground at Southwark, where he set me up with a desk plus a phone line. I got my speedway programme printer in Southend-on-Sea to produce me a small brochure called 'New Ski 3V' and I went for a week to the Alps to look at the chalets – two in Meribel Mottaret, one in La Plagne and three in Verbier (Switzerland).

Mike employed a girl to answer the phone and deal with sales for me and I was ready to do business. It was all very haphazard and not at all well-organised but I was so happy to be going ski-ing all winter that I allowed myself to be blinded and didn't pay too much attention to details.

We started to advertise and distribute the little brochure and some bookings started to roll in. Mike had told me to buy aeroplane seats from other, bigger operators as and when I needed them, so as not to undertake too much commitment. At first that seemed to work OK but soon I realised that it could create a problem, so I pre-bought 20 seats a week from a company run by Nicky Lunn, the grandson of Arnold Lunn, who started the whole package holiday business.

By now it was December and time for me to go to the Alps. Mike had helped me to employ staff to run the chalets and a resort manager to look after Meribel and La Plagne, leaving me to oversee the operation in Verbier. At the last minute I had a phone call from a girl who was to work with her friend to run Chalet Charmet in La Plagne. She told me that she'd had a change of heart and couldn't do it. Panic.

A five-bedroom chalet and no staff, with the first holidays only two weeks away. We sifted through all the application letters still in the office, phoning one after the other but with no luck. One letter was from a married couple who lived in Cumbria. We weren't looking for a couple but as a last resort I phoned them to offer a job. 'Oh, we're sorry, we've arranged something else now and we can't do it.' It was the same answer we'd already had a dozen times over. I went home that night a worried man.

I went back to Southwark the next day to continue the search and at about 10 o'clock the phone rang. It was Brian Sill, the male half of the couple. 'Look,' he said 'if you really want us, we can rearrange our plans.' I nearly whooped with delight and was about to offer the job when my office girl said: 'Hadn't you better meet them?' Crikey, so I should.

'Can you get down to London so we can talk about it?'

He agreed and the next day I met Brian and his partner Pauline at Euston station before taking them over the road to a café where we had a lasagne for lunch. They agreed to work for me in La Plagne but none of us realised at the time how important that decision would turn out to be.

Then it was time to travel out to the Alps for my first winter as a tour operator. On visiting the local business people in Verbier, including ski hire shops, the laundry and one or two restaurants, I discovered to my horror that the 'old' Ski 3V owed money everywhere and all of them expected *me* to pay! The debts were not mine and I hadn't bought a going concern – I'd only bought the assets of the company, which included the name.

It only took me 24 hours to realise that it was the name that was causing the problem. So it was no problem – I'd change the name. It didn't matter to me one way or the other what I was called. For a week or so I operated in the alps without a name because I was undecided about it.

In the week of New Year I left Verbier, where there were no beds to be had, to go and live just for that seven days in Meribel. While there I spent some time ski-ing with the well-off Thompson family who owned Blackpool Pleasure Beach. As I dined with them in the chalet we talked about finding a name for my company. Geoffrey Thompson suggested that 'Silver Ski' would be a good choice but I had some other ideas that I thought were better. We discussed it several times and at the end of the week, just before they went home, Barbara Thompson came to me: 'You know,' she said, 'my husband is a very successful businessman and if he says your company should be called Silver Ski, then you should take his advice.'

After they'd gone I pondered on her words of wisdom. 'She's right,' I said to myself and Silver Ski was born in the first week of January 1985.

How it was to change my life yet again.

Chapter 20 – That's snow business
SILVER SKI LIVES!

HAZAL, having married Steve Naylor, was living in a modern three-bedroom house, with an integral garage, in Acorn Grove, Larkfield, just on the edge of Maidstone. She was aware of the set-up I'd become involved in, sharing Mike Carter's office in London and the rather loose arrangement of collaboration between our two ski-ing companies.

Just like me, she knew nothing at all about the business of tour operating or package holidays. In spite of that, knowing that I was having a hard time trying to sell my holidays, she started to visit the office in South London to see how it worked and to make sure that my best interests were being served.

It didn't take her long to decide that the organisation was far from perfect and that Silver Ski would be better off being run from an office of its own. We spoke on the phone regularly and she suggested that when the ski season finished I should move my operation lock, stock and barrel to her home in Maidstone, where she'd set up an office in her garage. Knowing how well we'd worked together in business for the previous 10 years and having a high mutual regard for each other in spite of the divorce, I jumped at the opportunity.

Meanwhile, while I was living in Switzerland, lessons were being learned about how tour operating works and what makes chalet ski holidays so popular with the Brits. I watched carefully what other chalet operators did and made mental notes about what I saw. The London office were having difficulty selling many of the holidays at a decent price and one of the major reasons was because I had about 60 beds to fill each week – but only 20 aeroplane seats. There were constant problems trying to buy in the extra air seats needed and even if we could get them, the travel arrangements were very fragmented with guests arriving at all times of the day. Not satisfactory at all. We were knocking out holidays just to fill beds at any price and by the end of the season I'd done 40 grand in cold blood.

Sometimes you can learn things by listening to those who know but the quickest way to learn about business is to lose your dough. I'd done that in a serious way and at that point I began to wonder if it was actually possible to earn money in the ski business. Most sensible people would have chucked in the towel at that point but inside me is an egotistical streak that tells me that I'll make a success at whatever I do, no matter how the odds are stacked against me.

I sold a bit of property I owned and paid off the bank to keep the Silver Ski account in the black, moved the office into Hazal's garage and started to prepare for the following season. In the meantime it had struck me that I'd received several nice 'thank you' letters from clients who had holidayed in Chalet Charmet in La Plagne, the one run by Brian and Pauline Sill. At the end of the season I asked them to work for me again but they both said that they fancied doing something similar for themselves. Rather than lose their services I suggested that they might like to buy into Silver Ski. They very quickly decided they liked the idea and gave me £3,000 for a 10 per cent share, plus another £4,000 of working capital to help set the company up for the following season. They knew I'd lost £40,000 but understood the fundamental reasons why.

During the summer of 1985 I took out an Air Tour Operator's Licence (ATOL) with the Civil Aviation Authority. This enabled me to properly contract aircraft seats and sell holidays with those seats included. To obtain the licence I had to attend a sort of court hearing in the big C.A.A. building in Kingsway, London, where I was grilled by a panel of three senior personnel and I had to prove that I was a 'fit and proper' person to own a licence. Fortunately I succeeded.

Because of gross lies told about me to the chalet owners in Meribel Mottaret (these by a rival operator called 'Beach Villas'), I lost the two prime chalets there and had to replace them with another two in a far inferior position. It didn't help. However, I retained about 60 beds, so I contracted for 60 aeroplane seats every week, flying from Gatwick to Geneva. Now I knew that if anyone wanted to buy a holiday, I could at least get them there.

Our new office in Hazal's garage was set up very efficiently with a big wallchart showing every bed in every chalet on every date. This enabled us to tell at a glance exactly what was sold and what was still available. We use the system to this day – it's even more efficient than computer records.

In the late autumn we started taking part in various ski shows, including the big one at Earl's Court in London. In this way we distributed about 12,000 copies of our newly-produced brochure and therefore faced the second season with confidence. Brian and Pauline had proved to me that the idea of a husband-and-wife team running the chalets was a damned good one, so that summer we advertised for couples in all the ski magazines. It was a totally unique concept and Silver Ski was the only organisation to employ such staff. All the rest employed young girls. Not only that, we sought more mature people, those who, hitherto, had been ignored in the staff marketplace.

We then included ski guiding as part of our package, with a guide for every chalet whose services were free of charge. It was another unique concept never attempted previously by any other operator. These innovative ideas were eventually copied by our competitors but it took them several years to catch on. Even today none of the operators of any size offer the ski guiding service with a guide for every chalet. They find it too costly.

The 1985-86 season was more efficient and satisfactory in every way than our first one. Even so, at the end of the season we'd still lost 20 grand – a big improvement, but still a huge loss. By this time I'd run out of money and wondered how we were going to survive a third season. Brian wasn't a wealthy man. His previous career was as a manager in a shoe factory in Kendal, so he'd not had the business opportunities to earn any real money.

A lifeline was offered when I had a phone call from Henry Hitch, who was involved in Swindon Speedway. A man I knew casually and who appeared to be a sort of country gentleman, he was a keen skier and wanted to buy into the company and work alongside us. Since we desperately needed an influx of cash, I sold him half of my 90 per cent share for £30,000 and suddenly we had enough money to enter our third successive season.

We had acquired a few more chalets and the operation had started to grow, so it was just as well that during this time Hazal and Steve had moved to a bigger house in Grove Green Lane, Bearsted, on the edge of Maidstone. There we converted the roof area into a sizeable office with a big dormer window overlooking the lane.

The ski tour business gave me a whole new purpose.

I continued to spend my winters in Verbier, where I lived in a big, old chalet called L'Hiboudiere, which means 'owl-like'. All the timber wall panels were so erected that the knots in the wood were matched up to look like owl's eyes. And all through the chalet were ornaments and pictures of owls, hence the name of the chalet.

To avoid me taking up a saleable bed in the chalet, I lived in the loft area. It had no insulation and I couldn't stand up anywhere. The door to it was miniscule and I virtually had to double in half to get in and out.

My bed consisted of three mattresses on top of each other, covered by two thick duvets. Because it was so cold in there at night, I wore heavy pyjamas with thick socks and a woolly hat. It was amazingly warm dressed like that but I had to get up very early so that I could use the bathroom before the guests needed it. I didn't care, though, and enjoyed my life in the Swiss resort.

That winter we were just on the right side of breaking even and we began to see more light at the end of the tunnel with the thought that at last we might start to recover our earlier losses. We grew even bigger and in fact operated 15 chalets in our fourth winter, including a big one in a new resort for us at Villars in Switzerland.

Our expansion also included a lovely property in Meribel Village called Chalet Sam. It was owned by Christiana Ganivet, a petite divorcee who lived in Paris. Although she was every inch a chic Parisienne, she was actually of Russian blood. Her family, the Zbars, had escaped from the communist regime to settle in Paris during the war. She was a very sexy lady and despite not being in the first bloom of youth, she even succeeded in seducing me one evening – but it was a one-off, never to be repeated experience!

I had moved from Verbier to live in Chalet Sam so that I could ski in the huge Three Valley's complex, the biggest ski area in the world. We had nine chalets there so it made sense, business-wise, for me to move. In Chalet Sam I lived in a boot cupboard which measured just 5ft 5ins from wall to wall. Since I am half an inch less than that, I could just stretch fully out on my mattress on the floor, duly cut to size. Compared to my loft room in L'Hiboudiere it was luxury, indeed, but I still had to get up earlier than the guests to use the bathroom.

I bought a semi-detached house on the opposite side of the road to the office in Grove Green Lane and that made life easier as I was literally only 50 yards away. By now I had sold my interest in Rye House Speedway to Ronnie Russell for £30,000 so that I could give my full attention to Silver Ski. It was a sensible move and that year we earned a good profit by operating a total of 15 chalets.

It was onwards and upwards from there on, adding three more properties the following year and again enjoying a good profit margin. So confident were we about the future that Brian and I decided to move into a pretty French resort near Geneva called La Clusaz. We visited there several times looking for chalets to rent but with no luck. Then we found one that was for sale at what appeared to be a very keen price and decided to go ahead and buy it.

We used the profit from the previous season and ran a bank overdraft for part of the price on the optimistic guess that we'd pay it off during the next winter. Henry Hitch wasn't too keen because he would have liked to have drawn his share of our profits in cash in his hand. But we considered the future of the company to be more important and we only drew the most modest salaries. A sign of a split was showing. We each had different agendas.

The year of 1989-90 turned out to be disastrous. The pound plummeted in value, putting our French costs up by nearly 40 per cent. There was no snowfall from Christmas until February, making holidays harder to sell. To cap it all, the airline we had contracted with, British Island Airways, went belly up in January.

Before that time, having had a fall-out with our newly-appointed bank manager at Lloyds, Henry Hitch had persuaded us to place our account with Barclays in Sloane Square, London. It was his own bank and his family's huge fortune, involving an insurance company based on the Isle of Man, was handled there. Henry had plenty of influence – a factor which was to prove of huge significance as time went by.

Because of the problems we suffered that winter we were beginning to run short of cash and our overdraft limit of £60,000 was proving to be inadequate. I went home to Maidstone in January after British Island Airways had gone bust so that I could help Hazal in the stressful quest to find other aircraft to carry our people. We had 300 clients in the Alps with no flights to get them home, which was quite a problem.

However, with her normal quiet efficiency, Hazal had located an aeroplane available for charter sitting in Holland and arranged for it to fly to Geneva to bring the bulk of our customers home and fly the new ones out. The remainder we managed to fit onto other operators' flights. It was messy, but it worked, although in financial terms it was very painful.

I visited Barclays Bank to seek a bigger overdraft limit and had a good case to put to their manager. We'd bought a sizeable and valuable freehold property, the main cause of our cash flow problems. We'd had extraordinary bad luck which had restricted our income and on the face of it there were good commercial reasons for the bank to help us. But he flatly refused.

Little did I know at the time that Hitch had other ideas about the future of the company, which set us on a collision course. I feared that he could sell the whole Silver Ski operation to one of the major players, such as Crystal or Thompsons.

At that time my mother, almost 90, was in hospital, and not expected to live. So I certainly wasn't at my chirpy best when the ultimatum came from Hitch: 'Give me enough shares to control the company and I'll arrange for a £100,000 overdraft.'

I phoned Brian in France and we decided that we had no other choice. He sent me his letter to transfer some of his shares to Hitch and, with his letter in my hand, I was standing in Hazal's kitchen talking to her about it. Having made the decision, I stood there in tears as I could see my company – my baby – going into someone else's control. I was totally shattered and heartbroken.

Suddenly I heard Hazal's voice: 'What the hell's the matter with you? It's not like you to give up so easily – fight the bastard and tell him to get stuffed!'

I was taken aback: 'Christ, she's right,' I thought.

With Hazal right behind me I almost ran up the stairs into the office. Picking up the phone, I dialled Brian's number in Courchevel. 'Hello mate, I've got your letter but I'm going to tear it up. I'm telling Henry to stuff his head up his backside, somehow I'll pull us through.' 'That's more like it,' said Hazal.

It was about the third week in January, with about 10 weeks of the season still left. With all my experience as a salesman to call upon I sat behind my desk picking up the phone every time it rang. I sold a holiday to every person remotely interested. I sold at any price – I needed cash and I needed it quickly, so the price didn't matter. Most I sold at a loss but I sold them all and by April we had enough money to stay inside our overdraft limit and I'd beaten Hitch.

But to remove him cost us dearly. We had the chance to buy Chalet Charmet for a bargain price, ideal for our company portfolio, but we had to give it to Hitch in order to displace him. It meant he finished up with the value of seven times his initial investment of £30,000. It took us five years to pay off that debt but we got rid of him and it was as if a cloud had lifted off the company and from those dark days we flourished.

During 1990 I learned of a big restaurant building in the highest part of La Plagne that was for sale, freehold, for what seemed like sensible money. It was called Le Bon Coin, which literally translates as 'The Good Corner'. I went to see it and discovered a huge building, very well constructed, which had run a night club in the basement, a big restaurant at ground level and other rooms under the roof. It was a warren of a place and I immediately saw its potential as a ski chalet positioned, as it was, only 50 yards from the piste. But money was a bit tight, given all that had gone on with Henry Hitch, and my partner Brian – who by this time owned 20 per cent of the company due to the way the accountants redistributed the

Hitch 45 per cent shareholding – didn't want to take the financial gamble that the purchase involved. But I was confident and insistent, so he finally agreed to let me have my way.

I went to see the agent, Monsieur Paul DeVallier, at Plagne Centre and proposed a price to him about two thirds less than the asking price. He laughed at me: 'Look,' he said in his best English 'the owner's been divorced and is desperate to sell with his ex-wife pressing him for money, but he's not *that* desperate. It's a silly offer.'

'OK,' I said, 'but why don't you go ahead and ask him?'

With that he picked up the phone and spoke to the owner in very fast French – most of which I didn't understand. Putting the phone back on its hook, he looked long and hard at me. 'I don't believe it, he'll take your offer!'

So at just over £200,000 I'd bought a property of over 500sq metres in a prime position, probably worth, even then, nearly double that amount. I arranged a 10-year mortgage with the Banque Transatlantique, in Boulevard Haussman in Paris, borrowing the money in Swiss Francs because the interest rate for that currency was only about 2 per cent. By January 1991 the deal was completed.

Now I had to convert it into a chalet and I took the plans and carefully re-designed the interior taking care to maximise the use of every square inch. Working for me that winter were several people, all keen skiers, who had skills in the DIY department. One of them, my maintenance man, a Cockney from Dagenham, called Simon Gaywood, was a qualified plumber and electrician – City and Guilds and all . . . even though he was dyslexic. A very likeable young man in his 20s, who jumped at the chance of being involved in the project.

Others too volunteered their services, including Beverley and Steve Dickenson who'd run a chalet for me in La Clusaz two seasons earlier and Chalet Bonin, next door to the Bon Coin, in 1990-91. Many others pledged to come and help with working holidays during the summer of '91, which they all did. The work was massive and my original estimated cost of £30,000 nearly tripled in the end.

During the work process I went every Tuesday to Maidstone Furniture Auction in the town market next to the River Medway. There I bid for, and bought, loads of beds, tables, chairs and all kinds of furniture, some new some second-hand, loaded them onto a big Ford Transit mini-bus turbo charged diesel with a big roof rack and no seats. Then I'd drive it across France on Wednesday doing the 600-mile journey from Calais to La Plagne in eight hours, while eating sandwiches and sweets stacked in a box next to my driver's seat all the way there. I literally ate my way across France!

On arrival on Wednesday evening I'd then join the workforce to help with the conversion, returning to Maidstone at the weekend to man the office phone on Saturday and Sunday, then to repeat the exercise the next week. It was a busy time.

Slowly but surely the Bon Coin was beginning to look like a chalet rather than a deserted restaurant but the ski season was drawing near with still lots to be done and we all had feelings of panic as December arrived. Our first group of guests were due the week before Christmas and snow was starting to settle outside the chalet about a fortnight before their arrival. This served only to slow up the work even more as transporting things we needed up the mountain road became trickier.

It was a group of about 25 teenage college girls and several teachers who duly got off the plane and made their way by coach to the Bon Coin. As they were coming up the snow-covered mountain road, and only about 10 minutes from the chalet, the last wall heater was being screwed into position in the big lounge/diner. Once that was in place, we all put on our Silver Ski uniforms and went outside to wave a welcome to the coach as it turned the corner and came into view about 100ft below us. We'd won!

When we served dinner for the first time that night, with Bev and Steve in charge of the huge kitchen, some of us had tears in our eyes as we realised what enormous efforts our staff had made during the summer, with very modest financial reward, to make this meal possible. I was a humble but happy man that evening and learned the powerful lesson that true friends do things other than for personal gain.

As the company prospered we invested those profits into freehold properties in the resorts we worked in and finally ended up owning two in Val D'Isere, one in Meribel and two in La Plagne. The set-up of owning freeholds placed us in an enviable position in the market place since our overall costs were probably less than our competitors. In tough years that's invaluable.

Chapter 21 – French resistance
SPEEDWAY BUG BITES AGAIN

WHILE I had been devoting my efforts to Silver Ski Holidays, both of my children had been progressing in their chosen careers. Jackie had been concentrating her efforts into her love of horses and horse riding.

She eventually developed a stable and training facility on the Cambridge/Bedford border. Jackie and Dave Beech had eventually divorced and she married John, who was in the building trade. During those years her and David had produced two handsome sons, David and Tony, while the beautiful result of her marriage to John is their daughter, Danielle, so I became a grandfather at what I thought was far too young an age!

In the meantime Andrew had become a truly outstanding speedway rider of great skill and speed. He was a delight to watch and was one of the most exciting, young riders of his time. In 1986 he was called up by joint England managers Colin Pratt and Eric Boocock to make his senior Test debut against Denmark – even though he was still a second division rider.

It was a bold selection but I'd called up my old Rye House promoting partner and Hackney skipper Pratty to urge him: 'Do yourself a favour and pick Andrew.'

I knew my son's highly flexible technique, his ability to make tight turns, was ideally suited to Wolverhampton. Although England lost the match by two points to a then all-conquering Danish side, Andrew had contributed an impressive seven points – out-scoring seasoned internationals Chris Morton, Kelvin Tatum and Neil Evitts.

His most successful season was in 1987, when, aged 20 and riding for the Arena Essex team, he claimed no less than eight track records all over the country (including one at Stoke which has never been beaten), won several individual meetings, was top scorer in the league and won the National League Riders' Championship at Coventry almost exactly 25 years to the day after I'd won the equivalent championship at Belle Vue in 1962. It was cause for a family celebration.

Then, in 1988, he transferred to First Division Swindon, a move that ultimately proved disastrous for him. He suffered from a mysterious bug in both his engines which turned out to be hairline cracks – virtually undetectable – near the exhaust ports. The lack of speed against the world's top riders sapped Andrew's confidence and he became a shadow of his former self.

From time to time he showed his previous brilliance but he had become disillusioned with racing. The Swindon management had poor people skills and had no idea how to treat my son in order to produce the best results from him.

Above: Andrew in typically spectacular action for Arena Essex in 1987 – his most successful season.
Below: I'm back! – lining up with my son and the other Eastbourne Eagles.

Indeed, quite the opposite – their poor attitude pushed him in the wrong direction.

By the end of 1991 Swindon and Andrew decided to part company, so my friend Bobby Dugard, who owns Eastbourne Speedway stadium, took Andrew into the Eagles team. During that season it was run by a consortium who had transferred from Wimbledon to the Sussex venue.

I started to visit Eastbourne during 1992 to watch my son race and it soon became obvious that he was starting to regain his confidence and his scoring ability. But the management were losing money and it was also clear that things at Eastbourne had to change.

Winter came and we went ski-ing. Andrew was showing his prowess at the fairly new winter sport of snowboarding, at which he became an ace, eventually being generally acknowledged as one of Europe's top performers.

The Dugard family came for a two-week holiday and I ski'd with them every day. During the fortnight Bob told me that the Wimbledon consortium were ending their operation and suggested that I might like to become involved. It occurred to me that if Eastbourne folded my son would be out of work so, with that uppermost in my mind, I said 'yes'.

However, I placed a condition on my involvement. It was agreed that the promotion should be non-profit making with any surplus going into the development of the club and not into any individual's pocket.

Jon Cook, who'd been a junior rider there, was introduced to me as a person with administrative ability and I asked him to work alongside me, taking over the paperwork. He readily agreed and very soon we became great friends. His work was impeccable and we spent many hours together discussing the right or wrong way to promote successfully.

He was a quick and willing learner. First and foremost we needed a team that the fans would consider worthy of supporting and I went into the transfer market to buy the contracts of David Norris, Dean Barker and my son still owned at that time by Swindon. Bob Dugard purchased the contract of his own son, Martin, and with these top four performers the basis of a very good team was set up. Then I proposed to change the race day from Sunday afternoon to Saturday night on the basis that, in a seaside town like Eastbourne, sunny Sundays saw families heading for the beach, not to the speedway. The change certainly had a beneficial effect. The team did well and we were successful in turning the club into a financially sound enterprise even though surpluses were thin.

Sales in my ski business remained good during 1993 and the company continued to expand and improve. The ski season of 1993-94 arrived and all was going according to plan with no real aggravation. Hazal was running the office upstairs in her home, steadily becoming more and more knowledgeable and experienced, always helping the business to be more profitable. She looked after my interests in so many ways it was almost as if we were still married. It was a happy time.

During the late winter I decided to help my son regain his very best form. He wanted to change engines, so I purchased two new motors tuned by Otto Lantenhammer, the ace German, and also bought a new Toyota Hiace van to carry

Before he quit at the start of 1994, Andrew in flying form for the Eagles.

Andrew's bikes and other equipment. He seemed to have the perfect set-up.

Eastbourne's opening match of 1994 was at Coventry and I went there to watch with eager anticipation, expecting Andrew to put in a big score on his new engines. How wrong could I be?

Last away from the tapes in every race, he put in a dismal performance and I went home very disillusioned.

The next morning I was having a cup of coffee in Hazal's kitchen and Andrew walked in. He looked very sheepish. I looked at him with curiosity: 'What's up?'

'Well, Dad, I've thought about it a lot and I've decided to give up racing.'

It was a totally unexpected bombshell and I nearly fell over in surprise.

'What the hell for? What's brought this on?'

'I've thought about it for a long time and I just don't want to do it anymore,' he said.

Now I knew why he'd performed so badly at Coventry – he just didn't want to race, it was as simple as that.

I didn't try to persuade him to change his mind, unhappy though I was about his decision. Speedway is far too dangerous to be involved in when your heart isn't fully in it and I had to accept what he said.

Andrew has been a big mate of Gary Havelock since they both rose from National League stardom to become senior England internationals at more or less the same time – and they remain great friends. In 1992 'Havvy' became only the fifth Englishman to win the World Championship but success didn't bring him the rewards, financially or in terms of new sponsorship deals, he probably expected and deserved considering his huge achievement. It's my belief that this rubbed off on Andrew to some extent and, following his frustrating spell with Swindon, only added to his disillusioned attitude to the sport at the time.

The day after our chat in the kitchen I went down to Eastbourne to see Jon Cook and Bob Dugard. It was to relay Andrew's decision to retire followed by my own withdrawal from the promotion. Without Andrew there I had no incentive to remain involved.

Bob was alarmed. He thought I'd want the money back that I'd invested in riders' contracts. It amounted to many thousands of pounds and it clearly gave him great concern. But he needn't have worried. I didn't want the money back and I signed a document giving the contracts to Jon to ensure that he had a proper financial stake in the club so that no-one could steamroller over him. It was the least that I could do to help a young man who had dedicated his time and efforts on my behalf.

So my re-involvement in speedway promotion came to a premature end and I made up my mind that I would totally concentrate on my ski-ing business and try to forget about motorbikes.

It was as well that I did, because big trouble was looming in the winter sports industry and it related to the attitude of the French ski instructors. Most British companies provided some sort of ski guiding service for their clients, none more so than Silver Ski. We gave the best service in the industry with at least one ski guide for every chalet in our programme. It was a vital part of the package we sold and contributed heavily towards our success.

The legality of using guides who, although expert skiers, did not hold the French qualification, had always been a grey area. In the mid-90s the French government decided that such service was illegal. It was pure protectionism and came about after pressure from the French national Ski School (E.S.F.). Virtually all of our competitors immediately stopped providing guides and most were very happy to save the money, hiding behind the new law when questioned by their clients.

But I was very unhappy about it and decided to try to find a way around the new legislation. I visited Francois Chat, a top French legal expert in Chambery, to seek his advice. He considered that it was possible for me to continue providing ski guides as long as I could prove without doubt that my guides were not paid.

We jointly reached agreement on the ways we could achieve it. We published various items in our brochure and within our chalets and also produced a document to be signed by our guests. Then we had to find out for certain whether we were actually legal or not, and that was a very risky undertaking. It meant that our scheme needed to be tested in a French court-of-law and to achieve that we had to deliberately put our staff and ourselves in a position to be 'nicked' by the police.

The big risk was that, if we were found guilty of breaking French law, Brian, my partner, and I could end up in jail and our ski guides heavily fined. So it was a strategy that made us gulp a bit.

We spoke to our guides and told them of our plan, persuading them to wear their Silver Ski uniforms and to blatantly show that they were acting as guides to our guests, particularly if there were gendarmes in the vicinity. We *needed* to be nicked! But I was extremely nervous about it.

Sure enough, pretty quickly three of our guides were stopped by gendarmes and reported for illegally guiding without the French qualification. That qualification was, by the way, impossible to get unless you were French. The qualifications of other nations were not recognised.

Brian and myself received summonses, charged with employing illegal guides and the case was put before judges at the Halle de Justice in Albertville. The three guides, Brian and I presented ourselves at the big building in Albertville. There we were confronted by the prosecutor, a nasty anti-Brit who delighted in telling us that we were all going to jail and how pleased he was about that. He rubbed his hands together and reminded me a lot of Fagin in Oliver Twist. He even had a long nose! By the time we were led into the courtroom all five of us were fearful for our future.

The representatives of the E.S.F. presented their case but they were poorly prepared and even had some of the dates wrong, let alone actual facts – some of which were clearly invented. Our case, on the other hand, was watertight.

We were able to produce positive written evidence to support our claim that the guiding was provided on a voluntary basis and, because of this proof, all five of us were found 'Not Guilty'. We left the court walking on air – we had won! We'd beaten the racist E.S.F. members and, most importantly, we were able to continue giving our guests the full benefit they'd been used to. It was cause for celebration and celebrate we certainly did.

When our competitors heard about our great victory most of them started to provide guides once again but, in fact, although they got away with it because of what we'd done, none of them were actually legal. Unlike ourselves, they did not produce the paperwork to make what they were doing legal. As it happened, it all became quite academic since the European Court made France comply with common anti-racist law about a year after our court case.

It is fair to say that not all parts of the French Ski School were against our use of British guides. Some, as in La Plagne, openly supported us. It was, in our case, just a small body of anti-Brit militant instructors in Meribel who caused the rumpus. One of them owned two chalets which we operated and at that time he said to me that unless Silver Ski stopped their guiding activities he would end our rental contract. In my best French I told him to stick his chalets up his derriére!

Bev and Steve Dickenson, who had started working for me in 1989, first running a chalet in La Clusaz, then one year later the chalet Bonin in La Plagne followed in 1991-92 by the newly-converted Bon Coin, had become not only very good friends but vital people in my organisation. Bev became a resort manager with Steve as our chief ski guide. They made La Plagne their permanent home and by 1994 Bev had become our overall Alpine manager.

In August of that year their son Charlie was born and Bev came back to England for the actual birth, although it was always the plan to remain permanently in France. They all lived in Chalet Bon Coin and for two winters I rented an apartment for them just next door, so that Bev could look after her new baby son without having to worry about guests. Very quickly it became obvious that Charlie was to be an exact replica of his father, Steve. He was a big boy, like his dad, his blond hair and quiet manner making him a miniature Steve in almost every way. He became a great favourite with everyone.

In 1996 I decided that it was time for Bev, Steve and Charlie to have a proper home, so I designed a house to be built on the front of Chalet Bon Coin and obtained planning permission to build it. Just as when we'd converted the main chalet in 1991, I called on the DIY skills of any number of my winter employees and persuaded them to arrive in the summertime for working holidays. As soon as the snow melted in early June, we began the work.

I got a local firm to install the footings but from there on upwards voluntary or lowly paid helpers did the construction. I became a builder's labourer for the occasion and humped concrete blocks about as well as doing a lot of carpentry jobs. The whole enterprise took 13 weeks to complete and Bev, Steve and Charlie actually moved into their new two-bedroom house in September 1996.

One of the highlights of the build was the installation of a huge timber beam, half a metre square and designed to support the overhanging roof which was to cover the chalet's main entrance area. Our resident carpenter, Steve Alford, otherwise known (for God knows what reason) as 'Spank', had made the beam about eight metres long and fitted with two angled cross beams at the top end, which had holes in them to line up with holes in the new building blockwork. But when the time came to erect it, we didn't know how we were going to lift it into place. It was a huge chunk of timber, almost a complete tree trunk, only square, and its weight was far too heavy for us to manhandle it.

As luck would have it, one of our local French friends, Claude, who worked all year round for the ski-lift company as a maintenance engineer, came up with a solution. He 'borrowed' a huge forklift truck after work one evening and drove it up to the Bon Coin. There, aided by 'Spank', he wrapped a huge chain around the beam and slowly lifted it off the ground. It was at this point that we all began to appreciate just how big this lump of timber actually was.

It was a fact also recognised by the late summer holidaymakers living in the nearby apartments and hordes of them lined the area to watch in amazement as the beam swung up in the air, higher and higher. The two holes in the crossbeams had to line up perfectly with the holes in the top of the wall, while the bottom end had to sit square in the centre of the footings. With the huge chunk of timber swinging at an acute angle from side to side, it seemed an impossible task.

But bit by bit 'Spank' kept adjusting the chain holding it all up and with several of us helping to stop the swaying, the beam was steadily lowered in a vertical position with the bottom end directly over the one metre square footings. Everyone held their breath.

Finally Claude lowered the forks on the truck, dropping the beam into position. It landed with a gentle thud as 'Spank' twisted it to line up properly. As it landed our huge French audience applauded loudly and when we discovered the holes in the crossbeam lining up perfectly, we allowed ourselves to applaud too. Credit was due to 'Spank' who'd designed, measured and made it, for it couldn't have been any more perfect than it was.

During the ensuing years Charlie went to the local French school in Plagne Centre, becoming fluent in the local language as well as speaking perfect English. On many occasions we'd ask his advice on translation. He never let us down.

Two years after building Bev and Steve's house, we constructed a hundred square metres of underground rooms on the back of the chalet, together with an extension of the lounge. It was a huge undertaking which resulted in my enjoying the benefit of a nice, big bedroom and large bathroom of my own as well as a much bigger Alpine office and other rooms for staff as well. My winter home at 7,000ft was finally complete and even though I'm sure the building work I was involved in contributed to the arthritis I've suffered from ever since that time, its been a real pleasure to live there from November onwards every year.

My passion for ski-ing and the ability to enjoy the mountains has, without a doubt, made a very beneficial contribution to my health in later years. Even though when I arrive back in England every spring my face is coloured distinctly, brown at the bottom and panda-white eyes at the top, I can live with that!

Chapter 22 – Taxing times
ANOTHER NARROW ESCAPE

HAVING reached pensionable age I enjoyed, for the first time in my life, someone sticking some money in my bank account without me having to do anything about it. A very unique experience for me, as I'd spent all my life, from the age of 11, when I did my first paper round, earning my own living.

Whatever I had acquired, everything I owned, had been worked for, sometimes with the help of others and no-one more than my ex-wife, Hazal. She had supported me in every venture for over 30 years, no one guarded my interests more diligently and Lord help anyone who even as much as criticised me. She would go for the throat, sometimes to my embarrassment, because criticism doesn't particularly bother me.

On the other hand, I am probably Hazal's most loyal supporter and for good reason. Over the years she has proved to be my genuine best friend, a fact not always looked on kindly by others close to me.

Hazal was very keen for me to live a healthy lifestyle and encouraged me, not only to ski for the whole of every winter but also to visit the mountains in the summer to help improve some of our chalets – the physical exercise and clean mountain air were obviously of benefit.

But I didn't always stay healthy. I had suffered for a good many years with occasional painful indigestion. It came and went on varied occasions and sometimes it was so distressing that I'd roll on the floor sweating with agony. My 'cure' was to swallow dozens of anti-acid tablets but they didn't really help.

In the middle of one summer during the 90s I was due to drive a minibus full of furniture to La Plagne from Maidstone auction rooms but the night before I was feeling very groggy and physically sick. I didn't think too much of it and believed I'd simply eaten something that didn't agree with me.

So the next morning, still feeling a bit the worse for wear, I set off in the minibus for Dover and the P&O Ferry that would take us to Calais. On the ferry it was my usual habit to eat a nice meal and set myself up for the 600-mile drive to La Plagne and Chalet Bon Coin. On this day, although I filled a plate in the self service section, when I sat down to eat the thought of it made me feel ill and nothing went down. I felt sick all the way across the Channel.

After disembarking and driving out onto the auto route to Reims, I began to realise that my sickness was not going away and the pain in my stomach was very uncomfortable. I still had a nine or 10-hour drive ahead of me and, amazingly, looking at the situation in hindsight, I never ever considered turning back.

Pushing my stomach hard against the steering wheel in an effort to reduce the pain, I drove down through Reims *en route* to Lyon, my foot flat on the accelerator making the turbo diesel move at between 85 to 95 mph. I was just trying to get to Chalet Bon Coin in La Plagne as quickly as possible.

The miles hurried by and I stopped to fill up with diesel at a service station near Dijon. On getting out of the cab, I was overcome by a feeling of faintness and I began to realise that I might just have to stop driving. Then I realised that I'd need help so I made a phone call to Bev, in La Plagne, to ask her to organise a doctor to see me when I arrived. By now I felt sure that there was something quite seriously wrong with me.

Back in the cab, I continued to drive until I finally got through Lyon and on past Chambery to Albertville. From that point I drove on the dual carriageway to Moutiers, then on to Aime and finally up the winding mountain road into La Plagne. I was in a complete daze. It was a miracle that I didn't put the Ford over the edge and only God knows how I managed to steer all the way up to 7,000ft and the door of the Bon Coin.

When I got there Steve ran to the bus to help me out of the cab. He stopped me falling on my face and half-carried, half-dragged me to his own car. Once inside and with me almost unconscious, he sped down to the medical clinic at Plagne Centre, where a doctor had been waiting for me – obviously organised by the ever-efficient Bev. Steve helped me to undress so that the quack could examine me, which he did very thoroughly, even sticking his rubber-gloved finger up my backside to feel my prostate! I remember jumping out of my skin when he did that even though I was still very dozy.

When he finished the examination he made a phone call to Moutiers Hospital and told Steve to drive me there as quickly as possible. I don't remember the journey because I passed out soon after getting in the car. I woke up when several pairs of hands were lifting me onto a trolley, which was then wheeled into a big, bare room. There a doctor ran an ultrasound scan over my stomach. I thought: 'Christ, I must be pregnant – no wonder I feel queer!'

However, the doctor said to me in almost perfect English: 'You have gallstones, Mr. Silver, we must operate right away.'

I was too weak to argue and very soon I was being wheeled into an operating theatre, where he put me to blessed sleep and the pain drifted away. I woke up the next morning, the sun streaming through the hospital window, to find myself in a small ward with only two beds – the other one empty. Nurses whisked in and out but none said a word to me, they only spoke French. *'Pardonez moi, je voudrais parler avec le docteur, si possible?'* My French wasn't too clever but they understood me.

After a couple of hours during which I contemplated the bandages swathed around my middle, the doctor appeared. It was the one who had told me what was wrong the night before. 'You're a very lucky man,' he said. 'Look here,' and with that he undid the bandages to expose my belly. I looked down amazed to find what looked like a big zip fastener from my belly button up to the middle of my chest.

'What the hell is that?'

'Don't worry, they're clips to hold your wound together – they're better than stitches.'

'Bloody hell! It looks awful.'

'Well, look at this,' said the the doctor, producing a round glass container about an inch or so in diameter and two or three inches deep. 'That was in your gall bladder.' I peered to see a huge number of small stones, varying in size from almost half-an-inch long to tiny dots. 'Christ!'

'Yes, we had to remove your gall bladder entirely – you can live without it but we were just in time. Another couple of hours and we probably couldn't have saved you!'

His words hit me like a bullet. Two hours from death? Surely not? I looked down at my 'zip fastener' and suddenly felt very strange as I realised that, yet again, my Guardian Angel had looked after me. I heard myself saying, 'Thanks Doc, I'm in your debt for ever.' He walked away smiling and I settled down to spend the next 10 days bored as hell in hospital.

All of the profit we'd earned from the Silver Ski operation went back into the company. None of it was wasted on a high life for the directors. In fact, so modest was the money I lived on that it precipitated a tax investigation because the Inland Revenue inspectors didn't think I could live on the money the company paid me. Clearly they considered that I had some sort of hidden income I wasn't declaring.

It was actually quite laughable and when the lady investigating officer discovered two Swiss bank accounts in my name, she thought she had caught me out. At first I was astonished. I'd never had two Swiss accounts – only one which was used for transferring cash to pay the company outgoings in Verbier (Switzerland), where we operated several chalets.

She sternly demanded to know what the 'other' account was for. 'But I don't have another account,' I protested. She then produced the evidence – a bank document, clearly in my name, and I was dumbfounded. My inability to explain it must have made me look as guilty as hell. The lady, on the other hand, was now very smug, sure in the knowledge that she'd caught me. I didn't sleep that night.

The next day, with the inspector once again in my office, I made a phone call to my bank in Switzerland. Fortunately the staff there spoke excellent English and when I asked them about my account, it was very quickly explained that the Banque Populaire Suisse had changed its name to Credit Suisse, hence the two accounts.

The over-zealous inspector was visibly deflated but I laughed like a hyena. It wasn't a good move. Now she had the knife in me, determined to discover that I was 'on the fiddle'. She visited my modest semi-detached house to see if I had a Rolls-Royce in my garage or any other obvious signs of an expensive lifestyle, but she was disappointed.

My house only cost £65,000 in the late-80s, well below the average house price of the period, and my furnishings had all come from previous homes with nothing new or flamboyant.

So she turned her attention to France, thinking that this was where the fiddle was taking place. I produced photographs of my personal room in the Chalet Bon Coin

– certainly nothing to write home about – and explained that in winter time I dined in the chalet with the guests, my food being provided virtually free of charge in the general chalet holidaymaker's budget.

'Gotcha!' she said. 'You haven't declared the value of your room or your food in France.'

'But it has no value,' I protested. 'I still maintain my house in England. My room (in France) would not be suitable for letting because it's in the basement and my cost to the chalet budget is nothing. It's the same amount of money whether I'm there or not.'

My argument fell on deaf ears and she 'won' her case against me. When all was added up and calculated, my personal tax bill went up by only £1 a week – yet the investigation producing that result must have cost thousands since it had gone on for about six weeks. What a waste of taxpayers' money.

As I said, all our profits went back into the company and most of it was spent by buying freehold chalets in French ski resorts. By 1998 we owned five, all bought and paid for. Two in Val D'Isere, two in La Plagne and one in Meribel. One of the most recently acquired properties, a newly-built, nine-bedroom chalet in La Plagne, called the Topaz, caused me another dose of intensive pain.

I was due to be handed the keys by the developing agent during the first week of December, just before the season was to get underway and I met him at the front door. He was beaming as he held out the key for me to take. Stepping forward, hand outstretched, the heel of my shoe landed on a small piece of plastic which was sitting on a sheet of ice. Whoosh! – up in the air went my legs and I landed with my back on the corner of a concrete building-block that was lying on the ground behind me.

'Jesus Christ!' I was in complete agony with a broken rib plus heavy bruising all round. But I still managed to take the keys of the chalet even though I couldn't move. Somehow I had to get down the 80 steps that led to the building and it took what seemed like forever, every step a major achievement. It slowed me down a bit, I can tell you, and I didn't ski for about a month. Even when I did, my breathing was very painful but I put up with it and skied every day for the rest of the winter.

The pain had not entirely gone when spring came round and in fact it took about a year before it had disappeared completely. So when I hear about someone busting a rib, they have every ounce of my sympathy.

In general, apart from the aggravation of a fruitless tax investigation, this was a good period with business matters progressing very smoothly. The turn of the millennium was to herald a new era of high activity and a re-involvement in the sport I love so much – speedway.

Chapter 23 – Rebuilding Rye House

A NEW MOUNTAIN TO CLIMB

IWAS sitting in the office in Chalet Bon Coin one evening early in 1999 thinking about snow conditions for the next day's ski-ing when the phone rang. It was a call from a chap I didn't know at that time – John Stoneman.

He was a member of the Rye House Speedway committee, a body of people determined to see the return of the sport to the little stadium in Hoddesdon by the River Lea.

After I'd sold the speedway promoting rights there in 1986 the Rockets had been run by Ronnie Russell for seven years. He had lost money all the time before finally closing down in 1993. During that time the stadium itself had been acquired by Eddie Lesley, a greyhound enthusiast who introduced stock car racing there to replace the speedway activity after Ronnie pulled out.

Against that discouraging background, a bunch of speedway fans had grouped together and all stuck £50 each into a kitty to finance the re-launch of the Rockets. The general idea was that the team would not have a 'home' circuit but operate using other team's tracks as a member of the recently formed 'Amateur' Conference League, a sort of training league for new, young riders.

I'd read a bit about it in *Speedway Star*, which I'd continued to subscribe to throughout the intervening years. So when John Stoneman phoned me to talk about their plans, I wasn't entirely ignorant.

He had more than 100 members who had each parted with £50 and was talking to me simply to try and recruit me as a member for £50. I questioned him about the plan and was impressed with his businesslike approach. 'I won't put in £50,' I said to him, 'you need more help than that – I'll sponsor the team with £2,000 and if I can use my knowledge or influence to help, just ask.'

What fateful words they proved to be.

From that day onward my office phone rang every day when I came in from ski-ing and it soon became clear that this committee, well meaning and enthusiastic as they were, didn't have any knowledge about speedway promoting or running a team. I found myself giving advice and getting more involved.

They had planned to rent the Arena-Essex track for £1,000 a meeting, an idea I nipped smartly in the bud. 'You can't possibly afford that kind of expense out of the budget you've got – leave it to me, I'll sort something out,' I said.

The next day I put a call through to my two old mates, Jon Cook at Eastbourne and Dingle Brown, by then the promoter at Mildenhall. Both of them helped me as I had expected. Jon said we could run one meeting at Eastbourne, free of charge, while Dingle set up a longer-term facility in which we would use the Fen country track at the end of each of his own meetings for only £300 a week. The committee were over the moon at the sudden realisation that their dream of seeing a Rockets team back in action was about to become reality.

Springtime came and I returned from the Alps to find that the first match for the new Rockets team – led by Simon Wolstenholme, a reasonably experienced rider at Third Division level – was scheduled to take place at the Arlington Stadium, Eastbourne, within a couple of weeks. The day duly arrived and I presented myself at the stadium, meeting my old friends Bobby Dugard and Jon Cook and ready to enjoy seeing the new Rockets team in action. They faced a King's Lynn side composed mainly of novices, just as our team was.

The match began and it was soon obvious that nearly all the riders were a little out of their depth. Not much skill was on show, just a lot of enthusiasm. Crashes and wobbly riders was the order of the day with the King's Lynn kids looking the better of the two teams.

However, in the second-half of the match Lady Luck swung in favour of the Rockets and 'my' team ran out winners by an odd point or so. It was amazing and the Hoddesdon fans were delirious. Not only had they now got a team to support again, they'd actually won their first match. This was their idea of Heaven.

Now the committee were getting me involved and I was beginning to enjoy it. Very quickly I realised that we needed some more experienced riders and soon signed a polished performer called David Mason. I sponsored both him and Simon Wolstenholme via my Silver Ski company. This gave the Rockets a far more professional look and when we raced matches at Mildenhall, our results were very respectable.

During that summer, Steve Ribbons, another member of the committee, kept badgering me about getting speedway back into Rye House Stadium. He had apparently spoken with the owner, Eddie Lesley, whom he said was quite keen. One afternoon I arranged for Steve to introduce me to Eddie Lesley so that I could find out what the situation really was.

When I walked into the stadium to meet him, I couldn't believe my eyes. The pretty little arena next to the River Lea that I'd left in 1986 was no more. In its place was a rubbish tip.

Next to the entrance was a wire mesh enclosure in which were dozens of bashed-up cars, just how you would imagine a breaker's yard to look. The centre green had a winding tarmac track on it with lorry tyres all over the place. And when I walked into the long bar building, it was like walking into a house owned by Steptoe and Son. Muck, dirt, grease and grime were everywhere.

A few derelict scaffold tubes stood starkly against the River Lea backdrop where once had stood a grandstand for 1,000 people. Entering the snack bar under the small concrete stand was like going into the Black Hole of Calcutta. It was a dump.

I met Eddie Lesley, a small, slim man wearing a leather bomber jacket whose eyes were constantly mobile. Almost as soon as I sat down next to him in the dingy, long bar he made it clear that the stadium was for sale rather than for rent. The price started at £700,000 but within minutes had reduced to half-a-million.

But I was only interested in renting. Dog racing didn't interest me and neither did stock cars, so outright ownership of the stadium was the last thing on my agenda.

We spoke for a long time and discussed the physical aspects of operating the speedway, considering that the original track had now been put to tarmac for stock cars. Track-laying was something in which I had some expertise and I suggested that I could lay and lift a shale track on top of the tarmac for each meeting.

He was astounded. 'If you can prove to me that it's possible, we can maybe have a deal,' said Lesley and I left the dump of a stadium suddenly realising that I was allowing myself to become seriously involved in speedway for the third time in my promotional life. But I thought: 'What the hell – why not?'

A few enquiries among some of my old speedway friends, including Peter Thorogood who had helped me lay the Wembley track among other things, enlightened me about where I could buy red shale, or its equivalent, and I ordered 20 tons to be delivered to Rye House for the test of laying and lifting a track. It was, of course, only enough to do a small section but sufficient to see if I could achieve my bold claims to Eddie Lesley.

The day duly arrived and the lorry dropped its 20-ton load onto the tarmac stock car track. Then I realised, rather sheepishly, that I had no tractor or grading equipment, which meant we had to spread it all by hand – a mammoth task. A few die-hard fans were there to help and after about an hour or so we had it rough laid about four inches deep. I then got into my car and drove backwards and forwards over the shale, tyre-packing it to consolidate the material, which took about half-an-hour.

Everyone was content that, although very rough because of the lack of grading equipment, the material could form a satisfactory base for a speedway track on top of the tarmac. Stage one – laying – had been achieved.

Now we had to lift it and, again, with no tractor available, we went to work with shovels, finishing off with a mechanical brush lorry that I'd hired for the purpose. It left the tarmac clean and black, with not a trace of shale to be seen.

Eddie Lesley was impressed. 'It'll be a lot of work,' he said, 'but we can have a deal – remember though, I want to sell the stadium.'

After a bit of haggling I agreed to rent the stadium for £500 a meeting but with the option to purchase for £500,000.

The winter of 1999-2000 was the period when the speedway facilities, like pits, dressing rooms, warning lights and safety fence, had to be installed. Committee spokesman Steve Ribbons had assured me that he had plenty of volunteer labour to help with the work but this promise turned out to be hollow in the extreme and the few volunteers who did turn up from his source didn't do very much at all, though one or two were willing enough.

From out of nowhere came Peter Jordison, a local man who had helped both myself and Ronnie Russell in the past. He was retired and looking for an interest. Speedway was his first love and every day he would present himself for work with a smile on his face. His hands were invaluable. He turned out to be an ace and a good friend.

Hazal had gone to Rye House while I was in the Alps so that she could report on work progress. Before long she phoned me: 'You'd better get back here or speedway isn't going to happen. No-one knows what to do or how to do it. Steve Ribbons is full of promises but not much else and you're definitely needed here.'

I cut short my ski-ing season and made my way back to England and Rye House. Sure enough, very little essential work had been done and it looked as if we had a mountain to climb, only one that wasn't covered in snow!

My original plan had been to lay the speedway shale entirely over the 300-metre stock car track, hanging my speedway fence on the triple-cabled stock car fence using car tyres on the posts as a safety feature for the riders. However, the idea was kicked into touch by the Speedway Control Board inspector Ronnie Allen. He demanded that my speedway fence should be at least two metres away from the stock car fence – but what that meant was that my inner line had to be inside the tarmac track. It gave me a huge problem because there was a high kerb and different levels to contend with. At the time I was hopping mad but, as I'll explain later, it turned out Ronnie Allen did me a favour.

While the preparation was taking place, I was considering my position regarding the purchase of the stadium. The place was in such a state that I could see it being necessary to spend huge amounts of money on it and I really favoured finding a site in the general area on which to build my own, purpose-built stadium.

Steve Ribbons had introduced me to some councillors in Waltham Forest and they were initially very keen to have a speedway stadium there, on a big sports field next to the M25 motorway, and I was keen to do it. Sadly, it came to nothing so I was left with a stark choice: buy Rye House or not.

Clearly, it wasn't worth the half-a-million being asked but it was either that or put up with operating as a tenant in what was a dump of a place. So I bit the bullet and agreed a deal with Eddie Lesley to rent the place for the 2000 season and buy it outright the following year.

Meanwhile, I had the severe problem of laying a shale track partly on the tarmac stock car track and partly on the centre green. There was also the difficulty in designing a safety fence that would slot two metres inside the stock car posts. My main helpers in all the work, which included building a new pits facility, were Peter Jordison, a chap called Brian Turner and Steve Webb. My grandson, David, joined the team and he learned to drive the big Digger that I'd bought.

We'd planned to open on May 1, 2000 and we worked towards that date. One week before we had a practice run, laying the track and hanging our fence. It was a total disaster and it quickly became obvious that our fence had to be re-designed.

Brian Turner came up with the idea of making panels of fencing to hang on a straining wire, and we decided on that. There was no way we could open on May 1 and I put the date back two weeks, to Monday, May 15. Then it was hell for leather as we worked day and night to build our fence panels.

Finally the big day came, the track was laid, the fence in place and we were ready to roll. While all the preparation was going on Hazal had told me that she would like to be involved on the administrative side – an idea I was very thankful for. It was a fact that her help was certainly a huge plus factor and with her on the team, I didn't have to worry about that side of things.

The opening meeting was an outstanding success and a big crowd turned up to see the historic event. Speedway journalist John Chaplin, whose son Chris had ridden for me at Rye House in the early 80s, had written a piece several months earlier in which he said that speedway would never return to Rye House and that, if it did, he'd 'eat his hat'.

On that happy opening day we made him do just that, and he sportingly agreed to a 'hat-eating ceremony' before the first race. It was highly rewarding to prove him wrong and the big crowd loved every minute of it. So did I.

The day after the meeting we faced the job of dismantling the fence and ripping up the track, a much less pleasant job. We'd made great big pallets to stack the fence panels on and we lifted these off with the big digger driven by my grandson. That was the easy part.

Now we had to remove the shale from the tarmac track and were grateful that only about two thirds of the tarmac was covered. I used my tractor and blade and circled the track, gradually scraping the shale inwards until most of it was piled inside the stock car circuit, where I intended it to stay ready for the next week.

But lots of the shale was stuck to the tarmac and my tractor blade wouldn't shift it. We worked with spades but that was very hard work and took too much time. So I hit on the idea of washing it off with my big hoses normally used to damp down the surface before racing. This was a much better idea and we managed to get all the shale removed.

Even so, it took all day on Tuesday and was a huge amount of work with five of us hard at it. As the weeks went by and knowing that Eddie Lesley couldn't do much about it if he wanted me to go ahead with the purchase, I left more and more shale on the inside of the tarmac track. The stock car promoter, Mark Eaton, was not happy about it but he was helpless. I held all the aces.

We completed the purchase on July 14, 2000 – with a long-term lease until 2035 – and the next day I gave Mark Eaton notice to quit. I didn't want stock cars in my stadium or any other sports that might interfere with the speedway operation. I only wanted greyhound racing as well as speedway. The dogs had been run initially by Eddie Lesley and then by a local consortium called the Rye Owners and Trainers Association (R.O.T.A). That organisation made it abundantly clear to us, as soon as we were the owners, that they didn't want to be dog racing promoters and that we must do it ourselves.

This was a bombshell we hadn't expected but we dealt with it very quickly, applying to the National Greyhound Racing Club for a licence and trying to find out as much as possible about the dog sport.

We soon found ourselves up to our necks in extra work over and above the running of the ski-ing company. Life would never be the same again.

I was 68. Retirement was not on the agenda.

Chapter 24 – Team spirit

WORKAHOLICS UNITE

DURING 1999 Hazal and her husband Steve Naylor had decided to have an amicable split in their marriage and, although they stayed both married and as good friends, particularly as they both enjoyed raising their daughter Vicky, they each found new partners.

In Hazal's case it was Alan Smith, a highly-trained plumbing design engineer (who, incidentally, played a mean guitar) and he became a valued member of our Rye House management team, concentrating on the catering facilities in the stadium.

Soon afterwards Steve Naylor also threw in his lot with us – as an ex-rider he also had a love of speedway. So the four of us, aided and abetted by Peter Jordison, evolved into the team which ran the stadium. Steve looked after the dog track, as well as helping me on the speedway side, and he also drove the electric hare during greyhound meetings.

Most of my job involved the preparation of the speedway track and ex-committee member John Sampford became the team manager. He knew the rule book and the sport inside-out, so his knowledge was invaluable. I had been out of the game for long enough to have become ignorant about the riders involved, so John's input in that direction was vital.

Although our management team was an excellent set-up for the stadium, we also had to look after Silver Ski, especially as this company was providing all the finance for the stadium. It meant that that we had to call a halt to our plans for buying new ski-ing chalets and every penny we earned went into a big, black hole called Rye House Stadium.

Whilst I had recognised that the dump of a stadium I'd purchased would need lots of money to bring it up to an acceptable level, I hadn't realised just how bad it was. We soon discovered that there wasn't a single item in the place that was any good. It started with the drains, which simply didn't work at all, so there was a constant problem with sewage and rainwater right from the word 'go'.

I wondered how on earth Eddie Lesley had been able to operate the stadium with these kinds of problems but clearly he had. It must have been very uncomfortable. We had to renew all the pipework and install big sewage pumps to make them work. But when we'd finished, not only did all our toilets actually function, the drainage system also handled the rainwater from the speedway track very efficiently.

The next emergency improvement was to the whole electrical system. It was a total nightmare and we discovered that the actual supply of electricity from the National Grid was well below what we needed. So, with the help from some of our fairground

John Sampford gave us invaluable knowledge.

friends who lived on the Showmen's Winter Caravan site next door, we found a big 250 KVA mobile generator, which cost us £7,000, and we installed it at one end of the stadium. With that in place and a whole new re-wired system we could at least turn on lights without fusing the whole system.

And so it went on, one thing after another, but steadily we were replacing and renewing everything so that we had a stadium to be proud of.

At the end of year 2000, I'd got rid of the stock cars and their heavy triple-cabled fence was dismantled and taken away by Mark Eaton. He tried very hard to keep the stocks at Rye House – even threatening me with court action – but he had no legal, or even moral, agreement and he finally had to accept that his motor activities in Hoddesdon had come to an end.

Now I could lay a proper, long-term speedway track with a permanent fence and without the huge burden of our first season in which we'd had to lay a new track every week. It seemed like Heaven not having to do that.

The new circuit was bigger than the temporary one but was still one of the country's smaller tracks at 262 metres. The design was such that the riders could race with throttles wide open for four laps and the racing dished up every Saturday night was of the highest standard.

For that second season I kept the Rockets team in the Third Division, the Conference League, as I looked to train young riders for a future elevation into the Premier League (Division Two). Our attendance figures were very healthy and, all in all, apart from the huge cost of bringing the stadium up to scratch, it wasn't a bad year. Silver Ski kept pretty healthy and all of us were immersed in the world of workaholics, making each week seem like eight days and dealing with both businesses on a daily basis.

Of course, when winter came I still spent many weeks in the mountains but had to return to England much earlier than in times past because of my speedway commitments. Although my ski-ing season was shorter than I would have liked, it didn't stop me from enjoying the company of the guests. Each day I'd ski with them, making sure that they followed me to the best slopes and good mountain restaurants for lunch, helping them all to get the most out of their holiday.

Then each evening I would, like all the staff, enjoy our evening meal, cooked by the chalet hosts, around the big dining room tables, swapping tales of the day's exploits on the mountains. Quite often I'd get out my guitar, or perhaps my ukelele banjo, to entertain with some silly comic songs that I'd written such as 'The Ski Guide Blues' or 'The Slippery Slope to Nowhere.' Everyone, including myself, had a great time. My teenage aspirations to have been a stage entertainer had never really disappeared and in the chalet, with the right guests, I could just as easily have been appearing at the London Palladium. What a dreamer!

At the end of the 2001 speedway season we applied to join the Premier League and after an interview with the promoters' management committee, we were accepted. I was invited to attend the November promoters' conference being held in a big hotel in Edinburgh, where I met many friends of long-standing and lots of new promoters that I'd never heard of. Presumably, they had not heard of me.

Back in the groove in my BSPA blazer.

According to protocol, I couldn't attend the first morning's proceedings as this time was used to deal with the season's business just ended and therefore nothing to do with me. As soon as that session finished I was invited into the big room. On walking through the big double doors I found the tables set out in a square with all the promoters sitting around, the management committee at one end.

I felt a little weird as I walked into the room – the longest-serving promoter in the BSPA yet a 'new boy' on this occasion. As I walked to my seat there was a smattering of applause from some of the longer-serving members who knew me and I found it quite embarrassing but nice nonetheless. It was a modest welcome that I hadn't expected.

The vice-chairman, serving under Wolverhampton promoter and BSPA chairman Chris Van Straaten, was Alex Harkness, one of the Edinburgh promoters and a man quite recently in the business compared to myself and others. During business concerning the Premier League he would take the chair and took the trouble to put me in my place as a new member, suggesting that I should listen rather than talk. I didn't take too kindly to that and ignored his suggestion, making a mental note that here was a man who'd probably prove to be an enemy rather than a friend. In later years I've tempered that view but can't forget how disturbed I was by his condescending attitude at that time.

As a fully paid-up member of the Premier League I then had to put together a professional team worthy of support. Here my old friend Jon Cook was very helpful.

He suggested that I should consider a rider who'd appeared in his Eastbourne team but whom he wasn't intending to use in 2002. That was American Brent Werner and after a phone call or two I arranged to meet up with him at the Brighton indoor meeting in December. We quickly became acquainted and got along fine, so I was able to leave the Sussex coast with his contract in my pocket.

An Australian from Peterborough, Nigel Sadler, had been in touch looking to ride for the Rockets, so I purchased his contract from the East of England club for £10,000. More phone calls followed, in particular to Scott Robson, a northern-based rider on the 'available' list, and he became the third member of the team.

In all negotiations so far I'd been able to reach agreement with the riders within just a few minutes of meeting them, so I was confident that the pay package I was offering was at least as good as, and probably better than, those of my competitors. It was very important that my team did not end up as the chopping block of the league. In fact, the Rockets needed to be one of the better sides.

I elevated two of my Conference team members from 2001, skipper David Mason and West Country boy Chris Courage. Then I purchased the contract of the veteran Mark Courtney and added Scott Swain to the seven. It didn't look too bad a side but in fact, when push came to shove, their record wasn't as bright as it might have been and we ended up 13th out of 17 teams in the league. Hardly anything to shout about but at least we were off and running.

Our public didn't criticise and kept attending in large numbers, so we were reasonably satisfied with our first year at Premier League level.

In addition to our speedway and greyhound activities, not to mention ski-ing, our Rye House management team of myself, Hazal, Alan and Steve started during this period to take an interest in horseracing. Not that we were betting people, it was simply that my grandson, Tony Beech, had become an apprentice jockey.

My daughter, Jackie, had arranged for him to attend the National Training School where he passed out with flying colours gaining, at the end of it, a job working for one of Newmarket's top trainers, Mr. Bell. Tony worked hard in the yard, helping to ride the horses in training every morning. Then one day Mr.Bell gave him his first professional ride at Yarmouth and, naturally, all of us went up to the east coast track to see him in action.

It was an amazing and emotional occasion because Tony actually rode the horse into a good second place and came within a whisker of winning. We were all 'over the moon' and I really felt that my young grandson was on the verge of a great career. Jackie moved into a big house next to the racecourse in Newmarket so that Tony had every chance of success with his new career on horses.

Meanwhile his brother, David, the elder of the two, was pursuing a career as a plumber and he went to college to obtain all his certificates and worked part-time for a local firm. Both of them loved to ski with me in the winter and after a while left me behind in the ability stakes. My granddaughter, Danielle, on the other hand didn't take so easily to ski-ing, although she did eventually become good.

During the winter of 2002-03 we were doing a lot of improvement work to the stadium under the watchful guidance of Hazal while I was in the Alps. She and Alan came out to have a holiday and she told me that there was a big surprise waiting for me when I next went to the stadium. She was obviously very excited about whatever it was but didn't tell me in spite of my exerting a lot of pressure. I was very curious.

Springtime finally arrived and I flew back to England and quickly took myself to the stadium, eager to see the surprise awaiting me. When I got there and started to look around, there were quite a lot of improvements, most I knew about and none of which surprised me.

Then I opened the door that led to the snack bar under the concrete grandstand. WOW! – what a difference! Gone were the old cubicles, the wall lights and red chairs. Instead the whole

Good sign of things to come.

of the interior, brightly lit by hosts of fluorescent tubes, was decorated with pine tongue and grooved timber, just like an alpine chalet.

New purpose-built pine tables, with chairs attached, sat on the newly-slabbed floor. On my left a pine serving hatch opened up behind which was a brand new fish and chip frying unit, all polished stainless steel with white tiled surrounding.

Further along I saw a new pine counter with refrigerators behind and a permanent hot water boiler for tea-making at one end. I was astounded. This was a fish and chip shop to end all fish and chip shops – the ultimate in quality and design. No wonder Hazal was so excited and I certainly was surprised, delightfully so.

At that time, pleased as I was with the transformation, I had no idea just how successful this fast-food outlet would prove to be. I couldn't know then that our fish and chips were to become the talking point of speedway and a major factor in our financial success.

Big though the introduction of fish and chips was to our catering facilities, there was an even bigger event dominating the speedway scene at that time. The sport had begun in Britain at High Beech on February 19, 1928 and I'd already had the privilege of staging the 50th anniversary event at Hackney in 1978. Now the Veteran Speedway Riders' Association asked me to present a 75th Anniversary meeting and I got permission to do so from the Speedway Control Board, although they insisted that it take place in March, not February.

We scheduled it for March 1, 2003 as British speedway's big season curtain-raiser.

To accommodate what we expected to be a bonanza attendance, we had installed high timber terracing at both ends of the stadium, giving the whole place a comfortable 'enclosed' feel and providing excellent viewing spots for more than

Above: Food for thought – what a wonderful sight it was to see our brand new fast-food facility, including the most acclaimed fish and chip shop in the whole of British speedway.
Below: The third/fourth bend at Rye House today. Note the riders' safety fence, which I vowed would be among the safest in speedway after the tragedies we suffered at Hackney.

2,000 extra people. It was agreed that any profit from the meeting would be split three ways – one third to the Veteran Speedway Riders' Association, one third to the Speedway Riders' Benevolent Fund and the other third toward stadium improvements.

Interest was high in the weeks leading up to the event, which was to feature modern-day riders using pre-war machines from the 1928-1939 period and in particular a match-race between the legendary multi-World Champion Swede Ove Fundin and England's last World Champion and present-day star Mark Loram. Memories of the classic race I'd staged at Hackney 25 years earlier, when Jack Parker beat Malcolm Simmons, came flooding back to me and I couldn't wait for the great day to come.

For the preceding three weeks the weather was unusually bright and dry and I was able to prepare a track hard and firm to make racing easy for the riders using the old 'dirt' Duggies and Rudge machines plus the later JAPs so popular after the war.

But come the day and it poured with rain, making everything very uncomfortable. None of the riders complained and every race was completed. In the match-race the great Fundin shot out in front of Loram, just as he had done in his hey-day, only to suffer an engine failure on the final bend, gifting the race to a grateful Mark. Ove had travelled from his home in the South of France to perform and many other top riders of yesteryear were there to add colour to the occasion.

Only the rain put a dampener on matters. While the attendance figure was fairly good, there is no doubt that there were just as many who had stayed at home because of the rain and this naturally meant that the profits accruing to the VSRA and SRBF was far smaller than we'd hoped. That apart, though, it was a successful day with my own rider Scott Robson running out the winner of the main event.

Oh and yes, the new fish and chip bar proved highly popular – a positive sign of things to come.

RYE HOUSE 2009: Above – The senior Rockets (left to right): Myself with Luke Bowen, Linus Sundstrom, Joe Haines, Danny Halsey, Chris Neath (on bike), Tommy Allen, Andrew, Rob Mear, John Sampford. Below: With our National League Cobras – Standing, left to right: Lee Strudwick, Danny Halsey, Michael Bovis, Jamie Courtney. Front: Rob Smith, Ben Morley, Dan Blake.

Chapter 25 – From shale to snow
NATURAL BORN RISK-TAKERS

AFTER we had been running Rye House Speedway for about three years, Hazal had the idea of inviting all of our riders for a free skiing holiday so that they got to know each other socially before racing together as a team. The success of the idea has been phenomenal and the team spirit among the Rockets riders is now legendary.

But the trips to the Alps were not always plain sailing and we have had one or two very anxious moments. In 2006, two of my younger newcomers, Luke Bowen and Jamie Courtney, arrived in the resort on Sunday afternoon along with everyone else. I took all of them to the ski rental shop to get them kitted out and some of the more experienced skiers then took off up into the mountain to get their first taste of the snow, even though they were tired after starting their travelling day at about three o'clock in the morning.

I never noticed at first that both Luke and Jamie were not with us in the chalet. Then someone said that they had gone off with all the others – news that gave me cause for concern. Neither had ever worn a pair of skis, let alone been in high mountains on snow. The risk to life and limb, with neither of them having received a moment's tuition, was immense and as the hours went by without them making an appearance I started to gently sweat.

Finally, at about 5.00pm, the skiers returned but, horror of horrors, there was no sign of Luke or Jamie. They were alone on the mountain, not knowing their way around and with dusk falling rapidly. I was walking up and down with agitation and mentally I was in turmoil.

As the evening light finally disappeared I decided that I must report their absence to the mountain rescue people, the 'Pisteurs', wondering how I'd tell them that I had allowed two complete novices to go out alone. Just as I picked up the phone the pair of them swanned through the door, grinning from ear to ear and acting as if nothing untoward had happened. They had a tongue-lashing from me, I can tell you, but I don't think they took any notice. They were, after all, young speedway riders and risk was the name of the game as far as they were concerned.

I think it was during the same trip that our American star, Brent Werner, went off for a snowboarding day with my son Andrew. Brent, although not an expert, was nonetheless quite an able boarder. My son, on the other hand, was a top performer with a reputation of being able to tackle the most difficult slopes and areas and that was why Brent wanted to go out with him.

'Come on, Andrew, take me to something really exciting' and so he followed him up in the cable car to the top of the Grande Rochette mountain which towered

LEN SILVER

Above: Interviewing Tai Woffinden, one of the most talented youngsters we've had at Rye House in recent years.
Below: Andrew back in the blue and yellow Rockets racejacket at the start of 2009.

My good friends Michael Lee and Nicki are part and parcel of the scene at Rye House.

majestically over Plagne Centre. From the top station it was possible to follow several different marked pistes, ranging from interesting and fairly gentle 'blue' runs to a severe and difficult 'black', and Brent thought that Andrew would probably not decide on the toughest run.

Oh, how wrong he was. It had started to snow and visibility was rapidly deteriorating so he kept closely behind Andrew as he headed for the edge of the steepest black run. There he stopped on the top of a gully so steep that it looked almost vertical. The bottom was lost in the swirling snow and Brent said nervously to Andrew: 'Jeeze, you ain't going down there, are you?' Not a word came in reply.

Instead, Andrew suddenly leapt off the edge and disappeared into the swirling snow, carving his way to the unseen bottom. Brent stood shakily, looking down into the white abyss. Then, taking a very deep breath, he launched himself into the unknown, not knowing whether he'd ever get to the bottom – wherever that was.

His hands and arms were hitting the snow as he tried to keep his balance on the snowboard, praying that he'd stay upright. Faster and faster he dropped, the cold snow spraying all around him. At last the slope started to level out and the snowfall became thinner.

Andrew came in sight, laughing his head off as he watched Brent finish in a heap by his feet, thoroughly exhausted both physically and mentally. 'Did you enjoy that?' asked Andrew. Brent's comments went un-recorded.

A most important member of the Rye House set-up is the 1980 individual World Champion Michael Lee, whose father Andy had been a huge moto-cross star and was a great engine tuner. Mike had got involved with me through his love of skiing. It came about when one of my younger riders, Stevie Boxall, started to make good progress as a rider.

His skill and daring were unquestioned but, unfortunately, he had no idea at all about how to look after his machinery and in race after race his bike would let him down.

Mike and I were standing next to each other during a home meeting one day and watched as, yet again, Stevie's bike ground to a halt in the middle of a good race. I turned to Mike: 'If you can get that boy going, there will be several free ski trips for you next winter.'

'Do you really mean that?' Michael replied.

'Absolutely,' I promised.

In what seemed like no time at all Mike had produced an engine for Steve and had also cured all sorts of other problems on the bike, in particular the clutch. Wow! ... what a difference and suddenly we had a new star rider in our midst, helping the team to become League champions in 2005 for the first time in 26 years.

I kept my promise and Mike, along with his partner Nicki, who serves drinks in the bar at Rye House, have been regular skiers with me ever since. In fact, nowadays they actually run one of our best chalets, where Mike shows off his skills as a chef every evening. But during the day he normally skis with me, which is great.

The only trouble is, he cannot keep his competitive nature from influencing his approach to ski-ing and he simply will not allow himself to be the last one down any slope. He just has to get there first, so I find myself ski-ing much faster than I would ideally like to simply try and keep up with him. It's great fun but I seem to age 10 years every winter!

The friendship I have with Mike and Nicki is something I value very highly and there is little doubt that the excellent results achieved by my Rockets team has been in no small part due to Michael Lee's input.

I was delighted when Rye House regained the Premier League title in 2007, although it's not just silverware that brings me joy and satisfaction in speedway. It's also the progress of the many youngsters who continue to pass through the ranks – from our Cobras junior team, through the senior Rockets and beyond. Since the days, in the 50s, when Rye House was one of the foremost venues for training youngsters, under the watchful eye of Dickie Case and then, later, Mike Broadbank, I hope our reputation for producing good, young riders never fades.

Having said that, it gave me great pleasure to welcome back a Rockets 'old boy' at the start of 2009, when my 42-year-old son decided that he would like another crack at racing. In view of Andrew's 15-year absence from the track, I did advise him to think very carefully before going through with it and not to rush into a comeback on a whim.

But once he had convinced me that he was deadly serious in his intentions, I was happy to back him and to offer him the chance to return to the club he had left when he joined Arena-Essex in 1986.

It was a huge gamble on his part, though, because after such a long time out of speedway, no-one would have been surprised if he had failed. Anyway, at the time of writing, I'm delighted to say that Andrew's comeback season has gone much better than anyone had any right to expect.

Above: Looks familiar . . . even after 15 years Andrew shows that he has lost none of his spectacular skills.
Below: The welcome sign inside the turnstiles. Hopefully we'll add to the honours list in years to come . . .

Above: Marvyn Cox came through the Hackney training school to become a big favourite at Rye House.
Below: Having a laugh with Jackie Biggs and Hawks' team manager Maurice Morley.

Chapter 26 – Characters I have known
THANKS FOR THE MEMORIES

SPEEDWAY racing has been, for me, a life of absorbing interest. I have been able to influence many aspects of the sport over the years and although I had but modest success as a rider, it is in the field of management that I will probably be best remembered when I'm six-feet under.

My most rewarding times have been the ability to discover and help young riders to achieve their best. Silly as it sounds, my own failures as a junior rider in the mid-50s have helped me to achieve success in this area. I vividly recall how I was treated as a youngster at Ipswich when Group Captain Arthur Franklyn would look sternly at me just before my first race: 'Now Silver, what we want is points –not pile-ups!'

Never once in all my riding days was I ever assisted to acquire good equipment or helped in any way, despite showing huge promise when I began my professional riding career.

So I've carried these memories with me for almost 60 years and I try, wherever possible, not to let any young rider who looks promising go without the benefit of some help. Of course, I cannot help everyone and most assistance goes to those that seem to have the spark of success in their make-up.

In my days as the promoter at Hackney we used to run a Saturday afternoon training school. We had about 10 rather ramshackle old bikes, looked after by the constantly oil-covered Terry 'Bert' Busch, that were rented out and novice riders would queue up to use the track. Most were no-hopers but now and then up would pop a youngster with a bit of sparkle.

It was always a struggle financially to keep Hackney Speedway alive because, although our fans were the most loyal in the business, never moaning when we lost at home (a very regular occurrence), there really were not quite enough of them – about 1,800, on average, in my final year there in 1983.

But this was only because of the costs imposed on me by my landlords, Brent Walker, who took 15 per cent of the speedway gate receipts – a huge chunk of cash. They also enjoyed a big profit from their catering, none of it shared with me, and I also had to pay them an atrocious amount for electricity and water. Had it not been for these crippling overheads I reckon I would have done quite well there.

The fight to stay afloat made me acutely aware that any advance in income was to be sought after. Running our Saturday afternoon training school helped quite a bit in this respect and in latter years I introduced a unique package – a three-day training school for complete beginners. It was very popular and I used to earn up to £1,500 from it, which was very useful money then, I can tell you.

One fine discovery from our Hackney school was Kent-based Marvyn Cox, whom

Above: The spectacular Barry Thomas was such a huge crowd favourite for many years.
Below: With Dag Lovaas, who had his best-ever season in the sport at Hackney in 1974.

I signed as an unknown kid. He came through the ranks with me, firstly at Rye House and then to Hackney before joining Oxford and achieving success at international level. I found the progress shown by him and numerous others most rewarding.

But there were many who graduated from the training school at 'The Wick' into my Rye House team and it was these eager youngsters who took the Rockets to years of success on the track in the late-70s and early-80s.

It was a source of immense satisfaction to me that one of my best discoveries was my own son, Andrew. He was one of the most exciting riders in the business, very spectacular, hanging off his bike at full throttle and able to pass even the best of opposition from the back.

Naturally, it wasn't only the younger riders that gave me pleasure. I had the good fortune during my days at Hackney to enjoy the friendship and riding skills of many world class riders. Probably the classiest of them all was Bengt 'Banger' Jansson, a quiet Swedish star who was a World Championship runner-up in 1967 and whose last bend passes at the East End track were legendary. We've always kept in touch and I value his friendship.

The same can certainly be said of my Danish star Finn Thomsen, who captained the Hawks in my latter years at Hackney. A really polished performer, he now lives with his wife Suzanne and his two grown-up sons in southern Spain. We see each other regularly and Hazal and I are godparents to their youngest son, Raymond.

Many others come to mind, none more so than one of my longest-serving riders, Barry Thomas. He joined me as a young kid in an exchange for New Zealander Graeme Smith (The Corduroy Kid) in a deal with my old and valued friend the late Johnnie Hoskins, then the boss at Canterbury. No greater trier than Barry existed in the whole sport and my Hackney fans worshipped him.

I always knew that he could have gone on to achieve at the very highest level but, unhappily, he liked his beer too much and could knock back 10 pints without getting even bleary-eyed! He was, for me, the representation of what Hackney Speedway was all about. An exciting racer who diced with death without a second thought but for whom life was about living for fun. And live it he did.

Only the older speedway fans will remember Jackie Biggs, a slim and tiny Australian with superb skills as an engine tuner. He and his wife Sheila were very good friends and they helped me no end in my early days as a promoter.

Jack always claimed that I was the first promoter he ever rode for who only paid him the official pay scale. It was probably true because all of my riders received the same. It was all that I could afford in those days.

He used to tune the engines for Hackney's first 'heart throb', local boy Colin Pratt who had transferred to The Wick from Stoke where he had established himself as their number one rider. He quickly rode himself into that role with the Hawks too.

His expertise from the gate and a unique ability to sit tight round the inside line stood him in good stead. No-one else could get as close to the inside as Colin and he wore what we used to call 'Pratty's groove' in the track.

On Friday afternoons he always arrived at the stadium very early, usually when I was watering the track, and he would join me just to make sure that I didn't over-water HIS bit of the track. We became good friends and remain so to this day.

Without a doubt, the most colourful character and the one rider whose headline-making exploits put 'bums on seats' like no other was the controversial Garry Middleton, an Australian who had a big reputation as a 'bad boy'. He had ridden for Wimbledon and had constant public confrontations with the management there. When he came to me in 1969 under the old Rider Control system which operated at that time, everyone told me to avoid him like the plague. But, glutton for punishment as I am, I signed him for the Hawks.

He gave his all on the track but was always arguing against officials and referees in particular. It became a regular occurrence for him to jump over the safety fence, climb up to the referee's box and pummel on the window demanding justice! The crowd loved it and I didn't stop him – it was good for business.

Controversial and good for the crowd he certainly was, but he was never aggravating to me – except that every so often I'd find him using my office phone to call someone in Australia!

One day at Cradley Heath, an argument ensued in the pits between Garry (whom everyone called 'Cassius' because he was as boastful as world heavyweight boxing champion Cassius Clay) and the Heathens' Roy Trigg. It was over something quite trivial but, suddenly and to everyone's total amazement, Middleton pulled out a gun from his toolbox and aimed it at former Hackney rider Trigg.

We all went wobbly at the knees but I had to intervene as best I could without becoming a dead hero. After calming down the situation I found out that the gun wasn't loaded and Garry thought it was all a huge joke. But no-one else did. The irate Cradley crowd were ready to lynch him and a police van was used to smuggle him out of the stadium for his own safety!

That incident was typical of this volatile, larger than life, character and I was sorry when, after a comparatively short stay at The Wick, he was allocated to Oxford in 1972. As it turned out, they hated him there!

Another colourful character was Malcolm Brown, a youngster born and bred in Leyton, only about two miles from the track. He was born to be a comedian rather than a speedway rider and he kept his team place more for his humour among the riders and the team spirit he generated than for the actual points he scored.

A clever mimic, he pulled a really funny stunt one day to embarrass my friend, the late Maurice Littlechild, then the promoter at King's Lynn as well as being one of the five directors alongside myself in Allied Presentations. While on a Northern tour with the team Malcolm amused his team-mates by phoning Maurice late one evening: 'Hello, is dat Mr Littlechild?' said Malcolm in a voice as close to being Caribbean as he could muster. 'My name is Raz Mandu and I is a top rider from Jamaica. I want to get in touch with a Mista Silver to ride for de Hackney 'Awks. Do you 'ave 'is number?'

Now you have to appreciate that almost every promoter in those days was seeking a Jamaican rider because of the huge influx of immigrants from the West Indies who had come to settle in Britain during the 60s.

Above: Bengt Jansson and Garry Middleton celebrate our KO Cup Final victory over Cradley Heath in 1971, watched by Eddie Reeves and Dave Kennett. Below: Colin Pratt 'hugging' the white line at The Wick.

Above: Me with my Swindon counterpart, former racing legend Norman Parker (second from left), along with respective team captains Gerry Jackson and Barry Briggs, plus our start marshal George Maskell.
Below: With Tommy Price, my opposing team manager at West Ham in the early 60s. He became England's first World Champion at Wembley in 1949.

Maurice replied: 'Now my son, you don't want to go to that Hackney place. They wouldn't appreciate you there. Now I've got a much better track at King's Lynn where we'd really look after you.'

'Well sah,' Brownie replied, 'ah'll tink about dat one and call you later.'

Well by now all the Hackney riders were in fits having overheard the whole conversation.

Then Malcolm phoned me to tell me what he'd done. I couldn't stop laughing but decided to play along with the joke and the next day I phoned Maurice pretending to be very upset.

'What the hell are you doing trying to nick my rider, Raz Mandu – he'll put a thousand on my gate!'

'No boy, I wouldn't do that to you,' lied Maurice. 'I told him you were a great guy to ride for.'

His nose must have grown three inches like Pinnochio but I couldn't contain myself any longer and I started laughing like a hyena. Soon it emerged that I knew the whole story and poor Maurice was never more embarrassed in his life.

Malcolm had also been a member of the Royal Corps of Signals Motorcycle Display Team during his National Service and once or twice he gave some jumping displays for me as an interval attraction. Once he landed and bounced himself on his testicles – very painful – but it looked terrific and I entreated him to do it again even though he could hardly stand up! He did too. What a character! He now lives with his highly attractive partner, Donna, in Florida, USA, where he owns a night club.

It's hard to remember all the host of riders who rode for me in all those Hackney years. There are just too many to mention but I'll never forget being the first to employ a father-and-son racing duo in the same team together, when 'Gentleman' George Barclay and his son John both rode for me at Sunderland.

Three outstanding scorers were the quiet Bo Petersen from Denmark, little Dave Morton from Manchester, who'd first impressed during my time with Crewe, and stylish Norwegian Dag Lovaas. He scored many maximums so easily that you hardly even noticed him racing.

One who should have been good for my crowds was popular Swedish superstar Christer Lofqvist. He came to me in 1975 – via Poole and four years after my neighbouring track at West Ham had closed down. I confidently expected his ex-Hammers fans to follow him to my track only five miles away. Sure enough, they did for a while to watch the spectacular little speedster in action.

But then he started to go missing and he would disappear for days on end. Every now and then he simply didn't appear in the pits for his racing commitments, which was hugely embarrassing and bad for our results. After several unexplained absences I called a halt and sacked him.

Little did I know then that Christer was actually ill. He turned out to have a malignant brain tumour, from which he died a couple of years after he'd left Hackney. I always felt quite guilty about sacking him when I learnt the truth but, of course, that was with the benefit of hindsight.

When I look back over the years I find myself somewhat surprised that I have

February 1978 and I was a proud man to host the Golden Jubilee of British Speedway meeting at Hackney on that crisp, Sunday afternoon. Above: With the grand old man himself, Johnnie Hoskins, who invented our great sport back in the early 20s. Below: On that same momentous occasion, Belle Vue legend Jack Parker (on a two-valve Jawa), leading the 'dirt-track-Duggie' mounted Malcolm Simmons in front of a huge crowd.

actually been on first name terms with promoters and riders from every era of the sport, dating right back to the early days before I was born. The fact that I knew Phil Bishop, who rode in the very first English meeting at High Beech in 1928, and also the man who 'invented' speedway in Australia in 1923 – the one and only John S. Hoskins – sends a strange thrill through me. But these were not the only ones. Most of what might be termed the 'All Time Greats' have been, at one time or another, in my circle of friends.

Those great brothers, Jack and Norman Parker; England's first-ever World Champion Tommy Price; Aussie Test stars Aub Lawson and Cliff Watson; and not to forget my personal idol, Ron Johnson, who rode for New Cross just after World War Two. It was a touching moment in my life when I learned after 'Johnno's' death that he'd been buried in an unmarked 'pauper's' grave in Australia. Along with others I helped to ensure that his great memory was encapsulated for ever with a properly engraved headstone befitting a giant in our sport.

These and many others I got to know when I was a cycle speedway rider as a teenager just after the war. Although I was just a young Cockney kid, they treated me with the greatest respect – a fact which I appreciated then and do to this day.

Of course, after I took up racing as a career I became one of the small circle of the 'family' of speedway. World Champions were pleased to pass the time of day with me and it has always been a source of amazement to me that legends such as Ivan Mauger, Barry Briggs, Ove Fundin and their like treated me as an equal when in fact, on a bike, they could have given me 50-yard start and still beaten me.

Then, as I progressed as a promoter and team manager, I got to know so many star riders as well as those less fortunate in the ability stakes, and all on a wonderfully intimate basis.

They say you are a lucky man if you can call two people real friends. I've had hundreds and life doesn't get much better than that.

At the age of 77, I can't honestly say that I have many ambitions left to fulfil. It would be a dream come true for me, though, if I live long enough to promote British Speedway's 100th anniversary meeting at Rye House in 2028. If I'm not kicking up daisies by then, I will be 96-years-old. Having staged the 50-year Golden Jubilee of British speedway meeting at Hackney in February 1978 and the 75th anniversary event at Rye House in 2003 . . . well, I can still dream, can't I? It would be the ultimate honour for me, so let's hope my Guardian Angel is listening!

More realistically, I would like Rye House Stadium to be my legacy. My eternal hope is that generations of speedway supporters from all over the country will continue to visit our lovely, little venue by the banks of the River Lea for many, many years to come, and that they gain as much pleasure from those visits as people do today.

I'll very happily settle for that.

TRIBUTES TO LEN

HOW OTHERS REMEMBE

Compiled by Gareth Rogers

PROMOTING & MANAGEMENT

Former colleagues and rivals on the other side of the fence

VIC WHITE

Despite being the same age as myself, Len had already been responsible for setting up an East of London cycle speedway league when I first met him. The Warwick Lions wanted to enter but Len wanted to know whether we were good enough. A challenge match was set up on a neutral track with the Beckton Aces. When we only lost by eight points, Len knew we had something and so we were admitted.

I competed on track against Len – he was a hard bugger! – and knew him as an opponent rather than actually being friendly with him.

Me and Vic White in our Provincial League days.

Little did I realise how well we would come to know each other over the decades to follow.

It was obvious then that Len had outstanding administrative skills. He was not content to just ride but pushed through the development of the sport in East London and beyond. He made an impact. The seeds of Len's reputation as a shrewd and successful speedway promoter were definitely sewn way back then. He ran the (cycle speedway) Control Board and was instrumental in arranging the fixture list.

During the early years of the Provincial League Len was once again a racing opponent of mine – primarily at Exeter, where he was one of the best – and hardest – heat leaders in the division. In later years, we were opposing team managers during my spells with Long Eaton, Leicester and Coventry.

My son, Keith, had taken up speedway and rode for Len at Crewe in 1973 and 1974. By 1976, after a spell at Birmingham, he was ready to step up to the senior British League. There were various options but he elected to join up with Len again, this time at Hackney. Obviously, I'd travel with Keith to some of Hackney's matches and that's where I think a long-term association with Len developed into a friendship. I liked the way he promoted the sport, dealt with the public, and handled his team. It was during this period that Keith enjoyed the best performances of his career, climbing to Hackney No.1 and reaching the Inter-Continental Final in 1977.

I worked with Charles Ochiltree at Coventry and had great respect for him as a speedway promoter but where Len excels over the rest is in his 'hands-on' ability. Not just in practical terms, but in looking after every aspect of public and rider issues.

His current outstanding success at Rye House really brings that point home. His work ethic is exceptional – he's always on the tractor when I phone him! He not only faces up to a challenge, he seems to thrive on them.

Len is a promoter in the truest sense of the word. He is one of the greatest promoters in the history of the sport and certainly the best post-war promoter that British speedway has seen. He is also a warm and generous human being.

Despite the many times we have been elbow to elbow on-track and contenders off-track, we have never fallen out. Long may it continue.

REG FEARMAN

Len and I have been pals for more years than I care to remember. All the local boys supported West Ham Speedway in the late-40s and 50s. Len and I were no different, although we'd first met during my short-lived cycle speedway days.

It was the explosion of the Provincial League in 1960, the year I started to promote speedway, that brought us closer together. At that time Len owned a car showroom in Seven Kings and I'd often pop in for a cuppa when visiting my parents in Ilford.

When a British League second division was proposed during the BSPA's AGM in the winter of 1967-68, we both enthusiastically joined forces with Danny Dunton, Maury Littlechild and Ron Wilson and formed Allied Presentations Ltd. The object was to re-open defunct tracks and take speedway to new venues. Over the next few years we operated at Reading (at both Tilehurst and Smallmead), Middlesbrough, Rayleigh, Crewe, Rye House, Peterborough, Sunderland and Newcastle but not all at the same time. Our aim was to develop British talent. The fact that we also made money was a side issue and an added bonus. As a business partner, Len was extremely honest and reliable. A pleasure to work with.

Len and I were always optimistic and enthusiastic about opening new venues whilst remaining pragmatic. One, in particular, we looked at was Gloucester Football Club, which had a wonderful grass circuit around the outside of the pitch that could have easily been converted for speedway racing. Unfortunately, it was close to the mental hospital and the council objected. One person, in particular, thought we should also be committed for even suggesting the idea!

Len and I made several trips to ski together in Austria. He was as fearless going off piste as he was as a speedway rider. It's amazing the similarities between riding speedway and ski-ing.

One of the greatest showmen and entrepreneurs in speedway, Len has achieved far more than many other promoters. He always had respect from his riders and fellow promoters, which is most important. Len had been Great Britain and England team manager when he was called in by the Speedway Control Board to prepare the track for Wembley World Finals after the contractors, who specialised in laying tennis courts, fell down on the job.

Len was always an 'ideas' man coupled with being an excellent administrator, which held him in good stead when he formed the Silver Ski company which has gone from strength to strength over the years and allowed him to purchase Rye House Stadium. The two sports which Len loves and adores – speedway and ski-ing – are within his grasp. I'm sure that whatever Len turned his hand to, he would have made a success of it. When he was awarded the 'Lifetime Achievement to Speedway' by the fans and friends of Hackney Speedway, it couldn't have gone to a better person. I am proud to call Len a pal.

PETER THOROGOOD

I also got involved in cycle speedway as a youngster and this is where I first became aware of Len. I initially rode for the Manor Park Stars at a track on Wanstead Flats. Then the council were persuaded to build a track at Itchy Koo Park and the Manford 'Stars' – an amalgamation of Manor Park and Ilford – were formed. I saw Len ride but I never rode against him. His Stratford Hammers were in the First Division and he was an 'A' grade rider while my team was in the Second Division and competed against the Hammers' B team.

I became aware that he was a key organiser in the local cycle speedway league, including arranging indoor meetings. I also saw his early speedway outings in second-halves at West Ham

LEN SILVER

Peter Thorogood was a big ally to me in my Allied days.

and later riding for Ipswich at Rayleigh.

By the 60s I'd moved near to the Rayleigh Weir Stadium. It was announced in the local press that the sport was being re-introduced there in 1968 with Len Silver at the helm and that a demo race was being staged at the next stock car meeting. I took myself off to that and Len was walking by when I called him over and re-acquainted myself. On behalf of my next-door neighbour, who was an ex-West Ham fan, and myself, I asked about the chance of a job on the track staff. Len gave me details of a staff meeting and I went along and initially became the fuel and oil man.

However, as I lived very close to the track, I began to help Graeme Smith, the New Zealand rider, in his other role of preparing the track and getting the fence up and down according to stock car meetings.

Len then asked me directly if I fancied taking on the role of track curator. I said 'yes' and he gave me some rudimentary lessons before handing me the job. His problem was that he had to take a more active role in running Crewe for Allied Presentations. Maury Littlechild, the main promoter there, had become quite ill in 1972 and couldn't carry on, although, despite having to travel so far north each week, Len would still be at Rayleigh on a Saturday night.

Then he offered me the role of full-time general manager of the Rayleigh Rockets, so I effectively became Len's co-promoter from 1970 and helped to gradually build the club up. I learnt everything I know about the sport from Len – track preparation, team management, administration, presentation and the actual art of promoting, including being 'hands-on'.

When Rayleigh Stadium was sold for redevelopment at the end of 1973, we looked at moving the Rockets operation to Southend greyhound stadium and also a site between pylons at Rayleigh Spur, before casting the net wider. Rye House and Crayford became the candidates for relocation but there was an initial problem with the latter as permission to stage speedway at the little stadium in Kent had lapsed. Rye House, a renowned training venue but one which had never staged pukka league racing before, was to be the Rockets' new home from 1974. It certainly took a lot of adjustment and work but Len and I were up for it.

By this time Len had developed a new passion – for ski-ing. For years Charlie and Jean Mugford had chipped away at him to take it up. He became so keen, I remember one day at Rayleigh when Len, Dave Hoggart (Graeme Smith's mechanic) and myself were sheltering from the rain in a van on the centre green when Len said he would even pack up speedway to go ski-ing. Dave and I didn't take him seriously at the time. Little did we know!

Anyway, I went into Rye House during that first season and we shortened the track. Previously you came down the straight and practically had to stop before turning left. I recall that it was so soft during track reconstruction, the tractor sank into the first bend!

Also, when Bob Dugard came to measure the track size, it was actually too narrow so we had to adjust it again slightly. Rye House was a success and initially we had coach-loads of Rockets fans coming across from Essex while we also built up a more local spectator base.

During that first 1974 season together at Rye House, Len took me aside to say that Crayford was likely to become available after all. I asked him if it was being considered instead of Rye House or in addition to, and he confirmed that he was keen to run both. We discussed me managing Crayford in 1975 in partnership with him while he sought a new co-promoter for Rye House. Eventually Colin

Pratt was recruited and between 1975 and 1978 I ran Crayford for Len with former Rockets Laurie Etheridge, Pete Wigley, Trevor Barnwell and George Barclay involved. Ladbrokes took over the stadium after that and employed me as their speedway manager. The track was kept in business in 1982 by Terry Russell, who had sponsored Trevor Barnwell. By that time, Len had long since come out of Crayford to concentrate on Hackney, Rye House and his other interests.

As with Rye House, Len and I also shortened the track at Crayford and made it a spectacular small bowl of a circuit.

I also got involved with Len in assisting him with track preparations for the World Finals at Wembley in 1978 and 1981. The track for the 1975 final had been a 'dust bowl', leading to the incident where a fan climbed onto the track, got hold of a hose and started watering the first bend. The SCB had been responsible for organising Wembley track preparation until then but in 1978 it was handed to Len, as someone who had a fine reputation for preparing the perfect track.

The 1978 staging was not without its challenges and problems but 1981 was the one we'll always remember. With all the problems (described elsewhere in this book by Len) in dealing with a football stadium, this was a situation that had to be rescued by intensive work. It was a nightmare working there because of the FA. You had to walk all the way around the pitch to reach a job that needed doing on the other side. You were certainly not allowed to walk across the 'hallowed turf'. Even so, everybody agrees we eventually produced a surface that was raceable.

What of Len as a promoter and a person? He is certainly a hard taskmaster. I remember working for him on the Hackney track and we would continuously take a four-wheel blade around and around. I used to think, 'are we ever going to stop?' He was such a perfectionist and he expected you to go that extra mile too. The job had to be perfect. His work ethic is tremendous.

Len's man-management skills are also very good. His riders like riding for him – a recent example being Chris Neath electing to stay at Rye House rather than move up to the Elite League.

Len has also got time for the fans. He is approachable – in fact approachable to everyone. That is another good reflection on him.

He is by nature generous. He paid for my wife and our two children to join me at a promoters' AGM in Spain. When I had to help him out at Crewe, he didn't take it for granted but put me up in good hotels.

You certainly know where you are with Len. If he doesn't approve of something or somebody, no-one is left in any doubt. I remember Frank Ebdon, then a newcomer to the refereeing circuit, having a mixed meeting at Hackney early in his career. He turned up at the pit gate a few weeks later. Len asked him what he was doing, so Frank replied that he'd come to watch the speedway. Len told him in no uncertain terms that he wasn't welcome and should remove himself immediately!

Len has made a success of all his mainstream tracks. He kept Hackney in the top league for the best part of two decades. He took Rye House from a long-time training track to the home of the League champions in two separate eras under his control. He has made a splendid job of developing the Rye House Stadium since regaining control.

If there were more promoters like Len Silver around today, the sport would be much better off.

DANNY DUNTON

I first became aware of Len Silver when I turned to speedway promotion in 1960, although I did have a season at Long Eaton for Reg Fearman during that period too. Len was riding for Exeter. I became a promoter at Oxford with Ted Flanaghan at senior (National League) level, so didn't see much of Len at that juncture. Obviously once the British League was formed in 1965 his Hackney team featured in the amalgamation of the two leagues and we saw each other at BSPA meetings.

Then at one promoters' conference held in Stratford-upon-Avon, Maury Littlechild of King's Lynn got several of us together until the early hours to discuss forming Allied Presentations Ltd and helping to establish a new Second Division. This embraced Reg Fearman, Ron Wilson and Len, as well as Maury and myself.

Allied worked fantastically well and helped with things such as rider pooling and swap deals as new circuits were brought into the fold over the next few years. Eventually Reg had Reading, although Len and I pitched in there too. Ron had Middlesbrough, Maury had Crewe and Len had Rayleigh, while I ran Peterborough.

Len and Reg were both good organisers and everything ran smoothly. We met regularly at Hackney to sort out affairs. I think we had a positive impact on the sport at the time and lots of young riders started coming through to the benefit of British speedway.

All good things must come to an end, though. Eventually, and inevitably, there were differences of opinion, so we had a meeting at Crewe one day and parted amicably. Friendships were not lost through the split.

I've been to Rye House Speedway in recent years and am so impressed. So much work has gone into the venue – but that's Len. He has a fantastic work ethic. He is hands-on and doesn't ask others to do what he doesn't do himself. He works on every aspect and every angle of speedway promotion – be it rider management, public relations, or track preparation. He is an absolute perfectionist too.

Len Silver is more than a 100 per cent, true speedway promoter.

COLIN PRATT

I first met Len when I was doing my National Service and I'd started having some second-halves at Ipswich, where Len was riding under the management of Maurice Littlechild and Vic Gooden.

When the Provincial League started in 1960, Len and I did clash on track because I was at Stoke and he was riding for Exeter. When Stoke closed in 1963, I then signed for Swindon in the higher National League for a month in 1964 before joining Mike Parker's Hackney. Len then bought out Parker, took over and asked me if I'd continue riding for him. The takeover was a gamble for Len but he was brought up in the East End, plus he had the gift of the gab. I went on to make progress while riding for Len at Hackney for six seasons.

Len was always a good promoter to ride for. At times I'd say what I thought and Len would voice his opinions too. We didn't always hit it off but we never walked away from each other during that period.

He is a real promoter in the truest sense of the word. By what other words can you describe him? In my time at Hackney he came up with a number of weird and wonderful ideas.

He once said to us: 'We're going up to Scotland, riding at Middlesbrough on the way, followed by Edinburgh and then to Newcastle on the Monday. I'm not going to pay travel money but I'll pay for everything for you and supply the cars, plus trailer.'

Two cars were scheduled to go up and he picked me up at Stanstead Abbots on the way. The trailer that was carrying our bikes was like a circus trailer with iron sides, as if we had lions in the back! We'd only got as far as Buntingford, about 20 miles north, with Len doing the driving – you know, looking under the steering wheel because of his size! – when I spotted two of our bikes upside-down in the road behind us, with lorries narrowly missing them.

Eventually we did reach the A1 but got a puncture and Len took off with the police to get it repaired. We couldn't wait for him, otherwise we would have been late for the meeting that night, so we flagged down a lorry and put the bikes on that.

When Len arrived back at the scene of the mishap, there was only one empty car and trailer to be seen. Anyway, he followed us up to Middlesbrough and when he got finally got there it was deemed that the trailer couldn't go over 40mph because of the whipping action, so two or three bikes went

With the Hawks of 1967 – left to right: Colin McKee, Gary Everett, Malcolm Brown, Brian Davies, Bengt Jansson, Gerry Jackson, Les McGillivray and Maurice Morley (team manager), with Pratty on the bike.

up to Edinburgh on top of a lorry load of steel the next night.

Len tried various gimmicks to drum up interest in Hackney. Once he announced that whoever was the first to arrive at the turnstiles holding someone's hand, they would only have to pay for one person. We went to watch outside the stadium – and the first couple to appear at the turnstiles were two blokes! If anyone was going to try something new it was Len. There are promoters today looking for fresh ideas but there aren't many that Len hasn't already tried. He worked hard promoting on and off the track and we had some laughs with it too.

In 1968 we drew on points with Coventry, the eventual league champions, but lost the title on race points difference. So we did progress from when Len took it over in 1964 – from Provincial League to the top of the British League. This, with pretty much the same squad – the McGillivrays, Des Lukehurst, Brian Davies and, of course, Malcolm Brown. There was a good atmosphere around Hackney as a club. Of course, Len was a lively personality.

I do recall one incident in which we didn't see eye-to-eye and it led to me being suspended. He took most of the Hackney team along to race in an open meeting at Rye House – I think it was everyone except me. And Rye House was my local track. So I said to Len: 'When you go to Edinburgh next time, those seven you sent to Rye House . . . you had better send them as I'm not ******* going!'

He replied: 'You'll have to go.'

'I f****** will not!' I told him.

He then asked me if he sent Sandy McGillivray up to Edinburgh, would I ride at Newcastle? I confirmed: 'Not really. It's a bit unfair to send Sandy up there to do only one meeting and have to sit on the coach the rest of the weekend.'

He came back with: 'What if I borrowed a second-half rider up there – would you do Newcastle on Monday?'

I conceded: 'If you want me to, you can put my bike on the coach.'

They went up to Edinburgh and lost by two points. I set out to reach Newcastle by train and an announcement came over for me to meet Mr. Len Silver on the platform at Kings Cross station.

He travelled up with me and even bought me lunch on the way up.

But when I got to Newcastle the rest of the team didn't speak to me much. I went out and scored 11 (paid 14) points. Afterwards, I loaded my bike back on the coach myself and only Howdy Byford helped me when the time came to take it back off the vehicle.

I worked on my bike as soon as I got home to Harlow and that was that. Some of the supporters were not very happy with me when they found out why I didn't go., although some of them agreed with me.

Len did have me suspended for that incident. I was the first rider in the British League to be suspended for two weeks. I had to serve the suspension and wasn't allowed to take any guest bookings either. I didn't even know about my ban until my mother read it in the paper and stopped me on the way to Terry Betts' place to tell me.

I then told Len where to stick Hackney Speedway – I wouldn't be riding there the following season. But, as history shows, I did ride there all of the next season after all!

Yes, we had our clashes on occasions but Len always knew that I'd do a job for him. He did a terrific job in keeping Hackney Speedway going all those years.

Looking back, these were probably the best days of my speedway career. I only had half-a-season at Cradley Heath before the Lokeren accident in July 1970. Len didn't want me to go from Hackney. it was just that I felt like a change. In the end I was exchanged for Bob Andrews. There was no fall-out. I repeat, I just fancied a change. Len reckoned that Cradley bribed me to go there but they didn't. I didn't usually discuss money with a promoter until I'd already agreed to sign. I knew how to value myself anyway.

After recovering from my broken neck and other injuries I sustained in the Lokeren tragedy and having got myself fitter, I ran the practice and training sessions at Hackney for Len for about five years. That's where we found promising, young riders like Allan Emmett, Bobby Garrad and Karl Fiala. Len had Rayleigh at the time and I'd have to send four riders from the Hackney practice down to The Weir for his 'vultures race' that evening. Young Steve Clarke, who later got badly hurt at Boston, was one who progressed in this way.

As Len and I had never fallen out for long, I was able to be involved with him again not only at Hackney, but also in what we developed at Rye House. I remember Eastbourne coming there in my first season as team manager and hammering us. As I walked off the centre green that afternoon, I vowed that I'd build an all-English Rye House team that would challenge for the main National League honours.

As Len was also still running Hackney at the time, it was decided that he wore the Hackney hat while I wore the Rye House one. The big clash came when our teams met in an inter-league fixture, which was quite a laugh with people being accused of various things!

Len and I had a good relationship at Rye House. He did the programme while the secretary at Hackney sorted the pay out. My role was to prepare the track and manage the team. It was my first move into management and it proved a good foundation that served me very well later in my career at King's Lynn, Cradley Heath and now Coventry, as well as my work with the England team.

The Rockets finished 14th out of 20 teams in our first season together but by the late-70s I'd taken them to two runners-up spots and a third, plus a KO Cup win.

In 1979, we were competing with Mildenhall for the NI title and the matches between us drew big crowds. We crammed 6,500 in for our home match with the Fen Tigers that year.

The league decider at Mildenhall ended in controversy when Karl Fiala got knocked off. Len wanted to pull the team out and not contest the second-half. However, TSB were sponsoring the second-half so I said to him: 'Len, you can't do that. I feel as bad as you do about what's happened but we still have a responsibility to the other promotion.'

All set for a fun promoters' race at Hackney in 1977 – Bob Dugard (Eastbourne) and Cyril Maidment (Wimbledon) with Colin Pratt and myself.

I made the riders go back into the changing rooms and get kitted out again for the second-half. If someone has a sponsor and has worked hard to get it, I'd expect the same respect in return if it happened at my place but Len had been adamant that they should go home.

We did disagree on some matters but, overall, we ran Rye House successfully and we made money out of it. Disagreements happen in any relationship. He would let me have my head at times. He'd say: 'You have your way and we shall see.'

Me and Len were probably the first promoters to have a full team sponsorship when we got Infradex on board in 1976. There were eight engines and eight sets of leathers, plus trailers and cars. We were well ahead of our time with that deal.

The team that I left them with won the NL championship the following year. Hughie Saunders took over my team and successfully kept the same riders together.

At the end of 1979 I'd decided that the time was right for a change. I then sold out and came away for a year's rest before returning to the sport at King's Lynn in 1983. Len and I kept in contact, though. When I became joint England manager with Eric Boocock in 1986, we brought Andrew Silver into the England team for his Test debut. Len went to the meetings with Andrew. Sometimes, Len could be a bit volatile and people would say to me: 'You go and talk to him – you know him better than anyone else!'

Even now we stay in touch and talk over different things. I learnt certain skills from him, including how to prepare a track. Len had various ideas that he put into practice. Hackney was a very well prepared track, although sometimes it was over-watered. In my riding days, I used to arrive there early on a Friday afternoon to make sure that he'd got everything on the inside line right, that there was enough dirt on that part of the track.

As for what he has achieved at Rye House in the modern era, it's ironic to note that in 2005 Len won the Premier League title with Rye House and I won the Elite League with Coventry. We laugh about it. I tell him: 'They will have to go some to catch you and me, eh Lennie?' He'd taught me a few things and so it came good when we won those titles.

Didn't they look the part in their matching red, white and blue Infradex-sponsored leathers. The team that went so close to winning the 1979 NL championship – left to right: Ted Hubbard, Ashley Pullen, Kelvin Mullarkey, Hugh Saunders, Karl Fiala, Bob Garrad and Kevin Smith. With virtually the same side, we won it the following year.

When Stuart Robson wanted to leave Coventry and step down to the Premier League, we made the arrangements and it was my recommendation that he went to Rye House. It was unfortunate what happened to Stuart but he had been a good servant to Rye House in recent years. So Len and I have continued to work together more than 40 years after I became his first rider signing at Hackney in 1964.

Having previously lived near each other in Essex, with Andrew being at our house and Troy at theirs on occasions, we have been friends. So I regard Len as a friend as well as a BSPA colleague.

I have the utmost respect for Len. He is a goer for his age. For what he has achieved and continues to do in both speedway and ski-ing, I think it's fantastic. A lot of people would love to be doing what he is at his age.

Colin and I having words with Kelvin Mullarkey.

IAN THOMAS

In a sense, Len and I got off to a rocky start in 1970. Allied Presentations were opening Peterborough and I was opening Workington at the same time. We both applied for league status and we were both turned down.

Allied solved the problem by buying defunct Plymouth's licence from Wally Mawdsley and Pete Lansdale for £1,000, which was a fair amount of money in the early 70s. I took a different path by paying a £10 appeal fee and

Ian Thomas telling me where to go again!

putting our case to the Speedway Control Board. I won – and had the £10 returned.

This didn't please the guys at Allied Presentations and one of them – not Len, I should add – suggested to me that as I'd need their consortium in the future, I should cough up 50 per cent of the fee they had paid Plymouth. My reply was one word: 'B******s!' So, indirectly, there was some initial friction between Len and myself.

As my speedway experience rolled forward, I did pull professional strokes by a good interpretation of the rules and so did Len in his time. So I began to respect him for his nous and we tolerated each other, but I still didn't get on with certain other directors of Allied Presentations.

It began to turn for Len and me when I became involved with promoting the indoor meetings at Wembley Arena in 1979. By now I was the Hull promoter and the Vikings were due at Hackney a few weeks after I'd announced details of the Wembley event. I phoned Len and asked him if I could sell tickets and he flatly refused. Then I mentioned a 15 per cent commission and the answer was 'Yes!' I sold out my 500 allocation and paid Len in readies!

He was more than pleased with me that night even though I wouldn't give him a free ticket, as I felt that he'd made enough on our deal to buy one! We enjoyed the mutual benefit and started to get friendlier.

Over the years we have had disagreements, of course, but I have the greatest respect for him as a speedway promoter – with the emphasis on the word 'promoter'. Because that is what he is – a proper promoter.

He certainly doesn't belong to the 'open the gates and hope they turn up' brigade. Len works hard at it and all his speedway involvement. For a 77-year-old he is amazing and I've no doubt that as he enjoys it so much, Len will go on and on.

I have laid down an interesting offer to him which has been on the table for about five years. If he comes to Workington and gives us a George Formby-style performance on his ukulele, then I'll go down to Rye House and perform an illusion. Perhaps he's worried who I will make disappear! Actually, it could be a surprise appearance, so hopefully it will come together soon.

Overall, except for him prolonging BSPA meetings with his speeches (!), I have no criticism of one of the sport's outstanding promoters.

MARTIN ROGERS

Len is amazing, the great entertainer and trouper still going strong after all these years. A latter-day Johnnie Hoskins but maybe we should not be amazed.

He clearly still has that special ingredient of enthusiasm without which it is a waste of time promoting. I have always believed many of his contemporaries simply failed to recognise the fact that their enthusiasm reached a use-by date and that was the time to exit but too many didn't, clinging on without properly recalling what it was that made them successful in the first place. It was a mistake I was determined not to make when I was promoting which, incidentally, I got into with at least some help from Len.

I was reporting for Speedway Star when I first encountered Len in his early days at Hackney. I covered about five matches a week and the Friday night trip to Hackney consistently rated as one of the most enjoyable. It was a super racetrack then and the Hawks had a team which was entertaining and a promoter who knew how to put on a show.

As general manager at King's Lynn from 1973 I got to know him more when we attended BSPA general council and, later, management committee meetings. Especially after he moved down the road from me and we often travelled together. Colin Pratt, with whom he promoted at Rye House, was a long-time friend and near neighbour and after he built a place near Takeley, Len bought the block of land next door and did the same. Inevitably the three of us had a few 'brains trusts' about speedway and the state of the world and Len was one promoter who was aware of my ambition to be a promoter in my own right, rather than running King's Lynn on behalf of the then owners.

It was, I think, about 1978 when he, Pratty and I paid a surreptitious visit to Harringay to check out the possibilities of operating a team there. It had to be on the quiet because Mike Parker and Bill Bridgett were running the cars there and we didn't want to alert them to the possibility of bringing in the bikes. Although, in the event, nothing came of it.

The following year, Len and I went up to Scunthorpe to talk about the possibility of buying out Brian Osborn, who was promoting there at the time, but, again, nothing eventuated.

In my role at King's Lynn I had a number of dealings with Len, probably the best from my perspective being the transfer which brought Bent Rasmussen to Saddlebow Road in 1978. With Len and Colin's help we also had Rye House's Bob Garrad there as number eight in 1979. The following year my wife Lin and I bought Leicester and as Cyril Crane wasn't bothered about having Garrad back at King's Lynn, he came to Blackbird Road and doubled up very effectively for much of that season. We wanted to sign him outright but this time Len didn't want to do business and 'Bobby G' almost inevitably ended up at Waterden Road.

It was no secret that Hackney was never one of the big bucks clubs but I was genuinely shocked when Len sold up in 1983. However, we were more than preoccupied with our own problems as Midland Sports sold Leicester Stadium and delivered a peremptory kiss-off to our blossoming operation there.

The following season Len bobbed up in an advisory role for Oxford and we had a big confrontation at the end of a very close match at King's Lynn (where Lin and I had returned to buy the promoting rights) when the Cheetahs nicked victory in the last race. Fortunately it was handbags at five paces, spur of the moment stuff and did not forever poison our relationship! In fact, Len continued to be a valued friend probably the more so when Lin and I joined the ranks of the National League as promoters of Peterborough.

But a variety of circumstances saw to it that our continued involvement in speedway did not extend beyond 1988, the year in which we sold first King's Lynn, then Peterborough and moved to Australia.

I'm sorry to say that as the intervening years have flown by we have done no more than observe from a distance how Len has extended his own promoting career to such legendary proportions. That distance, though, does not diminish our appreciation of his past friendship nor, especially, the undisguised endorsement of the fact he has continued to orchestrate so much pleasure for so many.

CHRIS VAN STRAATEN

My first year of regularly attending speedway was 1961. I can remember Len vividly from around that time, including his victory in the 1962 PLRC. I always favoured riders who were flamboyant and a little bit different. He always came across as one of that breed. Len always had this degree of flamboyancy which I think he carried through to his promoting days. He just stood out. Although I was a Cradley fan, he was a rider whose scores you followed with interest.

I had my first promoter's licence at Oxford in 1978, having been involved in speedway administration at Stoke in 1973. At the first promoters' meetings I attended I was in awe of somebody like Len, who had immense knowledge. I think I learned a lot from him about promoting the sport just by sitting there listening and taking on board what he was saying.

During the time that he was away from the sport, I grew within the BSPA and by the time he came back in 2000, I'd been chairman for some years and continued in that role. His contributions to the promoters' meetings since he returned have been extremely valuable. If other promoters spoke for a quarter of the time Len does, the meetings would be much better, because a lot of people say nothing.

I also find that you can have an argument with him and he doesn't seem to bear any grudges. I have had some right run-ins in my time with Len and the next day we are as right as rain.

He does have strong opinions and it takes a strong chairman to control Len in a meeting. But I regard that aspect of him as a quality. I've also found that he always tends to look after the underdog even though at times he has been one of the most successful promoters. When he is in a room and providing input, he has consideration for the less successful members.

His longevity and vigour is amazing. He has to keep reminding us how old he is because he doesn't come across as being 77. Sometimes when I go to matches at Rye House, it's like being in a time-warp – but that is not meant as a criticism. Len retains old-fashioned values in the sport. His is a traditional promotion and I don't think there is anything wrong with that.

It is fantastic that after all the years in the sport he is still as enthusiastic as a teenager. Len certainly doesn't need to do it from a financial point of view and his time could be put to better financial rewards, but he clearly still enjoys speedway immensely. The time and effort he has put into a circuit like Rye House and the improvements that he has made, have been remarkable.

In the history of the sport there aren't many men who have made a more favourable impression than Len Silver has over the years.

TERRY RUSSELL

I first started watching speedway at Hackney in 1963, when I was taken along by my parents. I can remember Len as a visiting rider with Exeter. In a less colourful age for the sport, the Falcons' green and white chequered rugby jerseys and white boots stood out. To add to their flair, I particularly remember Len and Howdy Byford coming onto the centre green with a guitar rendition during the interval!

When Len took over as promoter at Hackney in 1964, I was in my early teens and lived at nearby Bow. Every Friday during the school holidays my mate Dave Beech and I would turn up at Waterden Road at 9am and help Len

Back in the Hackney pits in 1984 and in conversation with new broom Terry Russell.

throughout the day with tasks such as track-watering and then we'd sit in the Jeep with Len when he was tyre-packing. Having spent all day working at the track, the 'pay off' was to be able to be in the pits watching our No.1 Colin Pratt up close. Most people presume that I met Len once I became a promoter at Crayford in 1983 but I first got to know him almost 20 years before then.

LEN SILVER

I eventually became Hackney promoter in 1984 and that was quite an emotional moment considering my modest start at Waterden Road as one of Len's young helpers. In a later life I became chairman of the BSPA with Colin as a colleague on my management committee.

In 1983 it had been announced that Chris Shears was buying Len out at Hackney. This coincided with stadium redevelopment at Crayford, so I was looking for a new track for the Kestrels to race at. Chris had been associated with Ipswich and when I heard the Hackney announcement, I switched my attention to Foxhall Heath.

When Chris didn't go through with the deal at Waterden Road, Len phoned me to test my interest. He is very fair and straightforward to deal with in any negotiation and we did the deal reasonably quickly. Not only did everything fall into place with respect to moving my Crayford team to Hackney, but it was much more convenient to my Kent home and business, plus it was where it all began for me.

By the time he returned to speedway at the new Millennium, I'd become a senior figure in speedway myself, going from BSPA chairman to president. The fact that Len remembered me as a young teenager does not prevent him from addressing me as 'Mister President' and showing respect. We have a positive and mature working relationship.

I don't often go to Rye House because of many other commitments but I have to say what a wonderful job Len has done there with the stadium. He got a grip on the lease and made our sport the priority. His ability in preparing tracks has also been an influence on me over the years – from the days when he taught me to water a track properly as a kid.

When I opened at Hackney in 1984 he turned up at 4pm that afternoon to wish me well. When I continued with speedway at Hackney in 1996, despite the stadium being in receivership, he was a regular and welcome visitor on Wednesday nights.

Although it's always nice to see new young blood coming into the sport, it's also good to have the established promoters on hand so that we can tap into their experience. Len was there in 1965 when the two divisions amalgamated into the British League. He has immense knowledge of the sport and great perspective.

Rye House could be seen as a successful fish and chip emporium which stages speedway! He has income streams that most promoters don't but he invests to upgrade facilities. He is blessed with a loyal support team at Rye House but that loyalty exists because of his loyalty in return.

He is not perfect – he can be wrong – but the bottom line is that Len Silver is a bloody good promoter and that's how he will be remembered.

JON COOK

My first direct encounters with Len came through my association with Martin Dugard during his time when he and Andrew Silver were coming through the ranks to full England status. I knew of Len as the father of one of the sport's up-and-coming prospects. I was a great admirer – as were my circle of Martin, Dean Barker and Paul Dugard – of Andrew's riding style. Ivan Mauger had actually criticised Andrew, saying that he wouldn't progress with his all-action, dynamic style but we all thought Andrew was the coolest rider around, both on and off the track.

In 1991 there had been some radical changes at the Eastbourne track that I supported. Wimbledon Speedway closed down and transferred their operation to Arlington, where they became the Eastbourne 'Dons'. By 1992 Bob Dugard was good enough to advise me that he felt I had certain talents which meant that I should aim higher than being a mechanic. He offered my name to Peter Brown, who was the Dons' general manager, and I took on the role of the club's commercial manager. This gave me a completely new perspective on the running of a speedway club, particularly one which was struggling with being a hybrid operation.

Andrew Silver had been signed from Swindon but half-way through the season the riders were called into the office and asked to take a pay cut. This also involved tearing up their current contracts to go on a pay-rate triggered by a per-centage of the gate. It has always registered in my memory that it was Len Silver's son – no doubt with the insight of his father – who stated: 'Speedway riders risk their lives. Promoters risk their money. Not my problem!' Len Silver had promoted for many years at many tracks but kept them going.

Eventually the Wimbledon promotion couldn't carry on, so a formula was hatched between the BSPA and the Dugard family whereby the sport could continue at Arlington. Len had been a regular visitor and Andrew had been enjoying a successful season. After discussions with Bob Dugard, Len agreed to take the club on – but there was a difference. Len wanted the public on board. No 'Sugar Daddy' principle but everyone working together for its survival. I'd had previous contact with Len through his Silver Ski company's sponsorship of the Championship of Sussex meeting in 1992. Now, at the age of just 26, I was to step up to be his co-promoter and enter into a most informative and enjoyable period of my life. With backing from the Dugard family, we put together a fantastic team. To the delight of Charles Dugard we brought Martin back to the team along with other former Eagles' favourites in Dean Barker and David Norris. The Eagles were reborn and with Andrew Silver, Peter Nahlin and Stefan Danno in the mix, we laid the foundation of the club becoming a force at the highest level. The craic was good and under a tremendous promotion, the crowds mainly doubled from the dismal Wimbledon days.

But then something significant happened around about the fourth meeting into the season. Mick Corby arranged a junior meeting on a Saturday night for which he produced his own programme. Len saw both aspects as the way forward. Within one week we were producing our own programme and arrangements were in hand to upgrade the lights at the stadium.

For the programme, a duplicating machine at Silver Ski was utilised and information could even be collated on the afternoon of a match itself. The supporters' club assisted with assembling the publication and it was a true club effort. As far as Len was concerned it was value for money plus it was self-generating. This practice went on for several seasons and Len's brief stay at the club had an impact both on and off track. He turned the club around and added a valuable dimension to my own learning curve.

In 1994, Andrew Silver announced his retirement from the sport and some additional factors at Arlington dented Len's enthusiasm. However, I repeat that he laid the foundation which led onto League and Cup success for the Eagles in the 90s. For me, his coming on board was in another sense a life-changing experience. For in 1992 I'd returned from a trip to Australia and wasn't certain what my future direction was. I'd even considered emigrating but the prospect of working with Len Silver kept me at home and soon afterwards I met my wife Louisa.

By April 1994 we were married and our son Jacob was about to be born. Len agreed to be Jacob's Godfather. Remarkably, Jacob wasn't christened until 2002 and Len dutifully turned up for the ceremony at Shoreham Beach. Meanwhile, he never forgets Jacob's birthday and is most generous in sending a card and a cheque each year.

He has remained most generous in another sense. For as a firm friend he has been available for advice during my own promotional career. When I took the decision to seek pastures new with the Lakeside Hammers at Arena-Essex after many years at Eastbourne, I talked it through with him and we also discussed some problems with certain personalities in the background. I did unburden on him and he told me not to look back, but to have future perspective.

We are always capable of 'chewing the fat.' We may disagree on issues but it is never personal. I hold him in high affection. Len is a very special man and I'm proud to be able to call him a friend.

FRIENDS & PARTNERS

DENNIS DAY

I first got to know Len in the late-40s, when me and a group of mates from Stratford in East London rode cycle speedway at a track on a bomb site at Janson Road. We would meet up after work and race around, eventually forming a team called 'The Vikings'. This track drew quite a few lads from the local area. One day this younger lad turned up and, without a bye your leave, started pounding around. We thought, 'who the hell is this?' It was, of course, Len.

Once he got to know us and settled in, then he started to organise things. It was Len who decided we would become the Stratford Hammers. I wasn't so keen on the idea myself. Our team was very successful and became part of Cycle Speedway folklore, becoming very competitive at both local and national level.

Len and I became team partners – something we'd repeat in a speedway context years later. The whole set up got bigger and bigger as lads were attracted to our set-up from all over. We ran four teams and as parents became involved, we organised coach trips to race in other parts of the country.

Eventually Len went into the forces and I used to write to him. He got experience riding motorbikes and amateur speedway while in Egypt. When he came home, he declared that he was going to take up speedway, so I said that I'd go into the sport with him. I went to Rye House to practice. We also went up to Norwich in a big, old van to attend training courses run by Ossie Powell. Then both of us got rides at Ipswich. Johnny Davies – who had lost the use of an arm in a track crash – used to take Len and I around in a Chrysler pick-up truck. Eventually Len bought the truck, as it was more convenient.

I was signed by Ipswich in 1953 and Len followed. As second-halvers, we were competing for a team place. The consortium of local businessmen and farmers who owned Ipswich Speedway at the time had lots of money at their disposal. They could afford to buy in riders as tracks folded and it was hard to break into the team. Finally, Ipswich gave me the push and Len retired.

In 1963, my last season with the Falcons. Standing, left to right: Alan Cowland, Cliff Cox, Dennis Day, Pat Flanagan, Pete Lansdale (promoter). Front: Me and old pal Howdy Byford.

Subsequently I went to work with Len in the motor trade. We were good pals and our respective wives used to socialise together. When he opened a car showroom in the Leytonstone Road he offered me a partnership at £500 – but I didn't have 500 pennies! Eventually Len found a partner and they built up a network of showrooms over time, which became potentially good businesses to sell on.

Len eventually decided that

he was going to resume speedway, so we teamed up again and went back to Ipswich together. Vic Gooden was now the promoter there and a good one. We were in and out of the side and with the formation of the Provincial League in 1960, there came the possibility of us being loaned out or sold. I was in line to go but had a couple of good meetings for the Witches while my position was under review. Instead, it was Len who ended up being farmed out to Exeter and, before long, it was the making of him. I did soon join him at the County Ground, so once again we travelled around together.

By now Len had a new showroom on the Romford Road, in partnership with ex-Rayleigh rider Alby Smith. I, too, went there with Len and we had a very efficient working relationship, although he is a hard taskmaster. When you worked for him you were actually a salesman/cleaner, which meant having to wash the vehicles as well as sell them.

When we weren't busy, I'd work on our bikes in a small garage at the back of the premises. It panned out well for me, though, as I had transport provided.

Len quickly proved a big hit at Exeter but I wasn't doing that well for the Falcons and moved to Hackney. I'd finished second in the London Riders' Championship and the then Hackney promoter, Mike Parker, approached me. It was very convenient to switch there.

Then, in 1964, came an interesting development as Len bought a half-share in the club despite continuing to ride for Exeter for a while before it became obvious that he, too, had to ride for the Hawks. So we became team-mates at a third different club.

Unfortunately, I was in the race that finished his racing career. The truth was that nobody liked riding with Len because he never gave his race partner a choice over gate positions. However, though I was peeved in one sense to be asked to ride with him, at least I was used to him and we obviously got on well.

After another Hawk refused to be partnered with him, I lined up with Len for a KO Cup match against Exeter at Waterden Road. Being Exeter, it was also a bit of a needle match. We'd won the toss and chosen gates one and three – Len preferred the outside gate so I settled into gate one. We were out against Alan Cowland and Howdy Byford.

I didn't quite make the gate but came hard under the other three on the first bend. They all finished on the deck but I carried on. I had run into Alan Cowland, who straightened up and, in turn, took Len off and into Howdy Byford. I was excluded but Len hurt his shoulder badly and could take no further part in the meeting. In fact he never rode again.

I felt bad about it because he was my 'bosom pal'. Through working and riding together over the years, I'd spent more time with him than anyone else.

It wasn't long before injury brought my riding days to a close, in very similar circumstances. Hackney were racing at Newport when my team-mate Jimmy Heard took me into the fence on the first bend. My right arm was badly broken but Len didn't realise that at the time – he was imploring me to get back up for the re-run! I was 36 and decided that enough was enough, although I wished I'd carried on.

I moved from East London to Benfleet, Essex and also went on to work in the motor trade in what became the Tri -Central dealership in Chelmsford. Len had been my friend since he was a schoolboy, so I always kept tabs on his speedway career. I knew that he treated his riders well and would always earn respect in the sport despite divided opinions. You either like Len or you don't, but liking and respecting are different matters.

I'd heard about the success he made of Hackney and Rye House and I was very pleased that he became the England team manager.

Yes, we had our ups and downs. He used to call me the 'Leytonstone Independent', after our local newspaper, because I often disagreed with him! However, he was a good and generous friend – sometimes too generous to others, I must add. But that's Len.

EXETER

ALLEN TRUMP

They say that what impresses you as a youngster stays with you for life and as I get older my introduction to speedway as a 13-year-old remains as vivid now as it did some 48 years ago in those pre-Beatle days of the early-60s.

I was brought up in the 50s with my father's tales of speedway greats like Cyril Roger and Jack Geran and the mysterious Bronco Slade, a legendary local leg-trailer. So I suppose it was inevitable that in the summer of 1961 I finally found my way to St Thomas and the dinosauresque County Ground – home of the Exeter Falcons.

What I experienced there was the start of a love affair with speedway that has lasted almost 50 years and is due in no small part to Exeter's leading rider at the time, the intriguingly named Len Silver.

Those were reverential days when the press referred to riders as 'gladiators in leathers' and the intoxicating and long gone smell of Castrol R drew us back weekly for another fix. It was a time when riders wore open helmets and slightly scary leather face masks and when riders like Len and Colin Pratt wore the new fangled all in one 'monkey mask'.

So what do I remember of Len? Well, he was a large part of Exeter Speedway and my life for two years from the summer of '61 until his untimely move to Hackney as co-promoter in May 1964.

Known as 'The Banjo Kid', Len was a consummate entertainer, crooning and playing the banjo, and many times would be hauled out by Wally Mawdsley to entertain the crowd in the interval on the microphone. At Exeter in the 60s you got the speedway and an interval attraction, usually involving Len.

In 1961 Len was the top rider at Exeter but it was the following season, 1962, that he took off into the Provincial League stratosphere. The Provincial League, the equivalent of today's Premier League, saved British speedway in the early-60s and riders like Len, who started riding after the war, were the top dogs.

By the end of October 1962 Len was Provincial Riders' Champion, Silver Sash match-race holder and the Falcons had lifted the PL Knockout Cup after demolishing Colin Pratt's Stoke Potters at the County Ground. Some season!

Every Monday after school I'd shoot off home, get changed and then catch two buses to the County Ground and hang around the pits whilst Len and the rest of the riders went through the seemingly black art of preparing their bikes. Whilst some riders gave the impression of being approachable, Len gave off the opposite vibes to us 13-year-olds and we certainly got the message – keeping our distance! Looking back, of course, it was a workplace for Len and, in my role as Coventry co-promoter, I now know myself what a nuisance kids can be in the pits.

On the track it was a different matter – we owned him! The dapper Len, always immaculately turned out in glistening black leathers, never disappointed on the scary, wide open spaces of the County Ground. His riding style was languid, as if he was sat in an armchair, and he made riding the track look effortlessly easy. In fact, I can only remember him coming off a couple of times in nearly three years, a rare event that sent a shock wave through the crowd as enraged spectators harangued the besieged tractor driver and demanded to know what was wrong with the track.

In front of Exeter crowds that Elite League clubs would die for today Len became, dare I say, a little

Dressed in my Exeter blazer, I was invited back to Belle Vue for the 1963 Provincial League Riders' Championship. Here I'm presenting pennants to Stoke representatives Colin Pratt and Ken Vale.

predictable. Top riders like Norman Hunter, Ivor Brown and Colin Pratt came to the County Ground and left humbled whilst Len just kept on winning. Us ragamuffins on the back straight, four telegraph poles along from the pits, dreamt of Len being beaten into the first bend just so he would have to wind it on and effortlessly swoop around the insanely banked second bend – his favourite manoeuvre. If he didn't get by first time there was no need to worry – there were plenty of laps and bends still to come and it would take a good man to hold him off on the four-lap, full-mile circuit.

Season 1962 dawned with the Falcons by far the smartest turned out side in the league, resplendent in green and white rugby shirts and white boots. Len picked up where he left off with. For me, it was the start of travelling with the supporters' club to away meetings. The Exeter SSC was run by Mrs Kerr, a smart grey-haired lady who looked 80 to someone who was only a young teenager but, in reality, was probably only in her early-50s. She organised the travel and my parents agreed that I could go on the coach providing Mrs Kerr kept an eye on me. Well, that was all I needed and I travelled all over the country following Len and the Falcons.

There were highs like the fantastic night at Belle Vue in September 1962, when Len won the PLRC. The first wave of supporters' coaches left Exeter at midnight on the Friday and, some eight hours later, arrived in Manchester and a world I'd never experienced before. Second-hand furniture and pets being sold on the pavements and street after street of what appeared to be a huge second-hand market. So great was the demand for tickets that a second wave of coaches left the County Ground early on Saturday morning as well.

Then on to Belle Vue Zoo, where the monkeys came to the edge of their enclosure and people flicked lighted cigarettes to them. The monkeys picked up the ciggies and smoked them like the experienced smokers they probably were.

That night the atmosphere was electric and the 20,000 crowd was the biggest I'd ever been part of. The riders came out and were introduced to the expectant fans – Len in his smart green and white Falcons rugby shirt and immaculate white boots, the Falcons' race jacket glistening under the lights. My mate Dave swung his green and white rattle and three coachloads of Exeter supporters started chanting '1-3-5-7, Hear this roar from glorious Devon – E-X-E-T-E-R, EXETER!

And there he was, Len Silver in the exalted company of the top Provincial League riders of the day in what was the most complex individual meeting ever. Twenty four riders, each riding four times in 24 heats and then a final with the top four scorers. Len was imperious, dropping just one point to Edinburgh's Wayne Briggs, Barry's younger brother, and as the evening wore on it dawned on those of us in the massed green and white contingent that our man was in with more than just a chance.

After Len's nail-biting fourth ride he'd amassed 11 points and had qualified for the four-man final. The tension was almost unbearable as the four riders – Len, Brian Craven, Guy Allott and Wayne Briggs – settled at the starting gate. We were stood on the first bend and had a good view as Craven was away first, with Len and Allott locked together going into the first bend. Allott seemed to bounce off Len and fell heavily. The race was stopped for what today would be called first bend bunching. All four back for the restart.

In the re-run Len missed the gate and Briggs led into the first bend with Len in pursuit. It took two laps for Len to wear Briggsy down and roar past him. Then came a long two laps as Len avoided engine failure, a fall or the ever-threatening Briggs passing him. It was all over and our top Falcon was the Provincial Riders' Champion.

It was only recently that Len told me the impressive silver cup he was awarded that evening, and paraded on the tractor around Belle Vue, was snatched back from him by Dent Oliver immediately after the lap of honour and returned to the office.

I recall the exuberance as we got back to our coaches followed by the 10-hour convoy back to Exeter that arrived on Sunday morning. We knew what to expect when Len was introduced to the crowd the following Monday night and weren't disappointed. Over 5,000 fans were ecstatic and gave Len a rapturous welcome. After all, it was the first time an Exeter rider had ever won a trophy worth parading.

It had been only two seasons since Exeter re-opened and, looking back, those were halcyon days for Exeter Speedway as crowds that had averaged around the 3,500/4,000 mark suddenly took off to 5,000-plus after Len's championship win and formed the bedrock support for the next 40 years.

TONY LETHBRIDGE

Len Silver was a big hero to a generation of Exeter fans. In 1961 Wally Mawdsley and Pete Lansdale re-launched league racing at the County Ground after a six-year break.

The Falcons struggled in their early Provincial League matches in 1961 and the turnover of riders was rapid. Len made his first appearance in the Capstan Trophy individual championship but finished well down the order with four points. He had previously made one racing appearance at the track, for Ipswich in 1955 when he scored one point. Four days after the individual meeting he broke his collarbone at Rayleigh, where the Falcons lost 50-25.

Don Trevelyan, the local reporter for *Speedway Star and News*, quickly wrote off our new signing's chances, claiming that he was 'not much improvement on what the Falcons already had.' This brought a stinging rebuke from Dave Lanning, then Ipswich's press officer. Big Dave made it clear that Len would soon make Trevelyan eat his words.Even Dave probably didn't realise just how big a star Len was about to become.

HACKNEY

MALCOLM BROWN

I first met Len Silver in 1963 at Hackney Speedway. I'd been riding at the Rye House training school run by Peter Sampson. He told me to go and see Len at Hackney with the aim of getting a ride in the second-half. I went and met him in his office at Ilford in Essex, at the back of his used car showroom in the High Street. He said: 'What can I do for you?'

I replied: 'I want to ride for Hackney.'

He said: 'You do, do you, and who the hell are you?'

Obviously I stated: 'Malcolm Brown', to which he responded: 'Never heard of you!' I couldn't resist saying: 'You will!'

A rare serious moment with Malcom Brown.

Len confirmed: 'I like your cheek. I'll give you a ride Friday night in the second-half' – and that was the start of a great friendship which lasted all my speedway career and still does to this day.

I first became a Hackney team member when he told me that if I could beat Jimmy Heard in the second-half, then I'd step up to ride at No.7. Well, from that night in 1964, I remained a regular in the team until the end of '68.

Len was a great speedway promoter and showman. He lived and slept speedway. He loved every person who came through the turnstile. He wanted everyone to get their money's worth plus entertainment.

He made me dye my leathers purple, which was done by using bottles and bottles of shoe dye for my boots and leathers for each meeting. Len told me that becoming a showman didn't come easy so 'stop complaining!'

This was the start of me becoming the so-called 'Clown Prince of Speedway'. As Len had taken me under his wing, I had to do as I was told! It started when he told me he was buying me some new speedway riding boots from Lonstaffs, a motorcycle store in the heart of London. He made me walk around London for three hours with these boots on to break them in so that they would feel nice and be ready to wear in the meeting at Hackney that night. Did it ever occur to Len that my feet would be covered in blisters?

However, during the course of my time with Hackney I got the chance to get my own back on 'Mr Speedway'. The team had travelled up to Scotland to ride at Edinburgh and Glasgow. Following the first meeting we went to a party. After a few drinks, Howdy Byford, Les McGillivray and myself decided to call up Maurie Littlechild, who was the Kings Lynn promoter and a good friend of Len. Maurie always slept with the phone next to his bed. I phoned at 2.30 in the morning, he picked up the receive and, in a Scottish accent, I said: 'This is the Glasgow police, do you know a Mr. Len Silver?'

Maurie replied: 'Yes, yes – what's up?'

I said: 'We have the Hackney team in jail. Howdy Byford and Malcolm Brown were swinging around on a lamp-post naked and all the rest of the team were drunk and disorderly.'

Maurie answered: 'OK, I will call Mr. Silver and let him know since they are supposed to be riding in Glasgow tomorrow.' And then he hung up.

Well, the next morning, as we were leaving Edinburgh for Glasgow, we all said that we should phone Len and tell him that it was all a joke. We called and his wife answered the phone. She told us: 'Len isn't here. He had to fly up to Scotland to see if he could get the team out of jail.'

We all thought we were going to be in trouble with Len but when he arrived and saw all of us there, he exclaimed: 'Bastards! Now let's go out and win this match.'

One night at Hackney, Len found out that I'd been in the Royal Corps of the Signals Display Team (White Helmets) in Ripon, Yorkshire when I was in the Army. He had this idea that I should do a ramp jump through a large hoop of fire on the centre green at the next meeting. He got Don Smith, who was then the British Trials Champion, to build a ramp, which I thought was too high but Len thought wasn't high enough!

The night I was going to do the jump, he made me practice in the afternoon with Don Smith and his trial bike but without fire. He had put the announcement of the 'ring of fire jump' in the programme the week before, so there was no turning back.

There were three gallons of petrol poured over the straw hoop at the end of the ramp, which I thought was too much. Len explained: 'I want the crowd to see a lot of flames.'

He told me to ride up the ramp as if I was going to do it on the first attempt, but then turn away. I was then instructed to ride over to him on the microphone and tell him that I couldn't do it – which I did. He'd then ask the crowd: 'Do you want him to do it?' Then there were loud screams from the fans – yep, they wanted it!

Len announces on the mike: 'It's Friday at Eight. Let's do it. Off you go, Malc.'

They poured so much more petrol on the hoop, it was like the towering inferno. I went speeding up the ramp, kicked the bike out of gear by accident, went through the hoop, came down on the other side – front wheel first – and hit my balls on the tank. I was in agony!

Len calls me over to him at the starting gate where he was jumping up and down with excitement. 'The crowd loved it and they want you to do it again!'

I told him that I couldn't, as I had no balls. Len said: 'Of course you do, go do it again.' He then proceeds to inform the crowd: 'Malcolm wants to do it one more time!'

Ice packs helped me out later!

One thing Len loved to do was play his banjo. I recall one occasion when he took me with him to entertain the residents at an old folk's home. He was playing the banjo and singing while I was telling jokes to the 60-odd OAPs present. He told me to hand out speedway fliers to everybody while he was singing and playing the banjo. The flyer said: 'Make it a Date, Friday at Eight' and he reminded me to tell them that a bus would be provided to pick them up, if they wanted to come.

Well, Len was first up on the floor and he was dying on his arse! So after five minutes he passed the mic over to me as he walked off laughing. I told a few jokes but no-one laughed and after a few minutes I announced: 'Let's pass you back to Uncle Len' who was sitting on a chair next to the stage shaking his head. This must have gone on for 30 minutes or so, back and forth, between us. However, Len is a showman . . . and the show must go on!

Another time, Pathe News had been to Hackney Speedway to make film clips on the sport. When it was released Len made me and Brian Davies dress up in our leathers, push our bikes up the steps of the local cinema, greet everyone that came in and hand out Hackney flyers. Sure enough, Len turned up and told us to wait until everyone had left the building before we were allowed to leave.

I told him that it was getting late but he came right up to my face, stared me in the eye and stated: 'Malcolm, that's show business.'

One aspect I'll always remember is when we'd finished a meeting and would be having a drink with the other riders and the fans. We'd look down from the bar and see Len out on the track on the tractor, grading the track for the next meeting whatever the weather.

I had the privilege to come back to Rye House Speedway in 2005 and ride with Bengt Jansson, Keith White and Finn Thomsen in a fun 'race' during the Vic Harding Memorial Trophy meeting. I'd travelled from Florida, USA, where I now live, for the Hackney Speedway reunion which had been held at Paradise Wildlife Park the night before. It has been over 40 years since I'd first met Len Silver and I have many happy and great memories, plus some sad ones too. One fact I know for sure – he has not changed one bit. Speedway promoters and riders have come and gone but he is still up there at No.1!

I'd love to know how many riders have passed through his hands and have thanked him for his help. He is a great man and a great promoter. It will take a lot to fill his shoes.

PETER SAMPSON

It was the late-50s/early-60s when I first became aware of Len. You saw people but didn't necessarily know them that well. You would say 'hello' but you had no idea what their background was – you just knew them as faces. I knew of him as a rider and a pretty competitive one at that.

I can remember one particular race with Len overtaking me when I rode for Rye House at home. I can recall Len pushing my leg along. He was quite robust. I thought that I'd better move over and let him past!

With Pete Sampson at the Speedway Museum in 2007.

I have never known Len as well as I have, say, Colin Pratt and Dingle Brown because we're from a different area. I knew Len when he was at Hackney because when I packed up speedway I went into the coach business. We supplied the coaches for Hackney Speedway, running a coach service to Waterden Road from outlying districts. So we began to build up a business relationship more than the speedway side and that continued until crowds slumped and demand for coaches reduced accordingly. It was through Len that we transported the Russian and Polish touring teams around the UK. We used to take half of the seats out of the coach, load the bikes in and tour the tracks.

Len and I had a further association when I worked at Victor Martins doing welding and repairs. I used to serve Len, who would come into the shop in Tottenham to buy spares and parts.

I also sponsored Len's second-half events. At Hackney my company used to back the 'Golden Shoe' and at Rye House it was the 'Silver Shoe.' Myself and 'Johnny the Welder' made the steel shoes for the winners.

What's interesting is that life has gone full circle. I think if Dingle Brown hadn't mentioned having a Speedway Museum here at Paradise Wildlife Park, then perhaps I wouldn't be involved in the sport today. I know this is a wildlife park and a haven for all sorts of creatures but because we are close to Rye House, we're fairly close to where High Beech is, plus we're on the edge of London and former tracks such as Harringay and Hackney, it seemed a reasonable place to have the museum. No doubt some think that Birmingham would be a much better place to have it but the opportunity was here. We have the land.

We had the first couple of planning meetings and Len came along. I think he could see a reasonable opportunity. We get 250,000 visitors through our place during the season but I'd say that most of them have not been to speedway. Now if we could promote Rye House from here, I'd be very disappointed if we couldn't help to boost Len's gates. The other issue we've discussed is us both offering a one-ticket discount covering both venues – spend a day at PWP and go on to the speedway racing in the evening at a discounted admission price. Len doesn't have a closed mind and is therefore open to business ideas.

I have only been to the stadium twice since 2006 but I'm impressed by what Len has done there. He had worked extremely hard. As I've known Rye House for 50 years, I know it quite well!

I'm totally convinced that Len is not doing it as a get-rich scheme, but because he loves what he does. He is passionate about the sport. The crowds are not as large as I'd like to see for all the effort he has put in but he is still very enthusiastic. At his age he still wants to get up, get out of bed and get stuck in.

On occasions Len will radically reduce the admission price or offer free admission in order to get that secondary spend from the catering facilities he has built up. One occasion he had two thousand come in on a free night and there was, for example, more beer as well as fish and chips sold than normal. 'Get them in' is the motto. They also go away from Rye House happy – and that's another important point.

Paradise Park staged the Hackney reunion in 2005 attended by Len and many of his ex-riders and the organisers did remarkably well. With his input and advice on various issues with the Speedway Museum, Len and I are back in harness to a certain extent.

BARRY THOMAS

Len spotted me one night in 1969 when I was riding at Canterbury and his Rayleigh team were the visitors. He had a word with Johnnie Hoskins about my racing in second-halves at Hackney and by 1970 I was doubling-up between Canterbury and Hackney in both leagues. Riding for the Hawks certainly helped my ability as a Second Division rider and by 1971 Len had spoken to me about coming out of Canterbury and going full-time with Hackney in the British League.

I was happy at Hackney and got on well with Len. Waterden Road was a very good racing circuit because he really took a pride in preparing the track surface. It was his 'baby' and he worked very hard at it. I wasn't a gater and the track, with its banked corners, allowed me to come from the back. You could have a go and felt that you could win. It is probably why I did so well at Halifax – a big version of Hackney.

As a promoter, Len was very supportive. He'd stick by his riders – none of this chopping three riders at once and bringing another three in. There would be the odd change but it was all

Fighting Thommo's corner with the referee.

very stable. Len was a good all-round promoter whether he was watering the track in a pair of shorts or being out there selling the sport with great enthusiasm.

As a person, Len was fair and down to earth. To an extent he was very easy-going. Throughout a long career with him, I can't ever recall us having a cross word. Of course, as a youngster I loved the racing and didn't worry that much about the money. As I got older and wiser I realised there was money to be made in the game so when it came to pre-season deals I'd be pacing up and down for two hours before picking the phone up to start negotiations with Len. He'd suggest that we met up at a steakhouse in Stratford. There, in nice surroundings, we'd chat over the contract and agree a deal. We always both went home happy, although I'm sure that I never asked for enough!

On another occasion we were returning together from an away match and heading for Hackney Stadium, where I had to leave my bike. We'd reached the East Way near the stadium when the police pulled me up for speeding. Len said: 'Don't say anything, leave this to me.'

He leapt out of the car and, to my amazement, tore into the police officers. He stated that he was a taxpayer and they were public servants. He told them that to pursue our car was a public disservice and he requested that they confirmed their numbers. Talk about attack being the best form of defence! They let me off and drove away!

One of the funniest incidents came one night at King's Lynn. The viewing area was then close to the pit gate. I'd just walked out on track and was sitting on my bike, ready to pull my clutch in, when I instinctively became aware of an object about to land on top of me, so I reacted by putting my arms up to protect myself. Unbelievably, that object was Len! My action helped to break his fall. He'd a right bust-up with Cyril Crane, who punched Len so hard that Len fell backwards off the raised area.

Another time Hackney were racing at Wimbledon and we got thrashed. Now with Len it was not a case of heads down and off home. He announced after the meeting: 'Right, everybody follow me to the local steakhouse.' 'Everybody' meant riders, mechanics, family members and general hangers-on.

During the meal, which he paid for in full – and the bill wasn't cheap, he spotted a guitar up on the stage. So he leapt up and started entertaining all and sundry. He did a great job of lifting spirits that night– he was ever the showman!

When Len was England team manager he picked me to ride in a Test match at Norkopping, Sweden. We were all flying from Heathrow but Gordon Kennett and I missed the plane. Although we took the next flight out, the airport we landed at was 200 miles from Norkopping. I said to Gordon: 'We'll have to take a taxi.'

We eventually reached the team hotel and I popped inside to find Len. He said: 'No bother, I'll settle up with the taxi driver.' Of course, he thought we'd taken a cab from the local airport and had quite a shock when the taxi driver told him that he wanted the Swedish krona equivalent of several hundred pounds!!

The good thing about Len is that he saw the funny side of the situation.

FINN THOMSEN

Len is 77 but he looks healthier now than in the days when I was riding for him at Hackney. All the ski-ing he does is probably the reason for that.

When I left Wolverhampton in 1978 to ride for Hackney we moved down to Essex, not too far from Len, who lived at Takeley. As a promoter he was the best that I've ever dealt with. He was just a nice man. He was fair and being an ex-rider helped him to understand your point of view as well.

I had six very happy years at Hackney until Len pulled out of there in 1983. But in all the time since then we've kept in touch with him and Hazal. Suzanne and I saw them at the Hackney reunion in 2005 and again at Rye House Speedway last year when we returned to England to attend the 80-

Finn Thomsen enjoyed his time at Hackney.

year anniversary at my first club, Wolverhampton, whom I'd joined in 1974.

I also liked my time at Monmore Green but you never always got to see the boss. With Len, he was there for you all the time. Any problems and he'd always help you out. He was very approachable and there was nothing that you couldn't talk to him about. He wouldn't take offence and he was a good listener.

As a front man and showman, he is still way out in front of the rest. He was doing it when we visited Rye House most recently. Len is special.

He had a friendly approach but he should have been a bit harder on some people. His heart sometimes outweighed his obvious intelligence. Len loves his sport and he's a gentleman.

BO PETERSEN

I first became associated with Hackney Speedway and Len Silver when I came across for trials at the end of the 1977 season. Someone had spotted me riding in Jutland and recommended me to Len. I met up with him at the track and found him a happy and chatty character straightaway. He was very easy to get on with.

Hackney was also a very good racing track which Len took pride in. Everything went well and I was signed for the 1978 season.

Len's reputation as a track curator was well deserved and it was the reason he was invited to prepare tracks for World Finals. I could have a go at Hackney and my career progressed. Of course, it had its rough patches, too, but Len was a promoter who would help a rider if he had problems.

When I first came to race in Britain it was hard. You could race your guts out and not score many points, or crash and bend a bike. In that case he'd say: 'Send the bill to me.' Len could see that you were trying and, as an ex-rider, he understood what was going on. It took some of the pressure off. You could get that new wheel or those front forks that you needed.

There was a friendly side to the club – a family feel with Hazal alongside Len. He was also very loyal to his riders. If he put a team together at the start of the season, he stood by them and a rider would have to perform really badly to be moved out. He gave everyone a fair chance.

In 1980, after the tragic death of Vic Harding the pervious season, Len asked me if I'd like to tie-up with Ivan Henry, who had been Vic's mentor. I was living with a family in Leytonstone and it was good there but Ivan was very much like Len. He had a good heart and was also able to offer me very good workshop facilities. He was very supportive and my career went from strength to strength from 1980 onwards.

I've praised Len as a track curator but he was also a first class promoter, very good at getting people going. He'd get on the centre green mic and really get the fans excited. He wasn't popular everywhere, especially if a decision went against the Hawks that he disagreed with, and there were some quite heated incidents.

However, he was one of the most honest promoters I ever met. If he agreed something with you, then he'd always stick to his word. There have been bad promoters in the sport – those who even bounce cheques on riders and many who make late payments. Len might pay earlier than you expected but he never paid late. That's how it should be, for riders take the risks and a good promoter will keep you motivated.

I haven't a bad word to say about him.

I only moved on (to Swindon) in 1984 because Len sold up and the new club owner took Hackney down a division. I look back on my time at Hackney and with Len with great pleasure. It was where it all began for me and I have such good memories. It made a big impression on my life and those good feelings still remain.

TONY HURREN

Post-war speedway at Waterden Road enjoyed an unbroken run of 29 years but, had it not been for Len Silver, the sport at Hackney would not have lasted more than two seasons.

When Hackney joined the Provincial League in 1963 the team were playing to a captive audience. The only other track in London was at Wimbledon, in the south-west of the capital, so the newly-launched Hawks from the East End attracted a new breed of speedway supporter plus many from long-defunct West Ham and Harringay.

The Hawks played to large crowds and the atmosphere in the stadium was electric – so

Bo Petersen making another young lad's night. Health & Safety rules wouldn't allow it today, but the kids used to love to ride round with their favourte riders.

much so that West Ham re-opened for the 1964 season. The competition from the Hammers meant that Hackney Speedway's future was immediately in the balance.

In 1964 the Provincial League split from the Speedway Control Board and Hackney suffered a double blow when arguably its two most popular riders, Norman Hunter and Malcolm Simmons, opted to join the Hammers. The team also lost another two of its riders when Trevor Hedge and Tich Read returned to their parent club, Norwich.

Manchester- based Mike Parker opened Hackney in 1963 after closing both Leicester and Bradford at the end of the previous season. He was the type of entrepreneur who was happy when things were running smoothly but tended to throw in the towel when the going got tough.

West Ham were winning the battle for viewing figures and Hackney needed a man with dedication and flair to stop the rot. The season was in its infancy when Len Silver arrived, first as a co-promoter then as a rider and soon found himself in a Canute-like situation.

The situation was dire. I remember Len telling me that in his first few meetings at Waterden Road when much – maybe most – of his attention was taken up with his riding, the crowd figures that Parker gave him were so disappointing that he asked a friend to walk the stadium and count the number of spectators present.

When Len was involved in a triple pile-up in his opening ride against Exeter on July 3 it ended his racing career but, as luck would have it (to use his own book title!), it secured the future of speedway at Waterden Road for the foreseeable future.

With Parker and his sidekick Eddie Glennon rapidly losing interest in the Hackney venture, it immediately became obvious that local car salesman Silver was the main hope to bring some kind of stability to a sinking ship. Silver was always a showman as a rider with his white boots and ability to entertain crowds by playing his banjo, so it was no surprise when he harnessed that flair to his role as a speedway promoter.

Parker had fallen foul of the Hackney Speedway Supporters' Club. Silver quickly healed the wound, installed life-long fan Snowy Beattie as supporters' club secretary and soon convinced the public that he was in the entertainment business.

Silver was a young, untried and untested promoter but he quickly showed the speedway fraternity that the sport had uncovered a promoter with the flair of Johnnie Hoskins, Freddie Mockford, Ronnie Greene, etc – showmen who promoted the sport after World War Two and who, week in and week out, treated the fans as if they were at an opening night at the London Palladium.

The key riders for Hackney in 1964 were Colin Pratt, Roy Trigg and Les McGillivray with the crowd – and I use the word crowd in its loosest sense – roaring when Silver leapt into the air as they and other Hawks crossed the finishing line in winning positions.

The launch of the British League in 1965 brought an immediate increase in crowd figures as Hackney fans could see the sport's big names in action on a regular basis. However, there was still a major requirement to actively promote speedway at Hackney and Silver encouraged his supporters' club committee and other helpers to invite schools, youth clubs, cub and scout groups to witness racing at Waterden Road as guests of the club. They were generally with both their team leaders and parents and encouraged to return as paying spectators.

Silver also encouraged his supporters' club to mount floats in local carnivals, take stands at park fétes, distribute Hackney Speedway leaflets and so on. The boss was an incessant publicity seeker and was both directly and indirectly responsible for decorating – or desecrating – countless defunct windows and walls with Hackney posters.

He thought up the slogan: 'Make it a Date, Friday at Eight', created the 'Traxcitement' catchword, launched the mad scramble for the lucky 'two bob bit' that he tossed into the crowd after the rival captains had called heads or tails and at the last meeting of the season he handed everyone a calendar (with next year's opening date clearly marked) and gave the kids a stick of Hackney rock.

Silver was fiercely loyal to his riders and to those he knew were willing to put more into Hackney Speedway than they took out of it. Supporters, especially when they reach the dizzy heights of committee members, can turn fickle almost overnight. Too many of that ilk think they are in office to hinder the promoter rather than to help him. Silver was fortunate that in Snowy Beattie he had a club secretary who appreciated that the supporters' club's main role was to tangibly assist the promotion as well as to help the riders.

I worked with Len Silver for the duration of his stay at Hackney, running the souvenir shops and, for most part, writing the 'Hawkeye' column. He was no stranger to controversy and some would say that he courted it. I'm not sure if he encouraged me to, at times, be controversial or whether it was a case of my realising that I could get away with so being. I remember on one occasion when a rider moved from Reading to Cradley Heath, or vice-versa, I wrote that he had moved from the clutches of claptrap to the auspices of verbal diarrhoea. The man in charge at Reading was Dave Lanning while Dan McCormick was the promoter at Cradley. I'm not sure which one took offence but the remarks led to the only occasion when I got the guv'nor on a fizzer.

It coincided with the time that Silver accosted a referee at Swindon after Zenon Plech had been very harshly excluded for foul riding against one of the Robins' riders. Silver was up before the Speedway Control Board on four charges, was found guilty on three of them but was cleared over my indiscretions. He got a month's centre green ban and capitalised on that by standing on the terraces, complete with bobble hat, scarf and programme board.

On another occasion the bloke who wrote the *Speedway Star's* Ipswich report took a swipe at the Hawks. As a result, Hawkeye accused him of having an honours degree in gross stupidity. He took exception to the remark and made a veiled threat but nothing came of it.

Len was always a generous man toward people he liked and trusted. In the 60s and 70s he often invited my wife and myself out for dinner and on a number of those occasions the 'perennial World Champ' Howdy Byford, who was down on his luck at the time, joined us.

He always thanked me profusely for the input I had into Hackney Speedway and, as a paid part-time helper, I can say hand on heart that he was a pleasure to work for. We discussed matters in a businesslike way and in conclusion, always believed we came up with solutions that were to benefit the sport at Waterden Road.

However, he also had a temper and was often like a bear with a sore head when Ipswich were the visitors at The Wick. The Witches gave Hackney a few wallopings at Waterden Road

Making a very worthy presentation to the late Snowie Beattie, secretary of the Hackney Supporters' Club.

and their promoter John Berry used to get under Silver's skin. The word among staff on the nights in question was: 'Give Len a wide berth.'

Silver was an entrepreneur and a perfectionist. He insisted the show at Hackney started at the programmed time, his staff controller Steve Meddemmen knew that the boss expected rakers, pushers, starting staff, etc, to be well turned out and capable of doing the job.

His track preparation was immaculate and if a rider couldn't score points at Waterden Road, it was down to his own deficiencies and not the racing surface. When Silver arrived at The Wick in 1964 he was faced with arguably the worst track in the league.

Transformation didn't happen overnight but with the help of an enthusiastic bunch of fans, Hackney's racing strip quickly developed from what resembled a bombsite to a smooth billiard table – and a heavily banked one at that.

When spectators arrived at Hackney they saw Len immaculately attired but had they entered the stadium during the day or a couple of hours before heat one, they would have seen a guy stripped to the waist, with hosepipe in right hand, tending the track as if his life depended on it.

When he marched out ahead of the riders and staff to the tune of *The Magnificent Seven* it signalled the start of the evening's entertainment and that's what it was . . . entertainment. The riders were the fans' swashbuckling heroes but Silver was the impresario. The Hackney fans loved him although he took some stick from them during Hackney's more barren wooden spoon years. However, when West Ham or Wimbledon were the visitors, then the sight of Leapin' Len marching out was enough to set their fans booing their hearts out.

On one occasion I used a throwaway line in the Hawkeye column when I said: 'Tonight we welcome the Wimbledon riders, management and their fickle supporters.' This led to the emergence of a chap named Vic whom Hawkeye christened Fickle Vickle. The guy used to write copious letters explaining he wasn't at all fickle – then signed himself off as 'Fickle Vickle.'

One night at Wimbledon, Fickle Vickle accosted Len and said he had evidence to prove that the Hackney boss wrote the offending column under the Hawkeye pseudonym. However, Silver used his undoubted charm to convince the fickle one that he was not the author of the aforementioned column but, even when put under immense pressure, he refused to blow my cover.

With two of our biggest crowd favourites, Bengt Jansson and Zenon Plech, at the Hackney reunion in 2005.

Len Silver did not promote speedway for altruistic reasons alone. He did it to make a living but he enjoyed it. For him it was a labour of love and probably still is. It wasn't all roses promoting the sport at The Wick but, for Silver, the good times outweighed the bad. Of that I am sure.

Towards the end of the 60s it became obvious that there simply wasn't sufficient support in the East End of London for both Hackney and West Ham to survive. The Hammers had, in Dave Lanning, a man at the helm who had editorial access to both the speedway and national press and continuously made things uncomfortable for The Hawks by reporting that riders were unsettled and writing other negative stories about the sport at Waterden Road. It was to Len's credit that he and his helpers rode out the storm and West Ham went to the wall while Hackney carried on for almost two decades.

Len's enthusiasm was boundless and it rubbed off on others. His attention to detail was there for all to see. He promoted at Hackney for 20 years and for 18 of those years his thirst for the sport never wavered.

He was an emotional man and during his last two seasons in harness at Waterden Road I detected that some of his zest for the sport and the enjoyment he got from it was beginning to wane.

Len was devastated when Vic Harding lost his life in a racing accident at The Wick in 1979 but had appeared to come to terms with it, only for a similar fate to befall Reading's Denny Pyeatt in 1982. Those fatalities, plus a number of personal problems, seemed to knock the wind out of his sails and it was no surprise that he quit Hackney at the end of the 1983 season.

He carried on at Rye House for two seasons before bowing out of the sport and I believed that would be his swansong. I was a touch surprised when, in his seventies, his enthusiasm returned for a second spell at Hoddesdon – but the 'old boy' is as professional as ever.

Elsewhere in this book there will be many mentions of the hundreds of riders – stars and second-strings alike – who wore the Hackney body colour but, for me, Len Silver was the king.

My feelings were endorsed when the Hackney reunion party took place at Paradise Park in Hertfordshire in 2005, when more than 30 riders travelled from many parts of the world – Zenon Plech from Poland and Malcolm Brown from the United States, to name just two.

Len Silver was at that reunion which, of course, is something you would expect. Also present were: Barry Thomas, Bengt Jansson, Bo Petersen, Colin Pratt, Dag Lovaas, Finn Thomsen, Malcolm Simmons, Trevor Hedge, those previously mentioned and many other former riders. It was an occasion for big names but the accolades bestowed on Len Silver that evening showed quite clearly that he was – and always will be – Mr Hackney Speedway.

Terry Russell, Dave Pavitt, Ivan Henry and various co-promoters who succeeded him did their best to keep the show on the road and should be applauded for their efforts. But in the eyes of those people who watched speedway at The Wick, there was only ever one promoter of Hackney Speedway and that, of course, was Len Silver.

IVAN HENRY

I first really became fully aware of Len when my wife Bobby and I started going to Hackney in the late-60s. Until then we had followed only West Ham. We used to sit in the stands and eventually became friendly with Brian, Bengt Jansson's ex-mechanic.

When Vic Harding, who lived near us on Canvey Island, moved up to the Hackney team after a career in the National League, I said to Brian that I felt that with a bit of help Vic could do well. So Brian asked me if I was serious about that and set up a meeting for myself and Vic. It was a conventional cash sponsorship and from the off we built up a good relationship and became mates. He was outgoing and his family were similar – he and his sister Beverley were peas in a pod. I got on well with his whole family and Vic and I socialised together.

Ivan Henry helping Bo Petersen.

You can imagine how devastated I was by his death after the crash at Hackney. I was prepared to give speedway away but Barry Thomas spoke to me and said: 'We have got to carry on and so have you.' Len and Hazal got involved in talking me around and Len came to see me to discuss matters. Eventually, I agreed to sell Vic's equipment to Zenon Plech, with the money going to the Harding family. Then Len came back to me and said: 'You used to mechanic for Vic and so understand the equipment. Why don't you mechanic for Zenon for a while?'

I was, mentally, at a crossroads. I'd been involved and losing Vic was like losing a brother but Len can read people and knows when it's the right time to make a move. He took the opportunity to ask me to look after a young Danish rider he'd signed called Bo Petersen. Having lost a brother in Vic, in many ways Bobby and I gained a son in Bo.

Whereas Vic was a mate, Bo needed more care. We took Bo into our home and Len had given me a new direction in life. Now I was dealing directly with Len as a promoter, on Bo's behalf. He was hard but a pleasure to negotiate with. It never got heated. Once the offer was agreed, Len would never pay late and often paid early. In general, despite any trials and tribulations in his personal or business life, he was always upbeat and never moody. Obviously if he was working on the track, etc, you wouldn't bother him. However, he was mainly approachable and a first class communicator. That is why, in my opinion, he was successful in his car dealerships and, subsequently, in his ski-ing business.

Speedway as a sport doesn't make the best use of Len. The other promoters should all sit down and listen to him. He can take seven individuals and blend them into a team. He can make a club into a happy family. He can make rivalry healthy, but friendly.

He is also one of the greatest promoters of all time.

TONY McDONALD

I have a lot to thank Len Silver for because he played a big part in helping to make my childhood such a happy one and for encouraging my early passion for speedway – initially as a supporter of his beloved Hawks since the early 70s.

My heroes were Bengt 'Banger' Jansson, Barry Thomas, Dave Morton, Dag Lovaas and Zenon Plech but without a brilliant track to race on, with emphasis on the word *race*, Friday nights at The Wick would simply not have been the memorable experience they were. It could be argued that maybe Len prepared the Waterden Road track a little too fairly, because we won very little as a team in terms of silverware except the 1971 KO Cup and two runners-up finishes in the British League, in 1968 and 1980, and there was no discernible home advantage for the Hawks. Everybody loved racing at Hackney.

I don't know of a Hawks' fan who would have wanted it any other way. Len always prized entertainment above everything else and he still does at Rye House. All of us who grew up on the terraces of Hackney Stadium, thrilled by the best racing to be found anywhere in Britain, should be grateful for his ethos.

It spoke volumes for his skill in preparing a fine track that he was asked to take on Wembley after the dusty shambles of the 1975 World Final. Ole Olsen and Bruce Penhall were ultimately the heroes of the subsequent finals held there in 1978 and 1981, the last two staged under the fabled Twin Towers. However, Len Silver deserved the accolades too for providing the canvas on which these world class artists could perform so brilliantly.

I have the greatest respect for the way Len endured some tough times early on in his promoter's career at Hackney. Through sheer determination, more than a touch of streetwise East End nous and a brand of showmanship so badly lacking among promoters today, he established the East London venue as one of the most popular in the land. We didn't go to Hackney for the intoxicating smell from the nearby OXO factory, to drink the watery, overpriced lager in the bar, or to queue for hours at the end of the meeting to get out of the cramped standard car park, or run the risk of getting our car broken into by travellers along Waterden and Carpenters Road. We went to Hackney every Friday from March until October to watch the greatest spectacle on Earth!

After I'd joined the editorial staff of *Speedway Mail* in 1978, I got to know Len for the real character that he is. Suddenly I was in the privileged position of being able to phone up or approach riders and promoters for interviews and Len has always been very approachable – good copy. He's a promoter who has always understood the value of PR and projecting himself and his team, even if the Hawks' results didn't often give him too much to actually shout about!

In the late-70s at Rye House, though, he formed a terrific managerial partnership with Colin Pratt. A more professionally run team than the Infradex-sponsored Rockets you could not wish to see. With Kelvin Mullarkey, Hughie Saunders, Ted Hubbard, Bobby Garrad, Karl Fiala, Ashley Pullen, Peter Tarrant and co. providing great entertainment down by the River Lea on a Sunday afternoon.

It was thanks to his drive and high energy levels that he took on and made such a success of the England manager's job. A thankless, unpaid task, he was in a no-win situation when he took it on in 1973, just as England were beginning to emerge as the powerful force they became through most of that wonderful decade. England were so good in Len's early days in charge of the national team that you wonder what he really needed to do when he had stars like Peter Collins, John Louis, Ray

Wilson, Malcolm Simmons, Dave Jessup and Terry Betts to call upon. But talk to any of these riders now, as I've been fortunate to do through our retro *Backtrack* magazine, and the man-management technique of Len is not in question. He didn't need to tell them how to ride but the right words in the right ears invariably helped smooth the way for England to enjoy the most glorious period in its history. How we'd like to win three consecutive World Cups today. Just getting to the final again would be a nice change!

Len cared deeply about the sport, still does obviously, and his natural enthusiasm and passion always came through loud and clear in interviews I did with him. Mind you, if he didn't agree with something that you had written, or he'd read about in the press, he was never slow to let you know! Sometimes he may appear to overreact. He still contributes occasional letters to *Speedway Star*, admonishing a correspondent or reader whom he considers has got his or her facts wrong. But that just shows how much he still has the sport's best interests at heart.

For me, part of speedway died when Len, his enthusiasm for the sport clearly on the wane, decided to sell up at Hackney at the end of 1983. Having been used to seeing the world's best riders grace The Wick for the previous 13 seasons, since I started watching at the age of 11, I knew that National League racing, for all its youthful exuberance, wouldn't be the same. The track had changed (largely for safety reasons) and while the new-look Hackney Kestrels enjoyed success, I couldn't get too excited about the actual racing, which had been the true essence of Hackney Speedway.

There are thousands of people, Hackney and Rye House patrons from the present and past, who owe their love of speedway to Len and the impact his actions had on us. That's why, personally speaking, I considered it an honour when Len asked if our company, Retro Speedway, would publish this book. It had been in the melting pot for some two years, so it was long overdue and I'm just delighted that now hundreds – hopefully thousands! – of others from generations will come to know what Leonard George Silver has done for the good of speedway.

PAUL TADMAN

Len Silver . . . well, I guess he has mellowed a bit over the years but I think you either love him or hate him! You may be surprised to know that, initially, I did hate him.

My first taste of speedway was as a 12-year-old at Romford Speedway, in 1969. Massive crowds on a regular basis made the atmosphere at Brooklands Stadium electric, every week, for the three seasons that they ran. I loved Romford Speedway and still do. I was so passionate about the Bombers.

There were a group of people who were not very popular at Romford. Tony Childs of Crayford certainly springs to mind, as does the then Eastbourne promoter Dave Lanning, who lived locally, and, of course, the Hackney and Rayleigh promoter Len Silver. As a young teenager I hated these three people immensely. Whenever they went onto either the track or the centre green they were greeted with jeers and boos.

What I didn't realise then was what showmen these guys were. I, like all the other Romford faithful, had fallen into their trap.

When Romford, then latterly West Ham, closed the doors to speedway, I had the choice of either stop going altogether, go to Wimbledon (which had never been one of my favourite tracks) or go to Hackney or Rayleigh, both of them being Len Silver tracks.

Eventually, although extremely hard to bear, by the mid-70s I became a Hackney supporter and also that of sister track Rye House. As I started work, money enabled me to watch Hackney away. As I got more involved I became part of the Hackney Speedway Supporters' Club and this really change my attitude towards the man at the helm. I couldn't believe that Len seemed to be as unpopular at most other away tracks as he'd been at Romford. I thought it was just the Romford

At the Hackney reunion in 2005 – another wonderful occasion.

supporters that didn't like him – and I think that rather disappointed me.

I also began to realise that the riders who rode under the Len Silver banner were his adopted children. He cared passionately about them and still does. Len has always believed in every rider he has ever signed, although perhaps Timmy Jo Shepherd may be the one he made a slight error of judgement on!

When Len left The Wick and later Rye House, apart from a stint at Eastbourne I thought that was probably the last we'd see of him as a speedway promoter.

But when Rye House reopened, it seemed like he hadn't been away. He took over the reins and the rest, as they say, is history. He has transformed Rye House. To own your own track must have been one of Len's dreams when he ran Hackney. Oh, what a shame he never had the opportunity to acquire the stadium at Waterden Road.

Finally, I have to mention the Hackney reunion that Chris Fenn and I organised in 2005. When I suggested a Hackney reunion to Len in 2004, I initially had a lukewarm response from him. Len is the ultimate professional and we wanted to run our reunion in a similar way that Len himself would have hosted such an event. The job of tracking down riders and where to hold the evening were challenges we had to overcome. And we did eventually overcome many obstacles.

That summer's night of July 22, 2005 at Paradise Wildlife Park, the base of former Hawk Pete Sampson and home to the Speedway Museum, was a unique event. Those who attended will tell you that the atmosphere Len created at Waterden Road was reenacted at the reunion. Len flanked by Dag Lovaas and the other Mr Hackney Speedway, Barry Thomas, with the tossing of the lucky fifty pence piece before it was throw into the crowd. It was like a time-warp.

Those riders who had travelled from America, all parts of Europe and the UK all came to pay respect to the greatest promoter that speedway has ever seen – Len Silver!

TONY WEBB

During the early-70s I started a company called Shaleway, one of the original speedway spares services in England. Through my good friend, the late Vic Harding, permission was granted from Len for me to operate from Hackney and Rye House stadiums. This arrangement was the springboard of the success of the business and for me it was an ideal situation. I could watch speedway almost every day of the week, for I soon extended to cover Crayford, Mildenhall, Ipswich and Canterbury plus earn a reasonable living from it.

There was never a formal contract with Len. I was merely asked to look after his riders and give them good service. Hackney was one big family. Snowie Beattie often placed orders for equipment for the riders on behalf of the Hackney supporters' club. Bert Busch was always on call for the mechanical needs and the wonderful Kathy Pope catered for the repairs of leathers, etc. No other track was so well served in terms of background support.

I gained a greater appreciation of Len Silver, the man, as I witnessed speedway from the other side of the fence, noting the hardships of promotion. Beyond the tough exterior he really looked after his riders and his love of the sport was evident. I also made lasting friendships with many speedway riders that I still treasure today.

RAYLEIGH

DINGLE BROWN

It was at Ipswich in 1961 that I started riding second-halves, when Eric Bason was running the track. I progressed into the team but on July 16, 1962 I had a bad crash at Exeter and broke a thigh. Len Silver was riding in the same meeting for the Falcons. As I was laid up in hospital in Exeter for 10 weeks, Len used to pop in on racedays and visit me. That was very good of him, but that's Len.

I did return to racing in 1963 but suffered the same injury at Stoke. It was a period of long recovery and I didn't ride for several years, although I did have some meetings in France in that period. It was only the birth of the Second Division in 1968 that saw me back on a bike – for Len at Rayleigh Weir. I'd gone to a speedway 'do' at the Conservative Club in Hackney when Len approached me about signing for him at Rayleigh. I was pleased to do so and enjoyed several happy seasons as a Rocket after that.

Maury Jardine was the announcer at Rayleigh and one night he had a few scotches too many and was hanging out of the box on top of the stand belting out: 'Now who have we got in this race? It's Dingle, Dingle!' So one stand would shout my name and the other responded – to the tune of Bow Bells.

While Len and I did have our ups and downs, he was the guv'nor. He always paid on time and treated his riders properly. I had six happy years at Rayleigh before moving on to Scunthorpe for two seasons. At the end of the second year with them, I scored 10 points at Crewe. Len put his arm around me and asked me to consider returning as a Rocket but this time at their new home at Rye House. I was cheesed off with the travelling to and from Scunthorpe and liked the idea of a track near my front door. Unfortunately, in 1975, I had contracted sarcodosis of the lungs, which makes them contract and lessen the supply of oxygen to the blood. I didn't realise I had this medical problem at first and so I'd only compete for three laps in a race before getting out of breath and finishing last. It was an awful season for me and I packed up, although Len did get me to make a brief comeback for Crayford in the 1977 season.

During my Rayleigh career I broke my back at King's Lynn, just as I was getting involved in helping Len to sort out the fundamentals for introducing the sport at the East of England Showground, Peterborough in 1970. One freezing week in March I was up at the Showground with Len and John Poyser. We spent the first day removing a chain link fence and cutting down grass that had grown to two-feet-high. We'd started marking and laying the track out when I had my bump at Saddlebow Road and wasn't available to see that project through with Len.

I began working with him in the motor trade. He'd lost his driving licence and although I wasn't riding speedway at the time, I could drive him around. Our partnership worked well from the off. We used to go up to Warren Street to pick up cars and he was called 'Little Lennie' by the guy he dealt with at the site – a Danny de Vito look-a-like with a flat cap and a big cigar.

I remember Len was very taken one day by a Triumph Herald which, due to a lack of space – or so we thought, was parked in a corner so that you could only get inside via the passenger door. As Len rushed into the office to conclude a deal, I noticed that the whole of the driver's side was smashed in. I chased after Len and practically rugby-tackled him as he was preparing to hand the money over. You could say that Len was less than amused with the proprietor!

After a while Len was so busy running Hackney and his other speedway interests that he wound down his involvement in the car sales outlets while I diversified into a breaker's yard. However, we

Me and Dingle in our best dinner suits.

did work well together for a couple of years.

He did catch me out, big-style, one day. We'd been up at Warren Street on car business when he asked me what I was doing that night. He said that he was chairing a speedway talk-in at a pub in Barkingside and asked me to come along with him. Eventually he offered me dinner and got me to phone my wife Janet and explain what we were planning on doing. We got there and it was packed. There was a High Beech theme and they even had cine film of High Beech showing horses drawing the water cart! Jack Barnett and Syd Edmonds were among the speakers recounting tales of pre-war speedway.

Then Len announced that he would invite to the microphone a modern-day rider who would give a talk on speedway in the current era. I looked around and wondered who the hell he was talking about. Then he continued: 'Ladies and Gentlemen . . . Mister Dingle Brown.' I had to get up and give a speech! I said to him afterwards that I'd get him back for that but he chuckled and said that he'd been struggling to find anyone who would do it.

In the 80s I came back into the sport, initially as team manager at Peterborough. But by 1989 I didn't like the way it was being run and resigned. I was approached by Dick Partridge to get involved at Mildenhall, initially running training schools for him. When it looked like the club was going to fold after only 16 meetings in the new Third Division, I took it over and ran it for eight years.

When Steve Ribbons started to revive Rye House as a team, the supporters eventually got Len involved in their initiative. He rescued them from getting in over their heads, financially, and set up a meeting to discuss Mildenhall becoming their temporary base. I told them that they could run at the end of my fixtures but also asked where the money was coming from to pay riders, as the public had already coughed up to get in. Anyway they did raise the money and Len started to come to Mildenhall to watch the matches – it was good to see him again.

Len had always wanted his own stadium with his own bars and catering, so it came to pass that he acquired the lease at Rye House – and the rest is history. He gives 100 per cent in everything he does. He believes that is the only way. As a promoter, he is top drawer, one of the very best there has ever been. As a bloke, he is great company – he has had me splitting my sides with laughter.

He doesn't show any signs of quitting and long may he continue.

TERRY STONE

When Len reopened Rayleigh in 1968, I phoned him up to ask about the chance of a team place. His first reaction was to tell me that I was too old – I was 30 at the time. I stood my ground with him, though, and reminded Len that I hadn't actually ridden consistently throughout the past seasons. Some seasons had been spent in second halves and some on the fringe of team selection. He was good enough to relent and invited me down to The Weir, saying: 'We will see how you go.'

I did quite well in the pre-season practice and so he put me in the Rayleigh Rockets team for their first-ever (BL2) fixture against Plymouth. I got changed, stood in the pits and realised that I hardly knew any of the riders present – only Eric Howe from the opposition.

The new Second Division was terrific for British speedway and Len was part of that vision, which is much to his credit. Len was a harder taskmaster in those days and used to pump us up before races. However, as a promoter Len did help me out. I didn't have the money to buy top class engines so he allowed me to borrow cash and then pay back by spread deductions from my points money. He knew that I was going well against good guys on better equipment than me. Len would give you support if you needed it and he felt you deserved a helping hand.

With Terry Stone at the Speedway Museum.

Barring injuries, I rode for him throughout the last Rayleigh revival (1968-73) but didn't make the move to Rye House with the Rockets in 1974. I'd decided to retire.

In recent years I've been involved with the veteran bike demonstration races at various tracks. I have to say that Len is usually the only promoter to come around afterwards and say 'thanks' for putting on a show. He is appreciative, courteous and approachable and when I'm seeking track time for the Men in Black, he tends to go along with our requests.

I've already stated my regard for Len as a promoter but what adds respect to that opinion is that Len was a rider who became a promoter. That tended to be the norm in years gone by but today it's mainly businessmen dabbling in the sport without having served any form of apprenticeship. Can't ever say that about Len!

GRAEME SMITH

Len was the one who gave me the nickname 'The Corduroy Kid' because the first time he saw me I was at Weymouth with no bike, no leathers, no nothing – and I rode in a pair of corduroy trousers Somehow, he thought I'd make a proper speedway rider one day.

I landed in England from New Zealand in 1968 with 2/6d in my pocket and I think he felt sorry for me. He had a car lot and let me sleep in the office. He was like an uncle to me and he and his wife took pity on me after a while and let me move into their house. I was 18 at the time. Back home I'd been a customs officer but I thought I'd jump on a plane and try my luck in England. I was actually arrested on the plane at Wellington because they thought I was a draft-dodger trying to avoid going to Vietnam!

When I eventually got to England I went to Weymouth to learn how to ride a speedway bike. Len bought me my first JAP – for £100. Then I had to start paying him for it! I was working for him 24/7 to try to pay off the debts – selling cars and collecting cars that he'd bought. If you ask him now he'd probably say I still owe him 20 quid!

His wife, Vera, was a lovely lady. She looked after me when it came to bed and board and making sure I had a clean shirt and underpants.

Hackney was my first team and I was named at No.8, although I rode half a dozen meetings at No.7 when Alan Jackson was injured. When he regained full fitness, I went to Rayleigh and captained them in my first year there.

Len was a tremendous guy. He not only taught me everything I know about speedway but he was a good bloke as well. He kept me on the straight and narrow. I didn't know anybody when I came over to England and he looked after me, for which I'll be eternally grateful.

We did have a big coming together at King's Lynn, though, when I was riding there for Hackney. I had a reserve's three-ride maximum and he told me he was going to put me into the final heat of a challenge match for what was called a '1,000 Guineas Trophy'. The match was level and the promoters wanted it to stay that way, so that no-one would have to pay out!

I was told: ''You're going to go on your arse on the first bend'.

I said: 'Thanks for telling me – now, how much am I going to get out of this?

Needless to say, there was no money coming my way. So that was me out of the race.

When Len heard about it, he threw me out of the house! When we fell out it was a big one. But it wasn't vindictive. Len had his views and I had mine.

We got back together again when he asked me to ride for Sunderland in 1972. I'd had a 10.5 point average at Canterbury in 1971 and we'd won British League Division Two. Two weeks after the season ended I broke my leg and spent six months in hospital. I went back to Canterbury and was struggling to remain a heat-leader – and, for some strange reason, Johnnie Hoskins thought I was throwing matches, which couldn't have been further from the truth.

Anyway, he put me on the transfer list and Len got in touch to say that Sunderland were struggling for another heat leader. He offered me the No.3 slot there and the No.8 spot at Reading, who were in Division One.

He came up to Sunderland for the first two or three meetings then took more of a back seat and gave full authority to Colin Armistead, the team manager.

But the thing about Len is, he always knew what was going on. I used to travel back down south with George Barclay and by the time we got home, Len knew all the ins and outs of everything that had happened back in the North-East.

Len was another Johnnie Hoskins – a real showman. Never too proud to have his pants pulled down or be flour-bombed in front of 5,000 people, like they always did after the last meeting of the season. He was good with publicity as well. He got us on the BBC children's programme *Blue Peter*, riding around Hackney in 1968.

When I came to England I didn't have a driving licence, so Len loaned me an E-type Jag to take my test in. I failed miserably but Len still made the most of it. The next day it was all over the papers: 'Top speedway rider fails his driving test but watch out for him speeding round the track at Hackney tomorrow night!'

We used to go out after tea most nights and fly-post the whole of the East End of London with stickers on lamp-posts and shop windows, saying: 'Friday night, 8pm, Hackney Speedway.' He would do anything to get a bit of publicity.

One of his favourite tricks was to pick up a ukelele and do his George Formby impression, singing: *Grandad's Flannelette Nighshirt*. I wonder if he still does that…?

LAURIE ETHERIDGE

In the winter of 1967-68 our paths first crossed at Weymouth. I remember that it was a horrible, wet day and Len was down to see Graeme Smith and just happened to watch me in action. The next development was that Wally Mawdsley – who ran Exeter and was about to open Plymouth – told me that Len was interested in acquiring my contract and taking me to Rayleigh. As I'd expected to be going to Plymouth, this came as a pleasant surprise. Len told me that he'd created some personal history with me, because I was the first rider he'd actually paid any money to buy. He paid £200 to sign me from Exeter.

I enjoyed my time at The Weir with team-mates such as Geoff Maloney, Dingle Brown, Terry Stone, Mike Gardner, Barry Lee and Dennis Mannion. This was British League Division Two and I gained a regular team place. Len was a super bloke, very approachable and a fair promoter.

Within a season I was moved up to Hackney in the British League. Graeme Smith was struggling at Hackney in 1969 and I was going well at Rayleigh. Colin Pratt mentioned this to Len but I had my doubts. I was doing well and enjoying it. I liked the company of my team-mates and the fans. But once I went to Hackney I didn't regret it at all. I was full time with the Hawks from mid-1969 to 1974.

When I first went there I was a young guy and suddenly partnered with Colin Pratt, who was riding at No.1. I was in a team that included Bengt Jansson, Malcolm Brown and Gary Everett. Len would arrange access to the track during the week and we'd practice dropping the clutch and going flat out at the first turn. With Len's encouragement, I got to like the track and during meetings 'Banger' Jansson would tell me where I was going wrong.

A word of encouragement for Laurie Etheridge, who rode for me at Rayleigh and then Hackney before he starred in our relaunch at Crayford in 1975.

During my time at Hackney we had the 'Phyllosan Boys', with experienced old-timers such as Jimmy Gooch, Les McGillivray and Jackie Biggs on board – all guys in their forties.

When I switched to Crayford in 1975 I enjoyed a major personal career highlight in becoming the National League Riders' Champion. Len was a big influence on my victory at Wimbledon. He told me to have a new tyre for every race. It worked and I became the individual champion.

I'd now ridden for Len at three clubs – Rayleigh, Hackney and Crayford – and valued his time and advice. I recall a lean period at Hackney when I was struggling to score and said to Len that I needed a new engine. So he sorted that out straight away then setting up a system of deduction from my pay, according to whether I'd had a good week. He was very fair. If you made a deal with Len – that stuck. There was no hassle. You had confidence in him and that counts for a lot as a rider. He was also generous should we win away and would treat us to a meal out. There was a lot of bonding and team spirit under Len's management. We would stick together through thick and thin.

I have seen him since I retired from racing in 1984. In fact, just after I packed it up my wife and I went ski-ing and flew into Geneva airport. Jean spotted Len waiting to greet some people. He said: 'There is always someone you know wherever you go!'

Two years later, my local golf club organised a ski-ing trip to Meribel for 16 of us. By coincidence, they booked through Silver Ski without mentioning it to me. We were all in one chalet and we met Len again. More recently, I've seen him at the veterans' dinners and I went to the Hackney reunion at Paradise Park in 2005, where he was obviously the centre of attention.

Len has always been a happy person and that is my lasting impression of him.

CREWE

DAVE PARRY

I briefly overlapped with Len at Crewe Speedway both as a rider and, later, as a promoter at the same venue. Crewe had opened in 1969 and by season 1972 we were Division Two league champions and KO Cup winners under the promotional banner of Allied Presentations and the direct management of Maurie Littlechild. The championship team included Phil Crump, John Jackson, Dave Morton, Dai Evans, Gary Moore, Gary Flood and myself.

Len took over in 1973 after Maurie's death. To a degree, it was a case of wrong time, wrong place. The team was being revamped, with Phil Crump moving up with King's Lynn and Gary Moore retiring. Feeling disillusioned, I also retired early in the season, as I was becoming disillusioned, although that was no reflection on Len. Attendances began to fall and After all the team's big successes and stepping into Maurie's shoes, it was a tall order.

Dave Parry, one of Crewe's longest-serving riders who later became their promoter.

Eventually Len moved on and I became co-promoter for speedway's final fling at Crewe. This meant that I attended promoters' meetings, where Len was very good. He stood his corner and despite being regarded by some as being from a previous era, he actually wanted to move forward. He was forthright, honest and his experience was invaluable.

He has continued to be a larger than life showman in our sport and his promotional achievements at Hackney and latterly Rye House, in two different eras, are a reflection on his ability.

With a few more Len Silvers around this would, indeed, be a better sport.

GLYN TAYLOR

I first met Len in the close season of 1972-73, when I came over to ride for Peterborough which was part of Allied Presentations. One thing led to another and over a very short period of time – like a week from the day I got here, my father, Chum Taylor, had fallen out with Danny Dunton, the promoter at Peterborough. So, the next night, he said: 'We'll go over to Rayleigh and see Len Silver.'

At that time Len was also running Crewe, so he invited me to go up and have a ride. I had three second-half races, won two and ran a second place. Len than proclaimed: 'Right, you are in the team next week' – and I never looked back from that point.

It was a huge track at well over 400 metres. It was a proper speedway track, not a Dinky toy, but still 250 metres short of Claremont in Western Australia! It suited me down to the ground. It was a good track for me. I rode there and at the same time I was doubling up as No.8 at Hackney.

Len was always absolutely spot on. I remember one night having a bad crash against Workington. I wrote my bike off but Len made sure that there was another one there for me the next week. He has a good heart, outstanding. You hear the expression: 'He's a hard but fair man.' He's not a hard man – he has a heart of gold and he's extremely fair. He is a top class guy, full of energy and absolutely professional.

SUNDERLAND

GEORGE BARCLAY

I came across Len when I started riding. I went to Rye House for some rides. In those days Bill Mathieson ran it and he was a colleague and good friend of Len's.

Bill arranged for me to have second-half rides at Hackney but I'd only ridden in three races there when he phoned me to say: 'Look, West Ham are short of a second-half rider.' So I turned up at West Ham and tried to get a second-half, only to be told by their manager Dave Lanning to come back in six weeks.

Bill told me to ignore Lanning and go back to West Ham, as there was definitely a space to be filled after Neville Slee had been injured. I turned up again with my bike and stood there all innocent – Lanning was so puzzled. Anyway, he did give me a second-half race and I won it. Afterwards, Lanning ran into the pits stating that I had to sign after that performance.

However, told him that I was sorry but I must phone Len Silver first because he'd already been giving me second-half races. When I got home late that night, I duly called Len out of courtesy and explained the situation to him. He told me: 'Look George, I have three other riders – Gary Everett, Alan Jackson and Richard Greer – and you are all in the same bracket. What I'd suggest is that you sign on there and get stuck in. It's an opportunity for you.'

I sent Len a bunch of flowers for his wife to say 'thank you' for being straight with me. Dave Lanning heard about this and gave me the 'Gentleman George' tag. At a dinner-dance some seasons later, Len's wife Vera mixed it up and called me 'Lord George!'

I ended up riding for Len at Rayleigh for about half-a-season in 1970. At the end of that season Len also started to promote at Sunderland, on behalf of Allied Presentations. He got in touch with me and said: 'I'm opening Sunderland. Would you ride for me?'

Without thinking, I replied: 'Of course I would.'

Len will tell you that it was the only speedway club that was run within a whole day. I'd go from my house in Plaistow, East London to Len's place in the Harold Hill area very early on a Sunday and after loading my bike onto the trailer, we'd drive up to Sunderland for the afternoon meeting. The journey would normally take five hours but, with Len driving, it took only four!

I can recall a Tyne Tunnel story with Len driving a car full of speedway riders. We were in his Volkswagen and on the trailer were three bikes. Len holds the record for doing 100mph in the Tyne Tunnel with a full car, trailer on the back, while eating a cheese sandwich!

Once we'd arrived at the track, I'd go around on the tractor a couple of times to make sure that the track was all right, having done most of the main preparation work the previous Sunday. While I was doing that, Len would be getting everything ready for all the staff – turnstile operators, etc. Gradually the supporters and the riders would turn up and the meeting would start.

As soon as it was over, we'd get back on the tractor and prepare the track so that it was laid and basically ready for the following week's meeting. Then we'd get in the car and head for home. I'd drive the first part of the return journey while Len worked out the riders' pay and every item of administration relating to the meeting just finished.

He did all his programme notes – the lot – and as soon as he'd finished, we'd stop at a services and Len would take over the driving. I'd then compile my 'Captain's Comments' column for the programme, which nobody knew about until Russ Dent – our real captain – let it slip at a Sunderland

George Barclay reading the programme notes that he'd written in my car the previous week!

reunion that he hadn't written it himself! Russ was quite capable and had a great sense of humour but the reason I had to write the piece was because we had to complete those tasks on the trip home.

So that's how everything involved in the running of Sunderland was achieved in the one day. We made good use of the hours spent travelling home whilst there was plenty of time for conversation on the way up. He is very knowledgeable, especially about speedway, but he's such a fascinating person in general and has lived such an interesting life. It's amazing how quickly five hours pass when you're chatting away – I can't ever remember going to sleep during the journey.

Len is great company and a good conversationalist, someone you really warm to. A lot of people you never get close to but he is my kind of guy. Even now I like to talk to him but he has never got time, has he? I just fit into his brief moments. He's always whizzing here and there. If I talk to him at Rye House, we have to talk walking along because he's in the process of going from one task to another.

I had four seasons at Sunderland. It was a big commitment and there were times when I had to go up by train, getting picked up from Newcastle Station by the start marshal and taken to the track. Yes, Len sold the club and left me up there!

Len is a very approachable promoter and I remember saying to him one day: 'You know, Len, when you come into the pits and talk to me, especially if I've had a bad first race, it de-motivates me. It doesn't pick me up.' It worked for some but we are all different individuals. We are all different personalities and that's the wonderful thing about life.

Len replied immediately: 'OK, I'll not talk to you in the pits again'– and he never did. He wasn't offended at all and I admire that.

I spent years in management with a supermarket group. I always realised that every single person on your staff needs to get the same job done but you may need a different approach to achieve it. 'Would you mind doing that?' or 'Do that for me please.' There is a key to each person. I can't imagine that Len will bear a grudge but he says what he has to say.

I did once ask him why, of all his riders, he took *me* to Sunderland. He replied: 'You were the only one who was fool enough to do it!' Obviously, he said it with typical humour.

The task Linda and I had in raising the money to build the Speedway Museum came out of the blue – I didn't volunteer. Len was so enthusiastic about the museum. He has been so supportive but he did tell me bluntly: 'George, I admire what you're doing. I think it's a hard task that you have taken on.'

But with all the different activities that he allowed us to undertake at Rye House, we raised over £2,000 for the museum. There were a few problems along the way but they were overcome because of Len's positive and helpful attitude.

Len is an absolute genius on track preparation. He goes around on the knife, as they call it, to blade it himself. He got off the tractor one day in his suit and my Linda said to him: 'Len, you're the best dressed tractor driver'. He replied: 'And the best looking!'

We tend to recognise people in all sports by awarding them, for example, an MBE. In all sports and all walks of life there are people who, if they deserve an MBE, then Len Silver deserves a dozen of them. OK, he has earned his living from speedway but he has devoted a lifetime to the sport and he has never changed his attitude. He has never changed his love of the sport and he has never changed his approach to the people who bring the money into the game.

You never see Len slag off the opposition because they have won. I remember a rider came down from one team. He went straight on at the first bend and never turned at all. He took out one of the Rye House riders. The referee re-instated him and Len's words to the ref over the mic were: 'We do *have* to turn left, you know?'. It was his way of saying, this man didn't even turn. He always has a suitable word or phrase to defuse a difficult situation.

If it's been a good match he'll send both teams around on the tractor – and you don't see that at many tracks. All the lads out there are doing their best and they should be getting full respect for their efforts. If you go down with good grace you'll send the fans home a lot happier than if you send them away feeling angry and bitter. It's bad psychology and Len knows it.

He is a genius the way he uses nice words to press home a point. Someone else would need to lose their temper to try and get the same point over, yet probably wouldn't manage to. It is far better to treat people decently. I suppose that when you are as small as Len is in stature, it's good psychology!

Len can be fiery but he doesn't retain it. His 'university' has been life itself and he has used his experience very sensibly. What became his personality has almost created his legacy. People who initially dislike him end up loving him.

I think of his contribution to speedway, particularly where he has soldiered on at tracks where others would have folded and those tracks would have been lost to the sport.

However, the most outstanding facet that stands out about Len Silver is that all the riders I've ever met speak well of him. You can see this also among riders who come to Rye House, for some of them could go almost anywhere they chose. Take Tai Woffinden, for example. His father, Rob, is no fool. He wouldn't have sent his son to ride anywhere that was dodgy.

Len is someone that the riders love – you'll never hear criticism. They say: 'Len has always been great with me' or 'Len treats me well.' And that's a great credit to him.

Russ Dent – my locally-based Sunderland skipper.

RUSS DENT

The first time I got to know Len was when he was a rider with Exeter. But in 1971 he gave me a ring and said that he was opening Sunderland and 'would I ride for him?' After Newcastle closed I said that I wasn't prepared to travel to places like Cradley Heath or Belle Vue to ride. It just wasn't worth it.

He came up to see me and took me for a meal at the County Hotel in Newcastle, where he told me about Allied Presentations' plans for Sunderland. I was turning cartwheels because it meant that I could keep riding and not have to travel too far for my home track.

He was a typical Cockney – a flash character

but very generous. A bit like George Barclay – full of blarney!

He liked everything done just right. He used to tick us off about not having our leathers looking immaculate. A real showman – and he would tell you what you wanted to hear. He'd give you loads of flannel and tell you that he thought you were the best rider in the world!

We didn't see see him every week at Sunderland, because George Barclay did a lot of the behind-the-scenes work for him, like work out the pay cheques and that sort of thing. He might come up for a couple of weeks and then leave other people to take care of things for a while after that.

I liked the guy. When people ask me: 'Who was your favourite promoter?' I always say: 'Len Silver' because he'd been a rider and he understood what we went through.

GEORGE ENGLISH (Jnr)

When, at the end of 1970, Allied Presentations decided to transfer the First Division licence from Newcastle to Reading they wanted to run Second Division racing at Brough Park. However, the stadium management at the time thought that a lower level of racing wasn't appropriate for the stadium and speedway was temporarily lost to Newcastle.

In an attempt to keep speedway in the area, Allied decided to open up at East Boldon, an inferior greyhound stadium to that at Brough Park. Ironically the roles are reversed now. As one of the directors of Allied, Len was assigned to promote at the track, albeit from a long distance. It was very difficult because not enough people travelled to Sunderland from Newcastle to support the new venture.

At a supporters' meeting at the start of the season, my father – George English Snr – was asked to transfer his experience from Newcastle to Sunderland and take charge of the Sunderland Speedway Supporters' Club, which he did while also running the track shop alongside my mother. They also looked after the office on racedays.

With Len so far away, he had to delegate so much and one of those items was the distribution of promotional leaflets around the area. I remember vividly, alongside a small group of others, spending countless hours trooping around housing estates, pushing thousands of leaflets through letter boxes in an effort to raise the profile of Sunderland Speedway.

Only one rider has ever managed to persuade me to act as a mechanic for him and that was George Barclay. George used to travel up from London with Len, ride the meeting and then when the match was finished – pull the track back ready for the next week while Len was still busy in the office.

One week Len arrived in a new car and George decided we'd use it to tyre-pack the track. No problem – except someone had left the grader on the back straight and the idiot steering the car didn't see it and drove over it. That idiot was – me!

It was always a struggle to keep Sunderland afloat and Allied Presentations eventually sold out to Liz Taylor of Berwick. I still remember the Saturday morning when official notification of the sale came through. Len wrote to explain that he'd sold out to the Taylors and that he was going on holiday and could my father co-operate with the Taylors to ensure a smooth transition between the two operations.

CRAYFORD

BRYN WILLIAMS

'Been there, done it, got the T-shirt!' That's a phrase often bandied about and, in speedway terms, it's a fitting testimony to the lifelong involvement within the sport of a certain Len Silver.

Supporter, rider, team manager, track curator, promoter – you name it, he's done the lot but he's still every bit as enthusiastic about this wonderful sport of ours today as he was when I had my first close up encounter of him during his, and my own, involvement with the much-missed Crayford Kestrels.

Mind you, I've got to say that my first impressions of Len were not all that favourable! You see, as I recall, an appeal had gone out for volunteers to go along to the venue in London Road to help Len and his crew undertake some much needed work on the track, in readiness for the start of a new season. At that time, not only was I working full-time in the City of London commuting backwards and forwards daily by train, but I was also a part-time disc jockey at a rather plush venue near Ashford in Kent. OK, I confess I was the Welsh Wizard in Mr. Toad's Music Show!

Anyway on the Friday night prior to the day on which said track work was due to be undertaken, I had a gig and was plied with copious amounts of ale throughout by my audience who were obviously appreciative of my efforts.

Arriving home at dawn and having unloaded all the equipment, I snatched a couple of hours sleep in the chair before making my way to the hallowed venue in London Road, albeit feeling like death warmed up! An empty plastic bucket was soon thrust into my hands and I was politely asked if I could go out on the circuit itself and help by picking up any large stones. And so, despite my somewhat fragile state but determined to help, I embarked on my given task.

I was finding the going tough to say the least when Len, driving his tractor, stopped next to me and said: 'Excuse me, do you think you could possibly go a little bit faster?'

Ordinarily I'd have muttered a few oaths and gone home there and then but Len was so polite and pleasant that I carried on AND speeded up – well, attempted to! That is testimony to his man-management skills, I suppose, amongst his numerous other attributes.

I have admired all his skills a great deal in the years that have passed since our first encounter at Crayford Speedway and it has been an honour to have known him throughout.

I recall at the end of the 2008 season, when most promoters were packing their bags in readiness to fly off to the annual winter AGM, Len was at his beloved Rye House working hard to overcome the ravages of a previous day-long deluge on the Saturday, to get the circuit in fit condition for members of the Southern Track Riders' Association, young and old alike, to get out there and enjoy a full afternoon's racing.

WEYMOUTH

RAY COLLINS

Len Silver breezed into Weymouth in the winter of 1977-78 promising a new and more successful era for Weymouth Speedway, which had previously been far from glamorous despite its well respected and long-standing training schools. League-wise, the variously named Scorchers, Royals, Eagles and Wizards had invariably struggled with even a mid-table place seemingly well beyond the reach of any of them.

So out went the Wizards along with their unique but exceedingly drab purple and white colours. First up for the new era was a switch to red and white with the choice of a new name being left to a Supporters Club which, after a competition, settled on the 'Wildcats.'

With a new name and colours the loyal Weymouth supporters were immediately aware that the changes were not to end there. For a start, the notoriously rough and rutted car park surface was actually flat and smooth! Then, on entering the stadium, they found everything painted red and white with alternate red and white flags fluttering in the breeze on each floodlight standard around the track and red and white bunting everywhere else. Despite the weather, this was followed by a flawlessly presented meeting.

Len had made sure the opening fixture at Weymouth was the very first match in the National League that season so after the new Wildcats had beaten Barrow he was inevitably out on the centre green at the conclusion of the match to inform the crowd: 'I am proud to say tonight that the Weymouth Wildcats are top of the league!'

OK, so everyone knew it was only because no-one else had ridden, yet to the long-suffering Weymouth fans it was music to their ears and a wonderful finish to Weymouth Speedway's most upbeat night in years.

As well as his reputation as a showman, Len's expertise in track preparation was also apparent from the word go. With Eddie Lack installed as the new manager at Weymouth, the pair of them set about ensuring a billiard table surface to the wide open spaces of the big Wessex Stadium track. An entertaining team, lively presentation and top class track conditions – the Weymouth fans had never had it so good.

Despite having had a number of excellent riders over the years, Weymouth's teams had usually lacked a 'professional' image but Len's first major signing was a masterstroke. He brought in the experienced Midlander Malcolm Shakespeare whose approach and attention to detail immediately started to rub off on his younger colleagues. Shakespeare's win in that year's Seyco Trophy (Weymouth's annual major individual trophy) was universally popular with fans and riders alike.

Eventually the Wildcats finished 13th in a league of 20. Nothing spectacular for most teams, perhaps, but for Weymouth it represented a major achievement. With Danny Kennedy picking up the team's first ever national title (the Warners Grand National individual) it was little wonder that Len and the new regime were so highly regarded by the Weymouth crowd.

In any case that crowd was enjoying facilities which few had thought possible over the years. Len's enthusiasm and drive led firstly to the terracing of the whole of the area under the back straight cover, followed by seating. Along with various other improvements the resulting 1000-seater stand turned the whole place into an impressive stadium far more in keeping with the newly found overall professionalism of the club.

Although steady progress was being made, matters very nearly came to a dramatic and tragic halt one Tuesday afternoon in mid season. As spectators filed through the turnstiles later that evening on the first day of August for the challenge match against Stoke, they were astonished to see the tractor upside down on the centre green. Now the Weymouth crowd had had a light-hearted ongoing repartee with Len about tractors ever since he had commandeered the Weymouth tractor in an earlier season, done his own track preparations and then watched his Rockets claw back a deficit to win the match! Also, it was not unusual in those days for bikes to rear up and 'back flip' particularly at the starts. No doubt Len had done this himself on occasions.

This time, though, it was far more serious. There had been record rainfalls for the area in July culminating with the whole of a normal month's worth of rain falling on Weymouth in just a few hours the previous day. This made the rough and rutted centre green very treacherous and when Len went to drive the tractor away it became stuck and the body was flung up and backwards over the rear axle, with Len trapped underneath.

Eddie Lack was the hero of the hour as he immediately produced a crowbar from somewhere, rushed across, jammed it into the ground and against the tractor, then amazingly held it there to prevent the tractor shifting any more and crushing Len.

Despite the rapid response of the emergency services it inevitably took some time for the fire service to get away from their town centre base out to the stadium and onto the track. Through it all Eddie remained stoic and prevented the situation from getting even worse. It is fair to say that he probably saved Len's life that afternoon.

Oh yes, there were never any more Weymouth jokes about Len and tractors after that.

About the only time Len managed to upset some of the fans that season was with one of his public relations initiatives. To a great extent Weymouth relies on the holiday trade as one of its main industries and this has led to a sort of love/hate view of the holidaymakers (known as 'grockles') with them being essential to the local economy but paradoxically resented by some as outsiders who 'take over the town' in summer.

Obviously Len wanted to tap into the influx of summer holidaymakers and issued discounted tickets to local hotels, etc. All very well so far but, unfortunately, the tickets had the fatal words: 'holidaymakers only' actually printed on them!

Once some had fallen into the hands of some locals, there was uproar from a section of fans. Their view was: 'I pay every week and some f****** grockle gets in on the cheap.'

Len's PR had to go into overdrive to deal with that one but it says much for his personality that he soon had everyone back on side!

During the season Len negotiated to buy the stadium and at one time a deal looked very much on the cards but, eventually, it fell through. Such a deal would have secured a long-term future for Weymouth Speedway and it is interesting to speculate where Weymouth's standing in the sport would be today if it had happened. Certainly the potential was there and Len has since shown at Rye house just what can be achieved.

After such a successful first season the immediate future looked bright anyway but during the winter there came a bombshell when the stadium owners announced that new promoters were to be brought in for the 1979 season. Len Silver's successful, but oh so short, reign at Weymouth was over. He had come in promising a better club all around and he had certainly started to deliver on that promise. Unfortunately, instead of the complete rebuilding that he had envisaged, he was not allowed to get much further than stirring the cement.

ENGLAND

RAY WILSON

I got to know Len a lot better through the fact that he became a family friend. My Dad, Ron, was a promoter who formed a business association with Len through Allied Presentations but he was also keen on ski-ing. This led to a real bond between them.

It was a positive twist of fate that led us to work together as England manager and captain from the start of 1973. Len had known me long enough on a personal level to understand my traits. We were very much on the same level as people. We had the same sense of humour and we developed a good relationship.

This was a positive influence on the rest of the lads and we all gelled. Everyone got on and we didn't argue, for instance, over gate positions. We looked out for each other on track. It made that period in the 70s, when Len

Proud to stand alongside Ray Wilson on Test match duty.

and I were involved, the most successful in England's history.

Len was full of enthusiasm and had excellent man-management skills. He knew the different ways to talk to each of us and got the best out of us. He was also very approachable in turn. Unlike the senior promoters who had preceded him as national team manager, the likes of Ronnie Greene and Charles Foot, Len was not at all aloof. He'd come into the dressing room before a meeting and join in the banter between the lads. He was the first former rider to become England manager, which made an important difference to the way he handled us. He was, if you like, 'one of us.'

Len was an integral part of our success and we were consistently successful for a number of years at home and abroad. Even the big nights at Wembley, when the pressure was really on, were actually very enjoyable.

Many people will remember the final of the 1973 Daily Mirror International Tournament at Wembley, when we drew 39-39 with Sweden before Peter Collins went out and beat Anders Michanek in the run-off that they still talk about today. As skipper on the night, Len consulted me before it was announced that PC would represent us in the decider and it was a decision that I agreed with wholeheartedly. PC was the one showing most spunk on the night – it had to be him.

Obviously I knew Len best as a team manager but I was aware of his many other skills as a track curator and promoter. He prepared excellent tracks and I liked Hackney, where I often got bookings and won the Superama on one occasion.

As a person, Len is a real man. He calls a spade a spade. He tackles everything with enthusiasm and gives 100 per cent. He is sociable and good company. Len is the sort that you could meet in a pub and immediately get on with.

MALCOLM SIMMONS

It was Len who gave me my first big break at international level shortly after he became England manager in 1973, so I have a lot to thank him for really. I'd been in and out of the England side in previous years and they were one-off appearances.

From '73 onwards he picked me on a regular basis, including two Wembley appearances for England in that first season, and I never looked back.

Thinking about it now, it was quite a bold thing for him to do, because I wasn't even an established British League No.1 at the time – I was behind Terry Betts at King's Lynn and didn't become a No.1 in my own right until after I moved to Poole in 1975. He obviously had faith in me.

As team manager, Len was a good motivator. He had always believed in himself as a rider and he made you believe in yourself too. He always sent you out for a race feeling confident and I still see him using that ability to good effect with his riders at Rye House today.

Len was still riding for Exeter when I first came across him in 1963. It was my debut season in the sport with Hackney and my first visit to the County Ground, which most visiting riders had a phobia about. The sheer size and speed of the pace, with its steel fence and steeply banked corners, put fear into the hearts and minds of many visiting riders, including me. It wasn't until I joined Poole and we had numerous local derby matches against Exeter that I got my head around what it was all about. It was all in the mind because there was nothing wrong with the Exeter track.

But back in '63, when I was still just a very raw 17-year-old who'd come straight off the grass-track, I made a point of taking it easy on my first visit to Exeter – and that meant staying out of Len's way. He had a bit of a reputation around there for being very hard, which was fair enough, and he'd wipe you out if you got in his way. I never did!

I always enjoyed my visits to Hackney when he was promoting there. The track had been as rough as hell in that first season of '63 but after Len took over it rightly gained a reputation as one of the best tracks in the country.

Len did tend to get a bit carried away with the pre-meeting watering, though! You'd turn up there on a Friday night and find the track almost flooded, where he'd watered it so much. 'Turn that bloody hose pipe off!' I'd think to myself but no matter how much you complained to him, he just carried on watering anyway. For the first three or four heats, it was fine if you made the gate. But if you didn't, you came back in covered in wet shale.

But he knew what he was doing. After those early heats and the track had begun to dry out, it all came good. It was a fine racetrack, with lots of different racing lines. It was only in Len's last couple of years at Hackney, after he'd lost a bit of enthusiasm for speedway and the only line round there was way out by the fence, that it was anything but a top racing track.

It was certainly in great condition the night I won the 1977 Superama – Hackney's biggest meeting of the season – before I did my shoulder riding in Germany that summer. Doing a deal with Len to ride in his open meetings was never a problem. He'd haggle a bit at first but he always knew a rider's value and paid accordingly.

In 1978, I was invited back to Hackney to play a part in the special Golden Jubilee of British Speedway meeting one chilly spring morning in February. As England captain at the time, I was asked to face Jack Parker, a legendary England

A dry looking Simmo – he must have been gating well!

skipper of the past, in a race. Jack rode a two-valve Jawa while I had to ride a 1928 Douglas machine that the old leg-trailers used in thre pre-war era. I'd never been a leg-trailer myself or been on a bike like this one, so it was a bit of a challenge.

Showman that he is, before we went to the tapes, Len had a few quiet words with me: 'Jack's got to win!' he said and I was happy not to spoil the party by beating the old veteran who had made the British match-race championship his own during his Belle Vue days.

I missed the start OK but it wasn't easy to stay behind Jack as I couldn't help but catch him up at every corner! Still, he crossed the line in front and it was nice to be part of such a historic occasion.

I eventually returned to ride for Hackney in 1986 but Terry Russell had taken over there by then and the team had dropped into the National League. I certainly would've been happy to have ridden for Len Silver, though.

What he has done, and continues to do, at Rye House is fantastic and I wish I could do now what he does at his age. My partner, June, and I visited the track a few weeks back. I didn't try and have a word with Len or even go near the pits – that's not my style. We just paid to get in and watched the meeting in amongst the fans. They had new seats installed round the third/fourth bend and the facilities seem to improve every time I go there. That's all credit to Len.

DAVE JESSUP

As England manager, Len was keen on the job and wanted you to succeed.

He looked after us immensely well. We attended a particular meeting at Hackney. Just about all the team were there – it might have been an open meeting or something. He took us all out to dinner that night because we were flying out to Sweden first thing the following day for a Test match. I'll guarantee that he paid for that out of his own pocket.

Having been the England team manager myself, I know that there were no expenses from the BSPA to take riders for dinner or anything like that, so that example shows just how keen he was. Obviously we all appreciated the gesture and loved the opportunity to get together.

Len was super-keen. He wanted to win and he used the best riders available to him. He used all his knowledge on team selection. There were no favourites. If you were going well enough, then you got picked. That's how it should be.

At Rye House, without being critical, he tends not to see any wrong in any Rockets rider at all. Len is capable of looking through rose-tinted glasses these days! He is 100 per cent behind his boys and I can vouch for that.

He took me to a tribunal once because he claimed that I didn't make a *bona fide* attempt to race a team-mate in a heat during an individual meeting featuring one of his Hackney riders. At the end of the day he would have done the same as I did. Unfortunately for Len, he lost at the tribunal and I won because I *had* made a genuine attempt to beat the Hackney rider, but didn't try to pass my team-mate.

We didn't even fall out about it – I even think that I was in his England team at the time. He was just looking after one of his riders. He was prepared to go to a tribunal to gain an advantage for his rider.

As for the transition of Rye House stadium, this is *his* stadium. He makes it as nice as he can within a budget. Obviously there are not limitless funds but Len has put an awful lot of effort and money into it and it is reaping rewards. It looks nice and tidy, everybody appreciates it and the crowds are not going down as they are at some other venues.

As a promoter Len does promote it as well as anybody – if not the best, in fact. He likes to put on a show. Being a former car salesman, he could sell sand to the Arabs!

With my England boys before the World Team Cup UK round at Reading in 1981. Clockwise: John Davis, Gordon Kennett, Dave Jessup, Chris Morton and Michael Lee.

CHRIS MORTON MBE

Len was my England team manager in 1981. It was a tough for him to come back into that role in '81 because we'd won the grand slam the year before with Ian Thomas and Eric Boocock as joint-managers.

As it was, we finished second in the World Team Cup Final that year in Germany. It was a tough meeting which Denmark won for the first time in a while. That was a really good meeting for me — — I only dropped one point.

Len did a good job as England manager that year. His experience was always helpful and his enthusiasm. I've only got good memories of him as a team manager.

He still has a very positive image as a promoter and I wonder where he gets the energy from! What would he do without speedway in his life? He runs a great show at Rye House and it's a credit to him. He knows how to run a speedway team and he knows how to promote.

MICHAEL LEE

I acquired my first proper speedway bike from Len Silver. I was about 14 at the time and there was this ex-Garry Middleton machine advertised in *Speedway Star*.

My Dad, Andy, took me over to Hackney one Saturday morning in February. There were seven bikes on display but I wanted the one with the blue glitter guards. It was very attractive, a two-valve Jawa, as ridden by Garry in his Hackney days. The deal was done but I couldn't take it out on track at Waterden Road that day because it was too wet, so I had to try it out at King's Lynn later on.

I already knew who Len Silver was because Dad used to take me to watch meetings at Hackney as a kid. There used to be this flamboyant little man who puffed his chest out and led the riders on parade.

It was an excellent track to race on under Len's preparation and I also got an insight into him as a promoter. He ran an efficient set-up and you knew who was boss. If he came into the pits unhappy with track staff, they soon jumped to attention. He was respected by riders and officials alike.

He liked to book me for his meetings – not only when I was at the peak of my career in 1980 and '81 but consistently, because I tried to entertain. Len was a good businessman who saw himself putting on an entertainment as well as a sport.

Looking at recent times in our respective lives, we both spent time away from the sport. Our paths crossed again when Danny King signed for Rye House. I'd been involved with Danny and when I went to the Hoddesdon circuit with him I could see that Len had really put a club atmosphere in place. He took the squad on a ski-ing trip to help them bond together. He assessed the team overall and gave them both direction and targets. He would listen to their point of view and put his own over with subtleness.

I was pleased to be entrusted with looking after Steve Boxall and to take on the role of training instructor. After a difficult period in my own life I was given the opportunity by Len to regain some self-respect and I'm grateful for that. He became a good friend and I look forward to my Saturday nights in Hertfordshire.

I tend to concentrate on mechanical aspects with the riders and allow them to be spontaneous when it comes to riding. Occasionally Len will ask me to speak to a team member about maintaining a positive attitude to their racing but Len is the main psychologist rather than me.

He has also got me into ski-ing but he can zip past me regardless of age. Not only do I enjoy being on the slopes with him, but when night draws in we sit down and discuss life and the world at large. I have gained great insight through these chats and learnt a lot about business issues from Len.

You have to respect the way he took himself from the East End of London and really made something of himself in two different spheres.

He even managed to talk me into take part in a match-race with him at the 2006 Vic Harding Memorial meeting at Rye House. I swore I'd never get back on a speedway bike but Len held me to a promise I'd made the previous February. I thought he'd forget about it, but no chance!

I'd summarise Len as the great entertainer and a first class promoter who has been a positive factor in my life.

WEMBLEY HERO

A few hours after we'd met in the bath, a fully dressed Bruce Penhall salutes the Wembley crowd after winning the 1981 World Final. It was a very memorable occasion for both of us.

BRUCE PENHALL

I have some very fond memories of Len. I can remember the very first time I was introduced to him, back in 1977, when I was over for my first taste of British speedway.

My fellow American Mike Bast and I were over for the Inter-Continental Final round of the World Championship at White City and we were trying to get some second-half rides to ready ourselves for the big day without much success.

However, Len did let Mike and I ride after the meeting at Hackney and he was very gracious about it. In fact, he offered to let us ride at Hackney again if we wanted.

Of course, to me, I think he was the best track-builder in the business, having built the 1981 Wembley World Final track! Great for me, but perhaps not so good for others.

I've always thought Len was one of the fairest promotors there was – he always backed up that strong Cockney accent.

One of the true good guys of the sport.

THE PRESS

PHILIP RISING *(Managing Editor, Speedway Star)*

Not sure that Len Silver would enjoy being called 'old school' given what some might perceive that to mean but in speedway promoters' terms he is exactly that.

Len's service to speedway has covered the full gambit, from rider to promoter to England team manager, along the line adding his not inconsiderable voice to various layers of administration at the BSPA.

His distinguished riding career gave him a valuable insight into speedway and he was the perfect candidate to take up the promotional reins alongside Mike Parker at Hackney. Parker, and his loyal right-hand man Eddie Glennon, were from the North and while there is certainly nothing wrong with that, Hackney needed a Cockney sparrow type of character at the helm.

Silver fitted the bill perfectly.

Len, like so many of his ilk, had and still has a strong passion for speedway. He was, and no doubt still is, opinionated and never slow to speak his mind and that has not always pleased everyone. During my time as editor of *Speedway Star* I had many vocal disagreements with Len and his fellow promoters Wally Mawdsley, Reg Fearman and Danny Dunton. I didn't always approve of his style of managership of the England team and said so in print both for the *Star* and the *Daily Express*. But at least with Len you could have a discussion, however heated, and then move on.

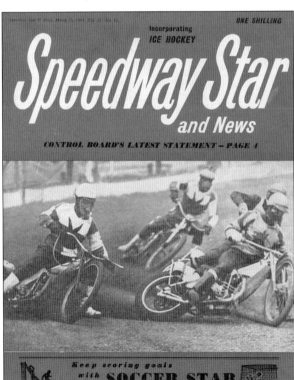

Since taking over at unfashionable Rye House and despite being involved with his skiing business, he has again shown what promoting is – or at least should be – all about. The stadium is neat and tidy, the track suited to entertaining racing. It's a proven recipe for success but one that is not always adopted by others in the business.

Len has devoted so much of his life and energy to speedway and for that alone the rest of us are in debt to him.

I made it onto the front cover of Speedway Star and News in March 1964. That's me trying the outside line at Wolverhampton.

RYE HOUSE

KARL FIALA

I used to go to Hackney Speedway as a kid in the late-60s where Colin Pratt and Les McGillivray were my favourite riders. I'm from Harlow and Colin Pratt was based there. He came to monitor my grass-track racing and, when I was 16, invited me to attend a training school at Hackney. That's when I met Len for the first time.

Eventually I progressed to joining my local club Rye House, where I don't need to tell you that Colin and Len were completely different personalities. Colin was very capable of geeing you up but Len could read people very well and knew when they were up for it.

I recall the climax of the 1980 season at Cleveland Park, Middlesbrough, where we had to win that night to secure the National League title. I was going for a 15-point maximum and it all went to a last heat decider. Len looked at me and didn't need to say a word – he could concentrate on my race partner.

I was leading at the first attempt to stage the race but it was re-run and I had to do it all over again. For a second time Len knew that he could leave it to me, and so I won at the second attempt. We took the necessary points to avoid having to win at Glasgow the next night.

Len was eloquent, he thought about what he was going to say and was shrewd with it. He was sensible, amiable and fair to deal with. For instance, when I became the team's No.1 he volunteered some extra help with my deal in providing fuel and oil.

I recall that in my early days at Rye House I stepped in to cover the absence of Ted Hubbard at a World Championship qualifying round in 1977 – and won the meeting. I was then given the chance of riding at No.7 for Hackney away at Birmingham. For some reason, I actually drove Len up to Perry Barr and during the match Len took exception to an unfair refereeing decision that went against us.

He was so angry after the altercation with the referee that he bashed the phone down so hard and the phone booth collapsed – in full view of the fans gathered around the pits area. Len had been correctly supporting his man but the crowd was upset and some of them were looking for him after the meeting.

Luckily, they didn't realise that I'd been his chauffeur for the day – so I smuggled Len out of the stadium with him ducking down on my back seat!

At the end of the season we'd flour and water him and then burn his trousers. He was always a good sport.

He's definitely the current 'Godfather of Speedway' and has inherited that mantle from Johnnie Hoskins whom I remember when I raced at Canterbury in my Rye House days.

Towards the end of the 2008 season I went to the stadium at Hoddesdon on my enduro road bike for a Sunday spin and caught the end of a meeting. How he has upgraded what was basically a modest arena. There he was – despite his age – full of beans, laughing and looking very fit.

I've been ski-ing with him in the past and he 's brilliant. He is an outstanding skier and that quality side of his life is, I'm sure, what keeps him fit and healthy.

I look back on the speedway phase of my life with great fondness. I retired at the end of the 1980 season having made it plain that I intended to do so. Nobody seemed to believe me. It was a wrench but I'd made a career decision and was seeking a new direction in my life.

At a Rye House social function in the mid-70s. With me (from back row, left to right: Ashley Pullen, Bob Cooper, Bob Garrad, Kelvin Mullarkey, Colin Pratt and Karl Fiala.

Len never contacted me as he presumed that I'd be back. So when Bob Garrard and Kevin Smith moved on and it became apparent that I wasn't gearing up for a new season, then Len did visit me and made a very flattering offer but I stuck to my intentions.

I was disappointed that articles started appearing saying that I'd let Rye House down. I repeat that I had made it plain that I was retiring from the sport to pursue new employment. Luckily there was no bad feeling between Len and myself and we've been ski-ing together since.

My final point on Len is his strength as a negotiator. You'd come away after having sorted your deal for a new season thanking him, when you'd only managed to get from him half of what you went in for. Definitely a silver tongue in more ways than one!

STEVE NAYLOR

I started at Eastbourne and then went to Crayford, where Len bought my contract for Rye House. I rode here for the Rockets for three years in the early-80s. He was the fairest promoter I ever rode for. If Len said that he would do something, he'd do it. You didn't have to ask. He is a very honest man.

He was a rider himself and so he understood how they reacted. When you had a bad day he never got on your back. When you had a good day he didn't praise you too much either. It was job done.

When Len finished with speedway in 1986 I never lost contact with him because of the ski-ing. When he returned to the sport I worked in

Steve Naylor leading Crayford's Barry Thomas at Rye House.

a warehouse, which I hated. Then I had the opportunity to come back and work at the stadium. Obviously, we have a great working relationship. We work very well together. Our interests are the same – ski-ing and speedway, with the Rye House link making it brilliant.

Len has transformed the place since coming back. The work and the effort that we've all put in here is backed by Len's energy. We just do what we have to do. Anyone coming here will see such an improvement since I rode here. He has got the enthusiasm for it and we all love it. We all work together as a team – Hazal and Alan, who works in the fish bar, we're all such a team. We want to do our best for Len and also for ourselves. It's a great atmosphere.

As a promoter he is one of the greatest of all time. There is not one rider who has ridden for Len who wouldn't do so again if they were asked. There is a lot to be said for that.

There is stability in his teams. Len will make a decision at the beginning of a season and he will stick with that team unless something really unfortunate happens. He'll never jack a rider and swap his team around for the sake of it. That's his decision and he will help them and encourage them to get through a difficult time. That kind of loyalty is unusual these days. If anyone hits bad times at some other tracks, out they go and in comes a foreigner.

I've been on quite a few ski-ing adventures with him. I've been ski-ing for over a dozen years myself but with no disrespect to Len, when you look at him you can't imagine him on skis. He is one good skier, I can assure you. We've had some great times in the Alps, like when all the team go out together and meet up. It's just being part of Rye House and Silver Ski.

The day that I originally walked in here as a Rye House Rocket began a very positive phase of my life.

KEVIN BOWEN

I was a Rye House Rocket myself in the early-80s. My Dad rode trials in the Army and my brother Keith, of Elmside Transport, had a go at speedway. It was something that I'd always wanted to do.

I'd been in a spot of bother and was a bit of a bad boy before I got involved in the sport. I moved back in with my parents and my Dad said: 'I understand that you've been having a ride at speedway? How would you like me to buy you a bike?'

That's really how it started off, when Colin Pratt and Len had Rye House in the late-70s. I was riding for Rye at home in 1981 when a kind person called Rob Grant (Berwick) knocked me up in the air and dislocated both of my shoulders. That was more or less the end of me really because the

Kevin Bowen – injuries cut short his career.

year before I'd injured my back. I'd just got married and I felt that was enough. The next thing I knew, I was going to be a Dad. That was my eldest boy – and then along came Luke.

I wanted my son to go to Rye House, whatever, because Len is an 'old school' promoter. You know that your wages are there every week, God bless him, and he is very much British. Len gives encouragement and he gets a great buzz from the boys as well, which is lovely. From time to time riders go through difficult patches with engines and bike problems but Len – and I don't think there is another promoter like him in the country – will be more than willing to put his hand in his pocket and help the lads.

As for his age, he amazes me. He is out there everyday on his tractor, sometimes for 10 or more hours. I think it's the thing that keeps him sane.

PETER JORDISON

I was a supporter at Rye House even in the days of Dicky Case. Bill Mathieson ran it as a training school for many years but he gave it up to allow the Rayleigh Rockets to move over in 1974.

I used to go as a supporter with my daughters, was on the supporters' committee and got to know Len a lot better. He was a dynamic promoter, building up the banking and working on the grandstand every Sunday morning. He once nearly lost a finger in a chain while flinging hooks over big girders and lintels. The whole site was pretty bare in 1974. The drainage was installed by Len with the help of Kelvin Mullarkey. Some of that system is still functioning today. I remember in the early days, when the Rockets raced on Sunday afternoons, he used to call it 'Sunshine Speedway'.

Len's a real hands-on promoter. He and I are the two old boys, working outside even when it's freezing. Even these days, he's still the first one out there in the mornings. We go down there on a Friday and then have a meal and drinks in the evening. Then we're back up at the track on the Saturday morning. Even if we've had a few drinks the night before, Len is always there ahead of us.

He will never slow down. We can have a meal on a Friday or Saturday evening and afterwards he'll nod off for 15 minutes. But he'll wake up in a flash and be back with it. He gets his energy back with just that short break. He'll go on and on.

Sometimes we sleep at the stadium on a Friday night, so that we're ready to start work early on the Saturday morning. You get up and he's already out there because the tractor is going around. He has not just invested money, but time, effort and knowledge.

As for the Rye House track, Len puts a lot of work into that. He is very thorough. The only way to do a track is to constantly go around it, grading and then tyre-packing. Even the visiting riders like Rye House because there isn't a bump on it – it's like a billiard table.

Len is good with words and writes his own programme notes. He has also ridden as well as prepared tracks to World Final level. He is a very clever man is our Len.

What he's done to the stadium is unbelievable. When we first went there the area where the fish bar is now was like a dungeon. That was eventually all boarded out and varnished. I can remember varnishing that at nights until my eyes were red.

It has become a major business and he's got the two fish bars operating now. These days it's probably the biggest you'll find in Hertfordshire.

When he returned to Rye he did say that he didn't know the riders as he prepared to build a team. That's when he became more involved with John Sampford. You ask John a question about speedway and he can answer it. They have made a good team.

There was a time when I didn't think Rye House would stage speedway again. With all respect to those who rekindled the Rockets, it needed some key figures to come in and drive it forward. Interestingly, Len's accountant advised him not to go back into promoting. We went for a spin on the tractor around the time I was involved while the original consortium were still running it. I told him: 'Much as I want you to go back, what you are going to do is stupid.'

In my opinion, he finally decided to do it because they told him he was wrong! Also, at heart, he wanted to do it. I don't think I had the confidence that Len had about the project. It wasn't going to be easy. But he is a hard worker and sometimes you can see the difference. We've arrived at away tracks and the home promoter isn't even there. Len can't believe it.

He is well aware of what the paying public expects from speedway today. He will tell you – you must have seating and cover. Len has a loyal band around him and that includes Hazal, Steve Naylor and myself. We are all happy down there. When he returns from his winter ski-ing activities in France each year, we know he'll be happy with our endeavours.

Forgetting any past issues in their personal lives, Len has great respect for Hazal, and vice-versa. He will also tell you that nine times out of 10 Hazal will prove to be right. Possibly, it's a woman thing! He will argue with her and if he thinks that he's right, he will get his own way. But if there are any doubts, Hazal has an influence on his decisions.

The first Rye House British League Second Division team after we moved the Rockets there in 1974. Left to right: Trevor Barnwell, Peter Moore, Pete Wigley, Peter Thorogood (team manager), Brian Foote, Les 'Red' Ott, John Gibbons and Steve Clarke, with Bob Young on the bike.

They have dual business interests because Hazal is a co-director of Silver Ski and Rye House co-promoter. She is a strong personality but is much softer than some people think. She's not the hard sort of person that people believe her to be. Hazal has a lot of good points. Both her and Len have a presence, that's for sure.

You don't talk to Len at a speedway meeting except about aspects of that night's meeting. He is focused on running that event – starting on time, for instance.

Len is, of course, of the older generation. He's not a computer man, although he sends and receives emails. He has trouble with his mobile phone on occasions, though! But he sticks to tried and trusted ways of communication-and there is a virtue in that.

The Rye House riders, even the younger ones, have a lot of respect for Len. In between the races they will come and stand with Len in that viewing area next to the pits. The riders will stand and have a little chat with him and he'll tell them what they have done and go over little things. You'll notice too that he will always take a walk around the pits once he is changed and all dressed up in his blazer.

I rate Len Silver as a first class promoter and I can't find a fault with him. Also we've become great friends. We are the two oldies in the middle of a younger support team. Sometimes we might take longer to do a job but we can still do it between the two of us.

Of his strengths, loyalty is certainly one of them. He doesn't suffer fools gladly, nor liars. Even if he doesn't like the content, he'd rather hear the truth. Telling a lie is one of his major pet hates.

He is still young at heart and active, despite being 77. Len promoted the 75th anniversary meeting of British speedway and he intends to promote the 100th anniversary meeting too. Johnnie Hoskins was very energetic for his age and promoted into his nineties. I remember Hoskins running across the Canterbury track and jumping over the fence to sort some supporters out who were causing a bit of trouble. He was in his eighties then.

In summary, Len is a first class promoter and a true friend.

JOHN SAMPFORD

My speedway roots run deep. My parents met at Rayleigh Speedway in 1950 and they took me along there in the 50s and 60s. I can recall Len becoming involved at Rayleigh after 1968 when it re-opened and I was aware that he was also Hackney promoter at the time.

The Weir Stadium boasted a 365-yard track where the bends were deep and the racing was good. As a family, we always enjoyed our time there. Then the stadium was sold for redevelopment in 1973 but, remarkably, Len was able to pull Rye House out of the hat and keep the Rockets running. Remarkable because Rye House had traditionally been a training track and had never featured in a professional league. It was a gamble but Len brought his promotional skill to it and totally altered it.

Initially, it was fair size and very flat. He made it smaller and banked the bends. As a family, we made the journey to Hertfordshire as faithful fans. Eventually I became involved in selling a variety of programmes from a stall and started to get a feel for what other clubs were producing. Len's view at the time was that fans only wanted a racecard. He was possibly correct but times were changing and other clubs' programmes were reflecting an expectation of higher standards of content and production.

Another problem was that Len took on most tasks himself and so didn't have that much time to spend on the raceday programme. So I offered my services to improve the content, starting with introducing some retro features. Once I'd moved more closely into being involved with my club, having been a fan for so many years, I had a different perspective as I became more aware of the personalities and politics involved on occasions. I stayed all the way to the end of Len's first era at Rye House in 1985, when he sold the club to Ronnie Russell.

Our paths crossed again when Steve Ribbons put together a consortium in an attempt to revive speedway at Rye House in 1999. I contacted Steve to offer my services again and one of his suggestions was that I became understudy to the team manager. Steve preferred an ex-rider to manage, with former Rocket Martin Goodwin a possible target.

Our first revival meeting was at Eastbourne against a King's Lynn Select. Steve announced that Martin might turn up but asked me to be on standby. Eventually I had to be pressed into service and we were 12 points down after six races. Then I realised it fell to me to do something about it! We won by a single point and I was in the frame of mind to take on the role.

Len became involved in the revival by invitation and helped the cause by pumping some money in. Eventually he took the opportunity to take up the lease on the stadium and the rest is history. The work involved, plus the cost, was daunting. Len spent £80,000 before a wheel was turned with commitment to plant hire, shale and a massive exercise in the removal of tyres and car parts.

Also, for the first season back at Hoddesdon, the stock cars still had a year left on their sub-lease and so the speedway track had to be laid and ripped up again every week. A formidable task for anyone approaching 70 but this is a meticulous man who is always prepared to go the extra mile. As he says: 'Others will go 50 laps on a tractor, so I'll go a hundred.' All riders like the Rye House track. Alan Mogridge used to say that he only came to Rye House once a season but always looked forward to it. He knew that he could race here.

Len is a generous man. I remember picking him up at the stadium to travel to an away meeting and he discussed having traced his family history back to Ebenezer Scrooge! Well, he is no scrooge with his silver when it comes to speedway and speedway riders. His successful development of the Silver Ski business has allowed him to help riders beyond the call of duty. Even struggling juniors have been lent engines in times of need. I've lost count of the number of times that Len has put his hand in his pocket to assist with things such as medical treatment, engine bills, etc.

He certainly runs the club in every sense. Everybody has their place. Conversely, Len and Hazal do not suffer fools gladly. Occasionally a rider may need a kick up the backside but Len will allow me to maintain my non-demonstrative style and will jump on them from a great height himself. He has told me to maintain my usual manner – I'm not one for ranting and raving anyway – and I appreciate his input and his reading of my character.

I hate losing as much as Len does. He is competitive but sometimes it doesn't seem obvious. With Len, he never gives up as long as it is still mathematically possible to retrieve a positive result to a match or an aggregate score. I can remember being at Somerset in 2002 and we were 10 points down. The tactical substitution produced a 5-1. Then, on advice, I dropped Nigel Sadler – who went ballistic – and put in David Mason, who went out and won that heat. It was a 5-1 and provided the platform for an eventual two-point win.

Obviously Len and I confer. I'd be a fool not to consult a man who has overseen Rye House and Hackney to the highest level before becoming the most successful ever England team manager. We work very closely together and I always tell him what I'm going to do before I put it into action out of courtesy. Sometimes I can tell whether he thinks it's a good move or something that he would not do himself. He'll turn around and look at me and then I'll think about my decision again before I do it. On occasions I don't change my mind, but on others I do. The times when that happens, more often than not Len is right.

There was one occasion regarding a tactical move that I recall in 2006. A rider had done nothing in his opening two rides and I thought there was no way I could give him a tactical ride but Len had already written the rider's name in his programme. I wasn't going to use the rider in question but he went out and won the race. Len always says, if we use my logic and his sixth sense, then we'll do fine!

As for bringing on young riders from the Cobras, he has an uncanny knack of promoting the right ones, perhaps because he's been a rider and he knows what is required. He knows when riders are ready and whether they have the potential to increase their average.

He is always planning ahead and looking at the green sheet figures for riders with the potential to improve. Tommy Allen and Steve Boxall would be in-house examples, whilst Tai Woffinden and Adam Roynon would be examples of looking elsewhere for young talent to bring in. Let's be honest, if Len genuinely thought a rider was ready for the senior team he would use him and not look outside.

To win the league title some 25 years on from the previous such achievement meant that Len was obviously 'over the moon'. Len is the guv'nor and I manage the team that he gives me – the team that he wants. Some riders will argue with me but not with him. It's respect more than fear.

What are his many qualities? Vision – the stadium has developed so much in recent years but he is now working through a new five-year plan. He does believe in investment – 'speculate to accumulate'.

He is very hands-on. He has a good back up team but puts in his fair share of work at the stadium. Len is a good all-rounder who can take on most roles at a speedway club. Obviously such a multi-faceted man is a complex character but he is a livewire and a living legend in our sport.

One of his greatest qualities is loyalty. He has a tremendous loyalty to riders and not just with his own team members. He does not necessarily offer the highest pay but the riders always get paid promptly. I recall at the 75th anniversary meeting taking the guaranteed fees for the visitors, such as Joe Screen, into the changing rooms before the event. The riders were very impressed. You can't fault him for that.

He is also good to the fans. Len's aware that a busy season with both Premier League and National League teams running means he has to be flexible on admission charges. On some busy weekends he has charged £1 for a one-off programme and reduced admission costs accordingly. So he maintains his gate and they still spend at the stadium.

A good promoter – definitely!

With Joe Haines (left) and Michael Bovis (right). It's important to spend time with lads who are keen to learn.

Wild horses wouldn't drag me away from vital track work that needs to be done. This was taken while grading the back straight at Hackney in 1971 but the same principles still apply today.

STEVE WEBB

I first started to work under Len at Hackney in 1974. I've been with him as a pit marshal and assisting him with tracks and stadiums ever since.

I actually moved to Hertfordshire in 1974 at the same time that the Rayleigh Rockets switched to Rye House. I worked in the pits at Hackney and they used to push the bikes off in those days, which they don't do in the modern era.

So I know Len Silver very well. He's one of the rare promoters who still prepares and maintains his own speedway track. To be with him is to learn about speedway. To be a part of his set-up – well, he has his moments! Perhaps, at times, Len can be too interested in what you are doing. However, working behind the scenes with Len is a very interesting experience. He treats us to restaurant meals and took 12 of us to the Farewell to Wembley Stadium Dinner in 2002. We met all the riders of the previous 50 years, including many former World Champions.

For a man of his age, he's a fun person. Mind you, to get him off his speedway track you have to wrench him off his tractor! He gets to Rye House at seven o'clock in the morning. He's here four or five days of the week and is always up first in the morning to get onto his track.

To be with Len and his entourage is a very fun affair. There are a lot of people who don't know that side of the business. If you are at Rye House on a daily basis there are some right telling-offs at times when we've done something wrong, especially if we don't do it *his* way! He's the boss through and through, but you can take it from someone with his knowledge and experience.

Many promoters are putting nothing back into the sport as far as producing youngsters is concerned. In the last eight years or so we have brought on quite a lot of our own riders from training schools to second-half races, week in and week out.

Rye House is a fun place. I'm still enjoying it.

CHRIS NEATH

I think it was in 2003 that Edward Kennett got hurt and I received a lot of guest bookings from Len. It was a track that I'd always ridden well on in the past. It went from there really. I seemed to click with Len and everyone else there. He made me feel welcome and it was somewhere that I felt I wanted to ride.

The opportunity arose for me to go to Rye House in 2004 and I've been there ever since. I didn't realise when I took those guest bookings how important Rye House would become in my racing career.

Len does such a good job with everyone. The club is just so family-orientated and I do feel part of the general family too. I think he appreciates the pressures and what is going on with the riders, so that's why he relates to us so well.

We are a young team and he is in his eighth decade but we don't think of him as an old fuddy-duddy at all. I like sitting down listening to his stories and he is such a great guy to be around.

With his passion and his enthusiasm, you wouldn't meet a person more dedicated to the sport – and to his ski-ing. The two loves of his life – Len always tells me that is what keeps him alive. Speedway in the summer and ski-ing in the winter.

It's the same when we go ski-ing. He's the first one out in the morning – 9.00am on the dot and waiting for all of us stragglers to get out of bed – and he's also the last one off the slopes as well. He has such vitality.

Our ski-ing trips are all part of the team-bonding exercise leading up to a new season. Again, that's down to Len and Hazal, plus everyone associated with the club. It's such an enjoyable place to be.

One day Len took us to a mountain that we'd never been on before. He warned us that he'd take us a little off-piste with an instruction to follow him. There was a group of about 10 of us.

He set off and we watched him go down this off-piste area – no problems. Next minute, we tried it. One's gone down, then another and soon it was like dominos. Len was then 75-years-old and he shot through with no problems, whereas us youngsters were buried up to our waists in snow. He had a good chuckle at us trying to sort ourselves out!

We also get together on occasions during the season. We have a meal in the pub over the road from the track. It's another part of the bonding process. It makes it such a good club to be part of.

As Rye House captain I would normally have to speak to the promoter on behalf of the team but there are never any real issues.

Sometimes he likes to get out on his water cart, which we are not so keen on. Len understands that we are having a bit of a whinge and it might annoy him but, normally, everything is positive.

In recent seasons we have won the Premier League title twice and been very together in that achievement. Len was so proud of us then, you could see a tear in his eye, especially after the last one when we achieved it in the play-offs and the championship was won on the night.

When we were crowned champions in 2005 we weren't even racing on the night – we just heard the results of our rivals. It's great that someone who has done so much in speedway should show his appreciation of what his riders have achieved all these years later. He has so many achievements himself, so that was a really nice feeling for all the boys involved in that team.

I've been very fortunate to have ridden for the best promoter in the Premier League in Len Silver and for Chris Van Straaten, at Wolverhampton, in the Elite League. I like to think that I've got to know Len on a personal level and I do have family connections through my partner. You couldn't meet a nicer person in general.

He is outstanding and I hope he continues in speedway for many years to come.

Top left: And the show goes on . . . I still get a buzz out of seeing the fans going home happy.
Top right: With skipper Chris Neath at the pre-match toss. Above: Chris with Tommy Allen.

Scott Robson

STUART ROBSON

I joined Rye House at the beginning of 2005. I'd ridden in a meeting at the end of the 2004 season – the Ace of Herts meeting – and won it. I spoke to Len not long after that and got sorted out pretty sharply for the following year.

Going from Coventry in the Elite League, which is a very professionally run club, to Rye House in the Premier League was a move to another well-run club. It was like a smaller version really. Colin Pratt and Len Silver work exactly the same way. They had worked together a lot in the past so, for me, dealing with one is very much like dealing with the other. They are very easy to get on with and very easy to deal with.

As for Len's man-management, I don't know anybody who has a bad word to say about the guy. No-one ever puts him down. He has everyone's respect and that's the way it should be.

TAI WOFFINDEN

I had plenty of choice of clubs to sign for at the start of my speedway career but I chose the best promoter and the best track in the Premier League. It's the same week in, week out and Len has been doing it for loads of years. He knows what he is about. In fact, he knows everything really. So what better place to come?

It's good that he enjoys speedway so much because he wants his team to do well. He wants a great team that people will come and watch. It's not that he needs it to happen – he *wants* it.

I made a good decision in 2007.

Luke Bowen, whose father also rode for me.

LUKE BOWEN

Len is not that old really. Obviously he's 77 but he is a lot younger in terms of his health and attitude, with loads of energy.

As a promoter, he's very fair and really encourages you to want to improve as a young rider.

I've been on his ski-ing specials a few times. They are amazing. We used to stay further down than where Len would be based in his main chalet. He'd come down on his own at nine o'clock every morning to meet us. Then he would take us all out on a day's ski-ing. Keeping up with him was a challenge! We were all over the place compared to him but it's a brilliant experience for the team.

My first effort on a bike was in March 2001 at a Marvyn Cox training school. From there it was six months of practicing and then Rye House signed me up. I've been in the Conference League and worked

Above: Tai Woffinden during his first season in the sport.
Below: Tommy Allen, another youngster making his way with the Rockets.

my way up. Obviously I've been blighted by injuries but that's speedway.

I love it down at Rye House. I'm only 10 minutes from the track, some six miles down the road. Len is a legend!

TOMMY ALLEN

Len is certainly an energetic and interesting man for his age. I've never known anyone to spend as much time on a track or at the stadium and the effort that he puts in.

I also think of our team in the last couple of years. We've had some good ones and won the league a couple of times. The effort that he puts in reflects in the boys.

We all have great respect for what Len is and what he is all about. The way that he treats the riders is the way he would wish to be treated if he were still a rider. It's always good to have a boss like that. I couldn't fault him.

ROBERT MEAR

I love being at this track – it's only 10 minutes away from my house.

Len loves racing and he loves to help you out. He does give advice but his best phrase is: 'Flat out off the line and into the first corner.' He says that wherever you are!

He is very encouraging and positive. He'll come up to you before a race and tell you that you're going to win it. That's what you want to hear, isn't it?

I was aware that he was a pretty good rider and I've seen some pictures of him.

On the snow he wipes the floor with the whole team going down the ski slopes. You can't catch him! Those ski trips are amazing, the best team-bonding exercises you could have. Obviously you are with your team mates all day up and down the hills then you go out and have a drink at night. You are with them the whole week. You do get along and have a bond with them.

Len is a lovely bloke, willing to help and you can't really fault him for anything.

DANIEL HALSEY

Everyone knows that Len is a great bloke. He always has a few words of encouragement for me. The advice is to be 'flat out'. It's always 'flat out' with Len!

He is awesome for a man of 77. He's one of the lads really and fun to be around.

LEN SILVER'S CAREER RECORD & MAIN HONOURS

As Rider, Promoter & England Team Manager

Len's League Racing Career Statistics

Year	Club	Division	Matches	Rides	Points	Bonus P	Total P	CMA	FM	PM
1953	Ipswich	SL	9	24	22	2	24	4.00	-	-
1954	Ipswich	NL2	16	45	43	8	51	4.53	-	-
1955	Ipswich	NL2	16	42	28	15	43	4.10	-	-
1956	Ipswich	NL2	21	82	45	9	54	2.63	-	-
1960	Ipswich	NL1	19	45	33	11	44	3.91	-	-
1961	Ipswich	NL1	1	2	2	0	2	4.00	-	-
1961	Exeter	PL	16	62	133	4	137	8.84	4	1
1962	Exeter	PL	28	119	270	7	277	9.31	6	1
1963	Exeter	PL	25	104	240	8	248	9.54	5	-
1964	Hackney	PL	7	24	47	4	51	8.50	-	-

Key:

SL – Southern League

NL2 – National League Division Two

NL1 – National League Division One

PL – Provincial League (Div 2)

Figures relate only to official league fixtures. Supplied by Matt Jackson & Hugh Vass.

Major Riding Honours

Provincial League Riders' Championship winner 1962
Provincial League Silver Sash Match-Race Champion 1962
Provincial League KO Cup winner (with Exeter) 1962

Len's Promoting Career Statistics

As a director of the Allied Presentations Ltd consortium of promoters, Len had interests in several tracks during the 70s, most notably at Crewe and Sunderland. However, our records here focus on the tracks where he has been regarded as the main promoter and figurehead.

HACKNEY

Year	Division	Final League Position
1964	PL	2nd (12)
1965	BL1	8th (18)
1966	BL1	14th (19)
1967	BL1	5th (19)
1968	BL1	2nd (19)
1969	BL1	19th (19)
1970	BL1	11th (19)
1971	BL1	7th (19)
1972	BL1	8th (18)
1973	BL1	16th (18)
1974	BL1	9th (17)
1975	BL1	17th (18)
1976	BL1	7th (19)
1977	BL1	16th (19)
1978	BL1	19th (19)
1979	BL1	18th (18)
1980	BL1	2nd (17)
1981	BL1	8th (16)
1982	BL1	7th (15)
1983	BL1	7th (15)

Hackney's 1971 KO Cup-winning team after victory against Cradley Heath in the final. Left to right: Laurie Etheridge, Hugh Saunders, Bengt Jansson, Eddie Reeves, Garry Middleton, Barry Thomas and Dave Kennett. We lost to Belle Vue in a thrilling final a year later.

RAYLEIGH

Year	Division	Final League position
1968	BL2	5th (10)
1969	BL2	5th (16)
1970	BL2	12th (17)
1971	BL2	5th (17)
1972	BL2	4th (17)
1973	BL2	18th (18)

The 1980 Hawks, who just missed out on the British League title to Reading. Left to right: Roman Jankowski, Keith White, Sean Willmott, Barry Thomas (on bike), Finn Thomsen, Bo Petersen and Zenon Plech. It was the second time we'd finished runners-up.

WEYMOUTH

Year	Division	Final League position
1978	NL	13th (20)

RYE HOUSE

Brent Werner and the boys celebrating our 2005 Premier League championship victory.

Year	Division	Final League position
1974	BL2	16th (19)
1975	NNL	14th (20)
1976	NL	5th (18)
1977	NL	2nd (19)
1978	NL	3rd (20)
1979	NL	2nd (19)
1980	NL	Champions (20)
1981	NL	16th (19)
1982	NL	6th (19)
1983	NL	11th (18)
1984	NL	8th (16)
1985	NL	13th (19)
1999*	CL	4th (7) *(home matches raced at Eastbourne, Mildenhall & King's Lynn)
2000	CL	6th (10)
2001	CL	4th (8)
2002	PL	13th (17)
	CL	4th (11)
2003	PL	14th (18)
	CL	2nd (13)
2004	PL	6th (15)
	CL	2nd (13)
2005	PL	Champions (15)
	CL	6th (12)
2006	PL	4th (14)
	CL	3rd (8)
2007	PL	3rd (15) Play-off Champions
	CL	6th (10)
2008	PL	4th (16)
	CL	7th (8)

Key:
BL1 – British League Division One
BL2 – British League Division Two
NNN – New National League (Div 2)
NL – National League (Div 2)
CL – Conference League (Div 3)
PL – Premier League (Div 2)
(The number of competing teams in each season are shown in brackets).

Major Promoting Honours

British League First Division KO Cup winners (Hackney) – 1971
National League championship winners (Rye House) – 1980
Premier League championship winners (Rye House) – 2005 & 2007
National League KO Cup winners (Rye House) – 1979
Premier League Trophy winners (Rye House) – 2005

Len's Record As England Team Manager

Len Silver is the only England team manager in speedway history to have led his team to three consecutive victories in the World Team Cup Final (now known as the Speedway World Cup). When he achieved the feat for the first time, at Wembley in 1973, the team rode under the name of Great Britain, although all five of his riders were in fact English – another historical first. For the wins in Poland (1974) and Germany (1975), his team rode as England.

To complete a brilliant first season as national team manager, Len also guided England to victory in the Daily Mirror International Tournament, beating Sweden in the final at Wembley.

World Team Cup Finals

World Team Cup Final Winners – 1973, 1974 & 1975
World Team Cup Final Runners-up – 1981

Test Match Series

1973
POLAND (U-23) 3   GREAT BRITAIN (U-23) 0

1974

ENGLAND	5	SWEDEN	0
ENGLAND	7	POLAND	0
ENGLAND	5	SOVIET UNION	0

1975

ENGLAND	5	SWEDEN	0
SWEDEN	0	ENGLAND	5
POLAND	1	ENGLAND	3

1976
No official Test matches were held this year, due to England's supreme dominance in world speedway and a lack of suitably strong opposition!

1981

| ENGLAND | 4 | USA | 1 |
| ENGLAND | 2 | DENMARK | 1 |

Overall Senior Test Match Record

Matches	Won	Drew	Lost
39	36	0	3

Index

As luck would have it . . .
I've reached the end and I'm still
in one piece!
Hope you found it enjoyable.
Many thanks for reading.

LEN
